Teacher-Made Assessments

Assessment is not only a measure *of* student learning, but a means *to* student learning. This bestselling book guides you in constructing and using your own classroom assessments, including tests, quizzes, essays, and rubrics, to improve student achievement. You will learn how to weave together curriculum, instruction, and learning to make assessment a more natural, useful part of teaching.

Find out how to . . .

◆ Ensure your assessments are fair, reliable, and valid;
◆ Construct assessments that meet the level of cognitive demand expected of students;
◆ Create select-response items and understand technology-enhanced items that are increasingly being used in assessments;
◆ Use constructed-response items and develop scoring criteria such as rubrics;
◆ Analyze student results on assessments and use feedback more effectively.

This second edition features updated examples that reflect the Common Core State Standards as well as other content standards and new, useful samples of teacher-friendly techniques for strengthening classroom assessment practices. No matter what grade level or subject area you teach, this practical book will become your go-to resource for designing effective assessments.

Christopher R. Gareis, EdD, is Associate Professor of Educational Leadership at the College of William and Mary, where he also served as Associate Dean for teacher education for more than a decade. He regularly works with school districts in the areas of classroom-based assessment, mentoring, instructional leadership, strategic planning, and teacher evaluation.

Leslie W. Grant, PhD, is Assistant Professor of Educational Leadership at the College of William and Mary. She has been a teacher, an instructional leader, and a content editor and item writer for a major test publishing company. She works with school districts in the areas of using data to inform decision making, classroom-based assessment, and effective teaching practices.

Teacher-Made Assessments

How to Connect Curriculum, Instruction, and Student Learning

Second Edition

Christopher R. Gareis and Leslie W. Grant

Routledge
Taylor & Francis Group

NEW YORK AND LONDON

Second edition published 2015
by Routledge
711 Third Avenue, New York, NY 10017

and by Routledge
2 Park Square, Milton Park, Abingdon, Oxon, OX14 4RN

*Routledge is an imprint of the Taylor & Francis Group,
an informa business*

First edition published by Eye On Education © 2008

Library of Congress Cataloging-in-Publication Data
Gareis, Christopher R.
    Teacher-made assessments : how to connect curriculum,
instruction, and student learning / by Christopher Gareis and
Leslie Grant. — Second edition
        pages cm
    Includes bibliographical references.
    Educational tests and measurements.   I. Grant, Leslie W., 1968–
II. Title.
    LB3051.G28 2015
    371.27'1—dc23
    2014041468

ISBN: 978-1-138-77610-4 (hbk)
ISBN: 978-1-138-77612-8 (pbk)
ISBN: 978-1-315-77341-4 (ebk)

Typeset in Palatino
by Apex CoVantage, LLC

Contents

Figures

Foreword

Writing more than sixty years ago, education icon Ralph W. Tyler argued that before anyone can teach another person anything, two fundamental questions need to be addressed: "What do I want that person to learn?" and "What evidence would I accept to verify that learning?" According to Tyler (1949), these two fundamental questions provide the basis of teaching and learning at any level of education.

Tyler further emphasized that these two fundamental questions show the essential relatedness of teaching and learning. Although learning occasionally occurs in the absence of teaching, teaching can never occur in the absence of learning. Tyler believed that stating "I taught it to them; they just didn't learn it" was as foolish as saying "I sold it to them; they just didn't buy it." Teaching, therefore, is not something a person could go off into the wilderness alone and do—not even if that person carried with them curriculum guides, textbooks, and lesson plans. If no learning took place, how could one argue that teaching had occurred? Teaching and learning are indelibly linked.

In recent years, we have made great progress in efforts to address Tyler's first fundamental question: "What do I want that person to learn?" In the early 2000s, educators in states and provinces throughout North America began to articulate standards for student learning. More recently those efforts have been extended in the United States through the development of the Common Core Standards in language arts and mathematics. These and other standards-based initiatives identify what educators want students to learn and be able to do as a result of their experiences in school. They have helped bring increased clarity to teaching and provide focus in efforts to improve students' learning.

Unfortunately, we haven't made as much progress in addressing Tyler's second fundamental question: "What evidence would I accept to verify that learning?" Our progress in the area of assessment—helping teachers develop better ways to gather accurate evidence on the most meaningful types of student learning—has been slow at best.

Numerous studies and surveys report that most teachers today are sorely lacking in their knowledge and skills regarding the assessment of student learning. Although many debate the reasons for this shortcoming, none deny that it exists. Researchers and practitioners alike also recognize that more than ever before, teachers today need strong assessment skills. They need to be able to make thoughtful decisions about the evidence they accept to verify student learning. In other words, they need to be "assessment literate." This means teachers at all levels need to be able to create assessments that accurately measure students' achievement of specific learning standards. They need to be able to interpret results from a variety of forms of assessment in accurate and valid ways. They need to be able to use assessments to diagnose students' learning problems and misunderstandings. And most importantly, they need to be able to craft instructional activities on the basis of assessment results to ensure higher levels of learning for their students.

What Chris and Leslie do so well in *Teacher-Made Assessments* is help teachers develop precisely these skills. They describe the technical aspects of high-quality assessments in clear and understandable ways, and then extend that discussion to the real world of teachers. They don't try to disguise the challenges teachers face in developing good assessments and in using assessment results to make a real difference in student learning. They don't try to make it sound easy or effortless—because it isn't. Instead, what they do is lay out those challenges, describe them in ways that make sense, and then offer teachers practical guidance in addressing those challenges.

As Tyler made clear, gathering high-quality evidence on student learning is fundamental to effective teaching. Using high-quality assessments to offer students meaningful feedback on their learning progress and guide their next steps in the learning process has also been shown to be one of the most powerful ways to improve student learning. *Teacher-Made Assessments* gives teachers the knowledge and practical skills they need to do better what they have always wanted to do: Help all of their students learn excellently. Teachers who follow the guidance Chris and Leslie offer on these pages will be glad they did.

Thomas R. Guskey
University of Kentucky

Reference

Tyler, R. W. (1949). *Basic principles of curriculum and instruction*. Chicago, IL: University of Chicago Press.

About the Authors

Christopher R. Gareis, EdD, is Associate Professor of Educational Leadership at the College of William and Mary, where he also served as Associate Dean for teacher education for more than a decade. He teaches courses in instructional leadership, classroom assessment, program evaluation, curriculum development, and instructional strategies. Chris began his career as a high school English teacher, taught at the middle school level, and also served as an assistant principal, principal, and assistant to the superintendent. Chris regularly works with school districts in the areas of classroom-based assessment, mentoring, instructional leadership, strategic planning, and teacher evaluation. His publications include articles, chapters, and books on the topics of teacher preparation, mentoring, teacher portfolios, teacher compensation, principal self-efficacy, and classroom assessment. Chris earned his bachelor's degree in English and East Asian studies from Washington and Lee University, master's degree in English education from the College of William and Mary, and doctoral degree in educational leadership also from William and Mary.

Leslie W. Grant, PhD, is Assistant Professor of Educational Leadership at the College of William and Mary. She teaches courses in educational planning, assessment for educational leaders, and program evaluation. Leslie has been a teacher, an instructional leader, and a content editor and item writer for a major test publishing company. She works with school districts in the areas of using data to inform decision making, classroom-based assessment, and effective teaching practices. Her publications include articles, chapters in books, and books on the topics of assessment, international comparisons of teachers and student achievement, and effective teaching practices. Leslie earned her bachelor's degree in history, Russian language, and Russian area studies from James Madison University, master's degree in educational leadership from Old Dominion University, educational specialist's degree in curriculum and instruction from the George Washington University, and doctoral degree in educational policy, planning, and leadership from the College of William and Mary.

Acknowledgments

A project like this book is never simply the product of the work of the names on the front cover. Our understandings, conceptualizations, and even our ways of sharing our thinking in writing have undoubtedly been shaped by countless others, far too numerous to acknowledge here by name. We recognize and value the influences of our own teachers—from kindergarten through graduate school—who have been instrumental in shaping who we are as thinkers, researchers, and writers. We also recognize and value the tremendous influences of the many teachers and school leaders with whom we have worked in school and district settings, literally around the world. These colleagues and friends helped shaped us as practitioners, and we hope that we have been true to our school-based roots with this book.

We also thank our students, most especially the many undergraduate and graduate students with whom we have worked in the School of Education at the College of William and Mary. These talented and committed individuals are comprised of aspiring pre-service teachers as well as experienced teachers preparing for formal leadership roles in schools and school districts. Their questions, explorations, and insights in the context of our classes have immeasurably contributed to our own learning. In particular, we want to thank the six graduate students—all expert teachers in their own right—who wrote and contributed the Teacher-to-Teacher excerpts in chapter 2: Lindsey Caccavale, Karen Cagle, Nate Leach, Katie Moore, Charley Shrack, and Ann Vinson. Additionally, we greatly appreciate the proofreading, feedback, and perspectives of three talented graduate students: Linda Feldstein, Mary Vause, and Leah Shy Wilson.

In addition, we thank the many teachers and educational leaders with whom we have had the pleasure to work in our home state of Virginia, in other states throughout the United States, and in other countries such as China, Singapore, South Africa, and Taiwan. It is through working with educational professionals that we continue to refine our work, ensuring that it is germane and applicable in the current classroom. Much of the revisions within this second edition are a direct result of our experiences with pre-service teachers, experienced teachers, and educational leaders.

We would also like to thank two gentlemen who respectively represent the ideation and the realization of the first edition of this book: James Stronge and Bob Sickles. James, who is an internationally noted scholar and speaker, has been a support to us both throughout our careers. He provided the moral encouragement to pursue this project before the first word was ever written. You might say James envisioned this book before even we did. And, if that is the case of James, then it is Bob Sickles of Eye On Education who brought that vision to realization. Bob was a gracious and understanding publisher who helped bring the first edition to press. In addition, we thank Routledge for seeing the value in a second edition of our book. Specifically, we are deeply appreciative of our editor, Lauren Davis. Lauren's firm nudging, gentle patience, clear direction, and helpful support were invaluable throughout the process of conceptualizing, revising, and producing this second edition. We also owe a debt of gratitude to Tom Guskey. Tom graciously agreed to write the foreword for our second edition, which is a great honor for us. We are so appreciative of his willingness to do this, but, even more so, we are appreciative of the model of integrity, commitment, and wisdom that Tom provides as he tirelessly and constructively contributes to the evolution of the teaching profession.

Finally, an endeavor of this magnitude would not have been possible without the love and commitment of our families. Leslie would like to thank her husband, Allen, and son, Matthew, for their continued, unwavering support. Chris would like to thank his wife, Molly, and their children, Hance, Isabelle, and Anne Ryan, for being blessed reminders of the most important things in life. Chris also thanks his mom, dad, sisters, and brother for continuing to be his deep anchoring roots.

1

Why Should I Assess Student Learning in My Classroom?

Teaching, Learning, and Assessment

How do you define *teaching*?

Take a moment to reflect on how you define this term that we, as teachers, use so often. Chances are that your definition of *teaching* in some way includes mention of another term: namely, *learning*. That's because the act of teaching is not complete until learning has occurred. It's similar to the age-old rhetorical question: "If a tree falls in the forest and there is no one there to hear it, does it make a sound?" We in the education field may well ponder a similar question: "If a teacher teaches but no students have learned, has the teacher taught?" This question helps bring to light an important point: *Learning* is integral to the act of *teaching*.

When we learn, we change. That change may be in something we know, something we're able to do, or something we believe or value. Thus, as you consider how to define teaching, you must also consider teaching's *results* and how teaching brings about those results. With this in mind, we define **teaching** as the intentional creation and enactment of activities and experiences by one person that lead to changes in the knowledge, skills, and/or dispositions of another person. Note that our definition does not presume that students are blank slates on which a teacher writes. In fact, we view learning as the creation of meaning both by and within an individual. More specifically, we define **learning** as a relatively permanent change in knowledge, skills, and/ or dispositions precipitated by planned or unplanned experiences, events, activities, or interventions. Thus, for the act of teaching to be complete, it must result in learning within another.

Assessment and Learning

As obvious as the relationship between teaching and learning may be, what is less obvious is the *evidence* of learning. For example, when a young child learns to walk, the evidence of learning may be quite clear: We see the child walking; therefore, we know she has learned. This is true of all physical skills: We can quite literally *see* the learned behavior. However, in schools, most of our learning objectives for students are cognitive in nature rather than psychomotor. In other words, so much of what we teach in schools and what students are to learn resides in the mind and is *not* as readily apparent as a child walking.

So if teaching necessarily involves learning, an important corollary follows: How do teachers know what their students have learned? Teachers need some way of *seeing* learning.

The way teachers see student learning is through a process known as assessment, and assessment, like teaching, is integrally related to our definition of learning. We define **assessment** as the process of using tools and techniques to collect information about student learning. In other words, assessment is the way teachers *see* their students' learning.

Assessment and Teaching: The Light Bulb

There's a familiar image that teachers use to describe one of the most rewarding phenomena in teaching: the light bulb. Perhaps you've used the expression yourself. You're teaching a concept that is difficult for students to grasp. You attempt to get at it one way, and then you explain it in another way. You have the students wrestle with the concept, and you have them try to apply it. Then, you begin to see an almost imperceptible change in the facial expression of a student or two. You scaffold the class's thinking and provide encouragement and feedback. One student says, "Oh, I get it!" Another student's eyes seem to say, "Ah-ha!" The *light bulbs* are turning on. One by one, students grasp the concept. And you, as the teacher, are relying on your students' facial expressions, body language, and incidental comments as information about their learning. In other words, you are gathering evidence of student learning in your classroom. You are assessing.

Teachers—at least the truly excellent ones—are teachers because they derive so much personal satisfaction not only from the act of teaching but from their students' learning. Teachers are driven by a desire to make a positive difference in the lives of others by helping others grow, develop, and constructively evolve into their potential as individuals. Whether it's through teaching a first grader to read, mentoring a middle school student through a personal crisis while still managing to help him master fractions, or engendering a passion for historical research in a high school student, teaching is the conveyance of knowledge, the development of skills, and the fostering of dispositions in ways that become enabling of and meaningful to the learner. It's this motivation for others *to learn* that seems to be at the core of why effective teachers *teach* (Stronge, 2007). Central to this relationship between teaching and learning is the ability of a teacher to *discern* that students are, in fact, learning. Assessment—whether informal or formal—is the means by which a teacher knows what students are or are not learning. Assessment is integral to teaching.

Curriculum, Instruction . . . and Assessment

In a formal educational setting such as a school, the act of teaching and learning is comprised of two essential components: curriculum and instruction. **Curriculum** is the set of intended learning outcomes for students (Johnson, 1965). Put more plainly, curriculum is *what* we intend for students to know, be able to do, and value as a result of learning.

It follows then that instruction is *how* we bring about learning. **Instruction** is comprised of the planned and unplanned experiences provided by a teacher that are intended to result in the acquisition of a set of intended learning outcomes for students. In short, for teachers in schools, curriculum and instruction are the stuff of teaching and learning.

However, curriculum and instruction alone represent an incomplete model of teaching and learning in the classroom. In addition to knowing *what* to teach and *how* to teach it, a teacher must also be able to discern *the nature and degree of student learning* at any given point in time. Figure 1.1 represents these three elements in a simple visual metaphor: a stool.

This representation of curriculum, instruction, and assessment illustrates the integrated nature of the teaching and learning process. Teaching is *not* a singular event that perfectly and inevitably leads to learning. Rather, teaching is a recursive, interdependent activity that relies on teachers to determine accurately what students are learning, to what degree they are learning, and what they are *not* learning. Teaching relies on teachers' ability to collect information about student learning to make decisions about what to teach and how to teach next. In other words, assessment is integral to decisions that classroom teachers must make about both instruction and curriculum.

Figure 1.1 A Model of Curriculum, Instruction, and Assessment

STUDENT LEARNING

CURRICULUM

What we teach

ASSESSMENT

*The nature and degree of
student learning*

INSTRUCTION

How we teach

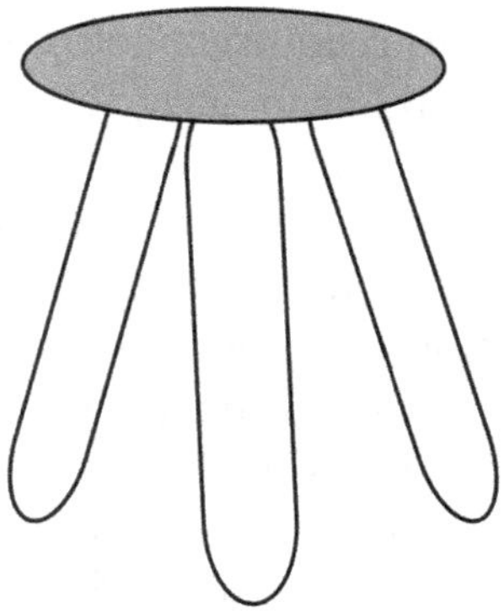

Understanding the integrated nature of curriculum, instruction, and assessment is one of the important foundations of effective teaching (Marzano, 2003; Stronge, 2007). However, it seems that assessment in the classroom is oftentimes unintentionally devalued. Consider some of the common misconceptions about assessment made by classroom teachers, shown in Figure 1.2.

Such common misconceptions about assessment in the classroom illustrate how the seemingly intuitive relationship among curriculum, instruction, and assessment (see Figure 1.1) can falter when teachers fail to grasp the various roles of assessment in the classroom. Without assessment, the act of teaching becomes a process focused only on the teachers' inputs of curriculum and instruction, as illustrated in Figure 1.3. Without assessment, student learning becomes absent from the teaching-and-learning process. If assessment is the means to discern student learning, then, in its absence, teaching becomes all

Figure 1.2 Teacher Voices: Common Misconceptions about Assessment in the Classroom

- ◆ "I give tests because I've gotta give grades."
- ◆ "Tests are a necessary evil: I hate giving them and students hate taking them."
- ◆ "Assessments don't have anything to do with teaching and learning."
- ◆ "Standardized assessments only require recall, so I teach recall."
- ◆ "My tests are valid and reliable because I use the test bank from our textbook."
- ◆ "I don't give my own assessments anymore because everything is tested with the district benchmark tests and the state tests."

Figure 1.3 Teaching and Learning in the Absence of Assessment

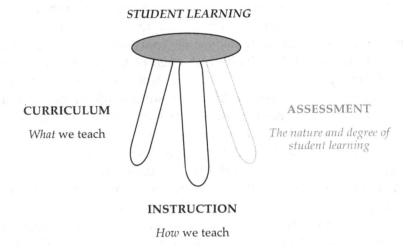

STUDENT LEARNING

CURRICULUM

What we teach

ASSESSMENT

The nature and degree of student learning

INSTRUCTION

How we teach

about teachers and their decisions and *not* about the students and their learning. As illustrated by the two-legged stool in Figure 1.3, teaching without assessment—that is, some means of determining the nature and degree of student learning—is about as dependable as a two-legged stool.

We do not fault teachers, though. In our experiences both as teachers and in working with teachers, assessment in the classroom is most often misused not for want of a conceptual understanding about the need to determine student learning but for want of a practical understanding about how to appropriately create and use assessments in the classroom. We begin to explore this next. Indeed, the focus and intent of this book is to help teachers create and utilize high quality assessments through better understanding the basic principles and techniques of assessment.

The Roles of Assessment in the Classroom

There are three fundamental roles of assessment in the classroom, and they are oftentimes distinguished by *when* they occur in relation to instruction:

1. **Pre-assessment** is the assessment of student learning prior to teaching.
2. **Formative assessment** is the assessment of student learning integrated into the act of teaching.
3. **Summative assessment** is the assessment of student learning at the end of some period of instruction.

Figure 1.4 provides a side-by-side comparison of pre-assessment, formative assessment, and summative assessment across a number of facets, including *why* to assess, *when* to assess, *what* to assess, and *how* to assess. This overview is intended to provide a comparison of the roles of assessment in the classroom and to distinguish each of the roles from the others.

Although this type of overview can be helpful, we caution teachers about interpreting Figure 1.4 too literally. In the day-to-day life of teachers, the fact is that the roles of assessment in the classroom oftentimes overlap. A 7th grade teacher, for example, may decide to use a discrepant event, such as students' observation of a three-leafed clover and a four-leafed clover, as a way to begin an inquiry-based model of instruction for a unit on genetics. During the portion of the activity when students are following their observations with possible ways to investigate the phenomenon, the teacher may informally assess students' abilities to generate hypotheses (Joyce, Weil, & Calhoun, 2015; Dean, Hubbell, Pitler, & Stone, 2012). In this situation, the teacher is using an activity that serves as both a pre-assessment of students' prior learning as well as a formative assessment to make decisions about the direction of the day's instruction.

By way of a second example, consider the classic term paper in a 10th grade English class. Clearly, a term paper—as suggested by the very name itself—is a comprehensive assessment of knowledge and skills developed over the course of an academic term. In this regard, a term paper is a summative assessment, and it often carries great weight in determining a student's grade for a marking period. Of course, the process of researching and writing the term paper is typically undertaken over a considerable period of time, with much direction and feedback from the teacher as each student completes various stages of the project, such as identifying a focused topic, conducting research, and developing a theme, followed by drafting, composing, and editing the paper itself. These processes and intermittent deadlines—as well as the teacher's close oversight, direction, and feedback to each student—constitute a series of formative assessments through which the student both gives evidence of her learning *and* refines her learning. Thus, the classic 10th grade English term paper suggests that assessments may serve roles that are both formative and summative.

With these two examples in mind, Figure 1.5 represents a more practical view of the three roles of assessment in the classroom. In this model, classroom assessment is viewed as a continuum along which the distinctions that separate pre-assessment from formative assessment and formative assessment from summative assessment become blurred. In fact, we contend that all classroom assessment is formative in nature in the following way: *All classroom assessment of student learning is ultimately intended to contribute to student learning.*

Figure 1.4 Comparison of the Three Roles of Assessment in the Classroom

	Pre-Assessment	Formative Assessment	Summative Assessment
When does assessment occur?	*Before* instruction	*During* instruction	*After* instruction
Why assess?	• To determine the prior knowledge and / or entering skills of students in order to plan instruction • To establish a baseline of learning in order to show student growth after instruction • To trigger previous learning	• To make instructional decisions in the near term • To provide honest, timely, specific, accurate, and constructive feedback to students • To develop students' capacity for self-evaluation and self-directed learning	• To judge the nature and degree of student learning • To communicate the nature and degree of student learning to others • To make decisions about the efficacy of curriculum, instruction, and assessment in the long-term
What is the extent of an assessment's coverage?	Either *focused* or *comprehensive*, depending on the intended use	*Focused* on discrete knowledge or a particular skill set	*Comprehensive* of some period of instruction and some set of knowledge and / or skills
What are the typical consequential outcomes of an assessment?	*High stakes* if used for placement decisions *Low stakes* if used for instructional planning	*Low stakes*—typically related to day-to-day decisions about teaching and learning	*High stakes*—can determine future placement, remediation, honors designations, etc.
Who primarily uses the results of the assessment?	Teacher	Teacher and students	Teacher, students, and third parties (such as parents, administrators, and guidance counselors)
How is the assessment typically done?	• pre-tests • interviews • class discussions • brainstorming activities • reviews of cumulative records	• observations of facial expressions, body language, and comments • handraising, thumbs up / down, personal whiteboards, exit cards, personal response systems, etc. • in-class guided practice • paper-pencil quizzes	• paper-pencil tests, quizzes, essays, and papers • projects, demonstrations, performances, checklist observations, and original creations • standardized tests

Figure 1.5 The Continuum of Classroom Assessment

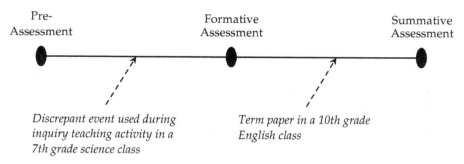

Assessment Matters: Improving Student Learning

Although the role of assessment in teaching has long been understood, what has been less evident is the effect that assessment practices in the classroom can have on the quality of teaching and the improvement of student learning. Does assessment matter in improving student learning? Research in recent years suggests that it does. Consider some of the research findings about assessment:

- ◆ Improved formative assessment practices in classrooms typically yield gains in student achievement roughly equivalent to one to two grade levels in learning (Assessment Reform Group, 1999).
- ◆ Teachers' use of feedback can have among the most statistically significant effects on student achievement as compared to other possible influences on learning (Hattie, 2009).
- ◆ How teachers conceptualize and use assessments in the classroom directly influences student engagement and learning (McMillan, 2013).

This sample of studies is illustrative of our growing understanding of assessment not only as a *measure* of student learning but also as a *means* to student learning. With all due respect to these researchers, however, the idea is not entirely new. Arguably, the practice of using assessment to improve student learning has been around as long as teaching has. Looking back a few millennia, we are reminded that Socrates's *modus docendi*—that is, his "preferred way of teaching"—was to *question* his students. What we now call the Socratic method essentially amounts to the use of questioning to assess students' understanding, guide their learning, and, ultimately, foster their ability to think critically. In other words, the Socratic method is a means of teaching *through assessment*.

Assessment and the Accountability Movement

The image of Socrates questioning his students on the steps of a public forum in Greece presents a benign image of assessment. Unfortunately, we live in an era today that many teachers consider far from benign (MetLife, 2013). In the contemporary public policy arena, the education profession has been strongly buffeted by the forces of the accountability movement. The emphasis on accountability in education is often traced to the seminal report of the Education Commission of the States published in 1983 titled *A Nation At Risk*, in which public schools in the United States were said to be characterized by a "rising tide of mediocrity" (National Commission on Excellence in Education, 1983, p. 5). Although schools in the United States have been subject to answering the call of citizens, business leaders, and policymakers to meet the real and perceived needs of society since as far back as Horace Mann's first organization of common schools in the 1800s, *A Nation At Risk* articulated for the first time a strident view from the federal government that public schools should be held to account for the academic achievement—and even the societal outcomes—of the educational process.

During the ensuing decades between 1983 and 2002, the federal government and the governors of all 50 states moved the nation toward an increasingly defined system of identified educational standards and accountability measures, leading to the passage of the landmark law *No Child Left Behind* (NCLB) in 2002 (Manna, 2006). Central to NCLB is its mandate for schools to be accountable for demonstrating that all students—regardless of race, gender, economic status, English language ability, or disability—achieve adequate yearly progress toward meeting a state's respective educational standards. Several years later, the federal government's demands for accountability reached even farther under the *Race to the Top* (RTTT) competitive funding initiative (Office of the Press Secretary, 2009). States were incentivized to develop a set of college and career readiness standards that would be common across the country (the Common Core State Standards), and states were also prompted to develop teacher and principal performance evaluation systems based on student growth or value-added models (VAM). And how is student growth to be demonstrated? Through performance on standardized assessments, alternate versions of which have been under development by the Partnership for Assessment of Readiness for College and Careers (PARCC) and the Smarter Balanced Assessment Consortium (SBAC).

We should say at this point that our aim here is not to argue the relative merits (there are many) and the erroneous assumptions (there are quite a few of these, too) of NCLB and RTTT as federal educational policies. Instead, our intent is to point out the effect that these policies have had on the role of assessment in the classroom. To state the case briefly, the confluence of the articulation of state standards, the advent of school and educator evaluation systems focused on measured student growth, and the profusion of standardized assessments has put an extraordinary emphasis on assessment as something *external to* the teaching and learning that takes place in the classroom. So, although our purer understanding of teaching and learning has us value assessment as *integral to* the educational process, the current era of accountability has shifted the thinking of many teachers to view assessment as something that is *done to* their students and, by extension, is *done to* teachers, too. In other words, assessment is viewed quite negatively by many teachers in the present day.

Teachers' impressions about standardized assessments are not without justification. Because standardized assessments have begun to carry high stakes for individual students, teachers, school leaders, districts, and states, a number of unintended consequences are becoming increasingly evident. Figure 1.6 summarizes some of the most insidious effects of high-stakes standardized tests associated with the accountability movement.

There's little question that the unintended consequences shared in Figure 1.6 constitute negative effects on our public education system. However, it's not our position that standardized assessments should be abandoned, nor do we advocate a wholesale dismantling of federal education policy. Standardized assessments, when administered and used properly, can provide valuable information regarding a student's, a school's, and a school district's achievement relative to certain legitimate, intended educational outcomes. There are a limited number of instances where the use of high-stakes assessments has led to positive effects, such as broadening the content of the curriculum, the integration of knowledge across the curriculum, and increased use of student-centered, cooperative instructional strategies (Au, 2007). But such instances are not the norm; therefore, we contend that informed professional judgment should guide the substantive revision of both policy and practice regarding standardized assessments.

Indeed, one of the aims of this book is to contribute to the diffusion of professional knowledge about assessment among aspiring and practicing teachers so that teachers can be excellent creators of classroom assessments and excellent consumers of standardized assessment results. With this in mind, it is helpful to consider how both types of assessments—that is, classroom assessments and standardized assessments—contribute to the process of finding out about student learning. Figure 1.7 presents a side-by-side comparison that helps illustrate the positive and complementary roles that the two types of assessments play.

Figure 1.6 Negative Unintended Consequences of High-Stakes Standardized Tests

Unintended Consequence	Explanation
Lack of test validity leads to incomplete and inaccurate inferences about student learning	Not all standards are able to be assessed on objective standardized tests; therefore, results on these tests can lead to inaccurate inferences about what students truly know or are able to do (Popham, 2005). Consider these educational outcomes as examples: ◆ The student designs and conducts an original scientific experiment. ◆ The student researches and composes a factually based interpretation of historical events. ◆ The student creates, orally presents, and defends a persuasive argument. Such outcomes are inarguably complex and represent the highest levels of cognitive behavior, yet current standardized tests are incapable of assessing a student's mastery of them (Wagner, 2008). Would anyone want to draw conclusions about a student's learning of science, history, or language arts without some such performance? We imagine not. *Thus, standardized tests ultimately provide incomplete representations of educational outcomes.*
The curriculum is narrowed	Continuing from the earlier explanation, when the standards that are actually assessed on a high-stakes test are narrowed because some standards (oftentimes the most important standards) are simply not conducive to being assessed in a standardized format, then there is the danger that teachers will teach primarily—if not exclusively—to the standards that are tested. This over-focus on the tested standards can result in breadth of coverage rather than depth of understanding (Clarke, Shore, Rhoades, Abrams, Miao, & Li, 2003). *Even more damaging can be the effect that some important curricular objectives do not get taught at all* (Wagner, 2008). Some teachers rationalize that it is better to over-teach a tested standard than to teach a non-tested standard. After all, they are not externally judged on students' performance on the non-tested standards. In some cases, schools and school districts make the decision to drop courses in non-tested subject areas such as art and music from the curriculum altogether!
Instruction is deadened	Rightly or wrongly, many teachers believe that standardized assessments are largely tests of recall and basic understanding. As their own performance evaluations become tied to students' performance on such assessments, teachers tend to teach to these tests and, therefore, also tend to teach less creatively (Nichols & Berliner, 2005). *Test-prep, scripted lessons, and "drill-and-kill" are instructional strategies associated with some teachers' misguided attempts to meet the challenge of high-stakes testing* (Kozol, 2005).

Figure 1.6 (Continued)

Unintended Consequence	Explanation
Lack of test reliability leads to undependable inferences about student learning	State standardized tests are intentionally designed to assess hundreds of thousands of students at a time in as objective a manner as possible, and to report results to state and district officials and to the public as quickly as possible. Typically, high-stakes tests consist of 25–50 or so multiple choice questions per subject area. *The reliability of such tests (that is, the degree to which we can depend on a student's score being a dependable indication of their learning) is threatened by certain limitations.* First, the limited number of items on a test (for instance, 30 questions to assess an entire school year of instruction in 4th grade mathematics) means that a content strand within a subject area may be assessed by one or two questions on the test. If a student misses (or gets correct) one of these two questions purely by chance, then an inaccurate inference about student learning is formed. Second, standardized assessments are single measures in time. Standardized tests do not provide for repeated measures to gauge the consistency of a student's performance over time. Thus, if a student performs poorly on testing day purely by chance, illness, unrequited love, or any other of a hundred reasons, then an inference about the nature or degree of his learning is undependable.
Some people resort to cheating	The higher the stakes, the more people have to lose. Therefore, the more likely some people are to cheat in order to avoid negative consequences that could result in the loss of income or one's job. A cursory review of a few major newspapers makes this point disappointingly obvious: ◆ Principals and teachers in five states resign after improperly aiding students on state exams (Magnuson, 2000) ◆ Teachers are investigated in cheating probe (Axtman, 2005) ◆ A director of testing is accused of changing student answer sheets and filling in unanswered questions (Burney, 2007) ◆ A superintendent is sentenced to prison for manipulating enrollment in order to boost performance on state assessments (Zubrycki, 2012) ◆ More than 130 educators in a large urban school district face disciplinary action for alleged cheating, tampering with public records, and forgery involving state exams (Maxwell, 2014). It is important to note that the cheating in these cases is oftentimes conspiratorial (that is, involving more than one person) and involves adult professionals. These people were willing to risk their livelihoods and, in the case of criminal conviction, their very freedom to falsify results. High stakes, indeed.

Figure 1.7 The Roles of Standardized and Classroom Assessments

Standardized Assessments Can Provide ...	Classroom Assessments Can Provide ...
Standardized conditions and, therefore, *comparison* among students, schools, districts, and even states	*Tailored or unique* assessments, which take into account the *particular characteristics* of students and the specific contextual factors of a classroom or school setting
Annual assessment information, which is indicative of *prevailing trends* among a population one year to the next	*Timely assessment information*, which is indicative of student learning over a particular instructional unit and progress toward mastery of either discrete or broad-reaching objectives
Validity in that they are typically aligned with the *state curriculum standards*	*Validity* in that they are typically more responsive to the *taught curriculum*—that is, the objectives that students actually had the opportunity to learn through instruction
Reliability in that they are typically constructed to be delivered under highly controlled conditions, objectively graded, and systematically subject to reviews to eliminate ineffective or inappropriate items	*Authenticity* in that classroom-based assessments often take the form of assignments that tap depth of content and breadth of skills—assignments such as extended writing and essays, projects, cooperative assignments, labs, demonstrations, and performances
Summative assessments of learning that are indicative of achievement of a comprehensive set of knowledge and/or skills, typically inclusive of a year or more of instruction	*Formative* assessments, the results of which may be used to provide timely, specific, constructive feedback to students and to allow teachers to make instructional decisions to support continued learning
High-stakes evaluation information that can be used to make judgments about the nature and degree of student, teacher, school, district, and/or state performance	*Low-stakes* (relatively speaking) evaluation information that can be used to communicate the nature and degree of learning to students, parents, teachers, and other education professionals

We should note that in Figure 1.7 we have looked at both standardized and classroom assessments in a decidedly positive way. To be sure, there can be drawbacks to either. However, neither standardized tests nor classroom assessments alone are sufficient to meet the needs of teachers to accurately and dependably gauge and thereby support continued student learning. Again, we contend that teachers must have proficient understanding and ability to employ both.

Assessment as a Professional Competency

Inarguably, assessment is playing an increasingly central role in education. Therefore, the imperative for teachers to understand and employ not only standardized assessments but, more importantly, classroom assessments is greater than ever before (Guskey, 2003; Guskey & Jung, 2013). Teachers must be as proficient in the area of assessment as they have traditionally been in the areas of curriculum and instruction. Indeed, we strongly contend that assessment must be viewed as a professional competency that every teacher should be required to develop and demonstrate for purposes of licensure. We're not alone in this thought. A review of state licensure standards for teachers illustrates the value placed on assessment as a professional competency. Figure 1.8 presents several examples of language from state licensure standards.

We should reiterate that the states presented in Figure 1.8 represent a random sample and that similar language is found in the licensure regulations among all 50 states. We should also note that we've presented excerpts only. In a number of states, the general language regarding assessment (as presented in Figure 1.8) is followed by specific responsibilities that comprise expected assessment practices of classroom teachers.

At the risk of oversimplifying a complex professional competency, we contend that there is a core set of knowledge and skills that all teachers should possess relative to assessment. We refer to this as **assessment literacy**—the ability to create and use valid and reliable assessments as a classroom teacher to facilitate and communicate student learning. More specifically, we hold that assessment literacy fundamentally involves a teacher's ability to:

- ◆ Articulate and unpack intended learning outcomes;
- ◆ Understand and appreciate the purposes and various forms that classroom assessment can take;
- ◆ Ensure the alignment of classroom assessment instruments and techniques to the content and cognitive demand of intended learning outcomes;
- ◆ Ensure the representative balance of intended learning outcomes on assessments;
- ◆ Create and use selected- and constructed-response assessment items and activities appropriately;
- ◆ Ensure that student performance on classroom assessments are not unduly influenced by systematic and random error;
- ◆ Use formative assessment techniques and feedback to progress student learning;
- ◆ Use student performance on assessments to communicate student learning to others and to make instructional and curricular decisions.

Figure 1.8 Sample Language from State Teacher Licensure Regulations Regarding Assessment

State	Excerpted Language from Licensure Regulations
Alabama[1]	Engages with colleagues to develop and refine common summative assessment options to demonstrate learners' knowledge and skills and to respond to learners' needs in relation to learning targets.
Florida[2]	The effective educator consistently analyzes and applies data from multiple assessments and measures to diagnose students' learning needs, informs instruction based on those needs, and drive the learning process.
Georgia[3]	Teachers understand and use a range of formal and informal assessment strategies to evaluate and ensure the continuous development of all learners.
Missouri[4]	The teacher understands and uses formative and summative assessment strategies to assess the learner's progress, uses assessment data to plan ongoing instruction, monitors the performance of each student, and devises instruction to enable students to grow and develop.
New Mexico[5]	The teacher effectively utilizes student assessment techniques and procedures . . . (A) Uses a variety of assessment tools and strategies. (B) Uses summative and formative assessment for remediation and instructional planning. (C) Maintains documentation of student progress. (D) Communicates student progress to students and families in a timely manner.
Oklahoma[6]	The teacher understands and uses a variety of assessment strategies to evaluate and modify the teaching/learning process ensuring the continuous intellectual, social and physical development of the learner.
Rhode Island[7]	Teachers use appropriate formal and informal assessment strategies with individuals and groups of students to determine the impact of instruction on learning, to provide feedback, and to plan future instruction.
Vermont[8]	The teacher understands and uses multiple methods of assessment to engage learners in their own growth, to monitor learner progress, and to guide the teacher's and learner's decision making.
Wisconsin[9]	The teacher understands and uses formal and informal assessment strategies to evaluate and ensure the continuous intellectual, social, and physical development of the pupil.

[1] Alabama Department of Education EDUCATE Alabama/LEAD Alabama. (n.d.). *Alabama Continuum for Teacher Development.* Retrieved from http://alex.state.al.us/leadership/Alabama%20Continuum%20for%20Teacher%20 Development.pdf.

[2] Florida Department of Education. (2011). *The Educator Accomplished Practices.* Retrieved from https://www.flrules. org/gateway/ruleNo.asp?id=6A-5.065.

[3] Georgia Systemic Teacher Education Program. (n.d.). *GSTEP Framework Guiding Principles.* Retrieved from http://www. coe.uga.edu/gstep/documents/index.html.

[4] Missouri Department of Elementary and Secondary Education. (2013). *Missouri Model Teacher and Leader Standards.* Retrieved from http://dese.mo.gov/eq/documents/StandardsInformationDocument.pdf.

[5] Teach New Mexico. (n.d.). *NM Teacher Competencies.* Retrieved from http://teachnm.org/experienced-teachers/nm-teacher-competencies.html.

[6] Oklahoma Commission for Teacher Preparation. (n.d.). *General Competencies for Licensure.* Retrieved from http://www. octp.org/general_competencies_for_licensure.html.

[7] Rhode Island Board of Regents for Elementary and Secondary Education. (2007). *Rhode Island Professional Teaching Standards.* Retrieved from https://www.ride.ri.gov/Portals/0/Uploads/Documents/Teachers-and-Administrators-Excellent-Educators/Educator-Certification/Cert-main-page/RIPTS-with-preamble.pdf.

[8] Vermont Department of Education. (2013). *Rules Governing the Licensure of Educators and the Preparation of Education Professionals.* Retrieved from http://education.vermont.gov/documents/educ_5100_licensing_regulations.pdf.

[9] Wisconsin Department of Public Instruction. (n.d.). *Teacher Education Program Approval and Licenses.* Retrieved from http://dpi.state.wi.us/tepdl/pi34.html#teacherstandards3402.

These competencies are our conceptualization of the key knowledge and skills that comprise assessment literacy, and we recognize that there are other assessment-related competencies that are important for teachers to possess (Kahl, Hofman, & Bryant, 2013). However, our focus is on the key competencies of assessment literacy upon which a more comprehensive set of professional practices of teachers and instructional leaders can then be built. Think of this list as being at the center of a set of concentric circles, where the next layer of competencies might include a teacher's or a principal's ability to develop diagnostic and benchmark assessments, to analyze standardized assessment results, and to empirically demonstrate measurable student growth (Kahl, Hofman, & Bryant, 2013). Additional, more sophisticated assessment literacies would extend in concentric circles beyond these in such a model—competencies that might be the purview of a district assessment coordinator, for example. Again, though, our focus is on the centrally important set of knowledge and skills that comprise assessment literacy for classroom teachers.

Strengthening Teachers' Assessment Literacy

How did most practicing classroom teachers learn how to assess student learning? There seem to be some typical scenarios:

- Some of us learned everything we know about assessing student learning by virtue of the fact that we were once students. In other words, we formed our understanding of how to assess students based on our past experiences taking tests and quizzes ourselves.
- Many of us completed one or more courses in instructional methods as part of our teacher preparation programs, and assessment was covered—to some degree or another—within the context of those courses. However, it may also have been that assessment was given a good deal less attention than was given to issues of curriculum planning and instructional delivery. Assessment in such courses is often given short shrift, if for no other reason than lack of time.
- For others, our formal training in assessment occurred within the context of a course in educational testing and measurement. But oftentimes in such courses, the focus is on the psychometric principles of assessment that, while important, are not necessarily translated into practical usage in the classroom.

Of course, there are others among us who have had the benefit of formal and effective preparation through a course or through professional development experiences. However, in our own personal and professional experiences as teachers and working with teachers, individuals with such preparation are *not* the norm. This isn't a condemnation of these teachers. (In fact, we are two teachers among those with little formal preparation prior to entering the classroom.) Rather, our anecdotal experiences with teachers have illuminated for us the need in the profession for current classroom teachers to develop their knowledge and skills in the area of assessment—that is, to strengthen their *assessment literacy*.

But our anecdotal impressions are not enough to undertake our writing (and your reading!) of an entire book on the topic. So, we look to other evidence of this need:

- ◆ The emphasis on assessment as a core teacher competency is relatively new. In 1983, a survey of state teacher certification standards revealed that only 10 states specifically required course work in assessment. The same was true in a follow-up study of requirements in 1989 (Wolmut, as cited in Stiggins & Conklin, 1992).
- ◆ As of the year 2000, only 14 states explicitly required demonstrated competence in assessment for teacher licensure, and only three required it of administrators (Atkin, Black, & Coffey, 2001). That means there's a strong likelihood that most current teachers who completed their professional preparation 10 to 30 years ago have gaps in their knowledge and skills regarding assessment.
- ◆ The Student Evaluation Standards, which were developed by the Joint Committee on Standards for Educational Evaluation, were not published until 2003. These standards provide a comprehensive overview of assessment competencies for educators, but more than a decade later, dissemination of the standards has been slow and the impact on practice not widespread.
- ◆ Educational researchers have identified assessment as a gap in the professional practice of classroom teachers (McMillan, 2013). In one study, researchers reviewed teachers' professional portfolios, which documented performance in five domains of teacher responsibility, including planning for instruction, instructional delivery, assessment of student learning, classroom management, and professionalism. Of these five domains, assessment was the area least adequately documented among teachers (Tucker, Stronge, Gareis, & Beers, 2003).
- ◆ Educational reformers recognize the shortcomings of many teachers' classroom assessment practices. For example, Schmoker (2006) drew the following conclusion based on his observations in classrooms across the United States: "It became apparent that student

assessment was surprisingly rare and haphazard. Students would spend days, even weeks, on activities without being assessed. A surprising proportion of student work was handed in but never returned—or returned weeks later, often without written feedback, and with no chance to revise" (p. 86).

◆ The United States is not alone. Similar concerns about teachers' classroom assessment practices exist internationally (O'Leary, 2008; Tierney, 2006).

◆ Research suggests that assessment literacy rarely seems to be the focus of professional development (Wenglinsky, 2000), and that professional development has not been particularly effective when it has been provided (Black, 2013; Popham, 2009).

◆ Even among new teachers, assessment is an area of need (DeLuca & Bellara, 2013). In a study of first-year teachers, assessment was the weakest competency on average when compared to the competencies of novice teachers in instructional delivery and classroom management (Good, McCaslin, Tsang, Zhang, Wiley, & Bozack, 2006).

From this brief review of findings from the field as well as from our own experiences from more than 25 years in the profession, it is evident to us that many teachers can gain from improving their professional knowledge and skills in the area of classroom assessment. Therefore, this book aims to help teachers become more competent creators, consumers, and communicators about classroom assessments in order to contribute to student learning.

Our audience for this book is, first and foremost, the classroom teacher. As former classroom teachers ourselves, we recognize that teachers are busy . . . very, very busy. A teacher might have 20 to 200 students to whom to attend on any given day; parents with whom to communicate; non-instructional duties intended to contribute to the smooth running of the school; and, somewhere in there, a personal life, too. So, we have sought to write a book that provides essential information, develops practical skills, and is written in what we hope is a professional but accessible style.

We should point out that this book is not a comprehensive tome on educational assessment, and it is not a scholarly epistle intended to change the way the profession views assessment. There are places for such works, and there are many excellent examples of them available to you. In fact, we reference quite a few throughout this book. But we have worked to write a book for current and aspiring classroom teachers who are seeking to improve their ability to determine what their students learned from them yesterday, or during the past week, or this semester.

We also have written this book with a practical understanding of the current educational context—namely, a greatly increased emphasis on and scrutiny of teachers' impact on student learning. With this in mind, the targeted audience for this book is teachers in K–12 schools, as well as the principals, assistant principals, and other instructional leaders of these schools. In our effort to keep this book to a manageable length, we have chosen to draw mostly on examples from grades 2–12 and from the core content areas of English/language arts, mathematics, science, and social studies. Nevertheless, the principles of assessment that we share are applicable to teachers in the early primary grades (K–1) and across all subject areas, including art, foreign languages, health and physical education, and career and technical education. We have also provided some such additional descriptions and examples, and this second edition includes a number of new examples that draw upon the Common Core State Standards (National Governors Association Center for Best Practices & Council of Chief State School Officers [NGA & CCSSO], 2010).

Another acknowledgement of the current educational context is reflected in our decision to focus on discussion and examples on teacher-made, classroom assessments. As we explained previously in this chapter, we define *assessment* as the use of techniques and tools to gather information about student learning, and we hold a broad view of what types of techniques and tools might be used for this purpose. Figure 1.9 presents several anchor points on what we have referred to as the spectrum of classroom assessment.

This spectrum is not intended to be comprehensive; rather, we offer it here to represent our understanding of assessment. Assessment is sometimes undertaken as a technique or strategy, such as reading facial expressions, observing student activity, or asking questions and then having students reply orally or perhaps with a thumbs-up or thumbs-down. Such techniques gravitate toward the left of this spectrum and would be characterized as being less formal and less objective but more integrated into instruction and more formative in terms of a teacher's ability to integrate student performance into progressing their learning immediately. At the other end of the spectrum, there are techniques and also tools or instruments that are more formally

Figure 1.9 The Spectrum of Classroom Assessments

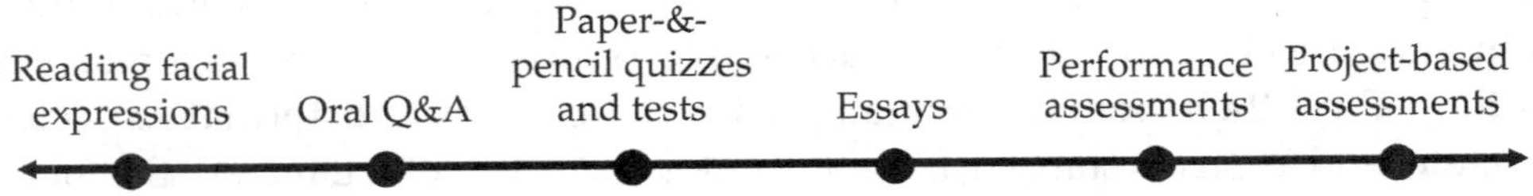

Reading facial expressions — Oral Q&A — Paper-&-pencil quizzes and tests — Essays — Performance assessments — Project-based assessments

structured, typically are more comprehensive, and require more involvement on the part of students to complete and on the part of the teacher to create and to evaluate. The middle of our spectrum includes some well-known tools or instruments of classroom assessment—quizzes, tests, and essays. When well made, such tools can be tightly aligned to the intended and taught curriculum, can provide some degree of comprehensiveness, can provide valid and reliable evidence of student learning, and can be an important source of feedback.

Classroom assessment can and should take many forms (Guskey, 2009). And an important related point is that the basic principles of assessment are applicable to all of these possible techniques and tools. For purposes of illustrating the key principles of assessment in this book, we will most often refer to teacher-made tests. A **test**, as we are using the term in this book, is a deliberately designed, representative set of written questions and/or prompts to which students respond in written form, intended to measure the acquisition of certain knowledge, skills, and/or dispositions. Admittedly, this is a rather weighty definition, but the basic concept of what a classroom test is intended to do is simple enough: A teacher's test is intended to determine the nature and degree of student acquisition of a set of intended learning outcomes after some period of instruction. Given the prevalence of tests as a very common means of determining student learning, our focus is on the characteristics of and basic principles for constructing good tests for the classroom. However, the principles and techniques presented throughout this book can and should be applied to the full spectrum of classroom assessments, which we will also address throughout.

Finally, we should also explain our larger aim with this book. Simply put, our intention is to influence the professional practice of as many teachers as we can so they can ultimately teach more effectively and, therefore, their students can learn more successfully and more meaningfully. In other words, we hope we can teach teachers—including pre-service teachers—something useful and valuable through this book. And we hope it helps teachers, in turn, to teach useful and valuable things to their students.

Overview of the Book

In keeping with the aim of the first edition of this book, the second edition is intended to be a practical and accessible resource for classroom teachers as they align their own assessments with the content and format expected of state and district standards-based curricula. We've organized the book into seven chapters:

- ◆ Chapter 1 provides a rationale for the focus of the book situated within teaching and also within the current context of the accountability era.
- ◆ Chapter 2 lays out a foundational understanding of key principles of assessment, focusing on the concepts of validity and reliability in both theoretical and practical terms.
- ◆ Chapter 3 presents the process of constructing assessments as seven steps, and it illustrates the critical task of unpacking a standards-based curriculum and designing classroom assessments that are aligned in content as well as in the level of cognitive demand expected of students. In this second edition of the book, we have also extended the practical uses of a table of specifications to critique and strengthen current assessments and to conceptualize a unit assessment plan. In our work with in-service teachers during the past several years, these uses and skills have been particularly valued by teachers and school leaders alike.
- ◆ Chapter 4 explains and illustrates how to create selected-response items, with a particular focus on multiple choice items, and also introduces characteristics of technology-enhanced items that are being used increasingly on state assessments.
- ◆ Chapter 5 explains and illustrates the use of constructed-response items, with special attention to short answer and essay prompts and the development of scoring criteria. A new conceptual model is introduced in this edition to guide teachers' creation of constructed-response items and assessment activities.
- ◆ Chapter 6 illustrates a process for analyzing student results on an assessment and describes the crucial role of feedback in making use of classroom assessment results to support student learning.
- ◆ Chapter 7 expands the focus of the book by describing a number of specific ways in which classroom teachers—equipped with meaningful understandings of the purposes and means of appropriate classroom assessment—can constructively influence the professional practice of other educators in their schools and districts.

Throughout this second edition, we have updated references, included new examples, and integrated samples and insights that we have garnered from our continuing work with classroom teachers literally around the world. We continue to learn so much from our colleagues in K–12 schools as we work with them to strengthen their classroom assessment practices, and we sincerely hope that you find the second edition of *Teacher-Made Assessments* relevant to your practice as a professional teacher.

2

What Makes a Good Assessment?

Assessment and Learning

As a student, did you ever take a test that you simply thought was unfair? Maybe the questions seemed so complex that you couldn't figure out what was even being asked. Perhaps none of what you studied seemed to be on the test. Maybe you were so distracted by another student in the class that you couldn't concentrate during the test. Perhaps you received a lower grade than you expected because you suspected the teacher's answer key was incorrect. Whatever the scenario, there were likely some rather predictable results from the test experience. First, your grade on the test was probably not what you hoped it would be. Second, you probably felt frustrated by—and maybe even angry about—the experience. You probably felt your grade on the test did not accurately reflect what you actually knew about the content being tested.

If you have ever had a similar experience, you understand the basic principles of good assessment in the classroom. Namely, when a teacher uses a test, quiz, project, performance, or some other assessment to determine the nature and degree of student learning, the teacher must ensure that the assessment is both *valid* and *reliable*. These two terms are, no doubt, familiar to you. But, as commonplace as the terms are and as frequently as teachers may use them, teachers oftentimes flounder when specifically applying these principles to their own construction and use of assessments in the classroom.

In this chapter, we explore what it means for a teacher-made assessment to be valid and reliable. We should point out that our intent is neither a comprehensive nor an esoterically nuanced explanation of these concepts. Instead, our intent is to help you refine your *practical* understanding of both validity and reliability so that you can apply these principles in your day-to-day responsibilities as a classroom teacher constructing and using your own assessments.

Validity and Reliability in Everyday Life

People use the terms *valid* and *reliable* all the time, and not just in educational settings. For example, an informal conversation between friends debating the merits of a local politician's tax proposal leads to one of the friends responding to the other, "You can't say that. Your point's just not *valid*!" A woman at the counter of the cell phone kiosk says to the salesclerk, "I'm not happy with my phone. I never know when I'll have reception and when I won't. It's just not *reliable*." In common, everyday situations like these, the terms *valid* and *reliable* have generally understood meanings. Consider this:

- When we say *valid*, we're likely to mean *truthful, suitable, legitimate, applicable, convincing,* or *compelling*.
- When we say *reliable*, we're likely to mean *dependable, consistent, stable,* or *error free*.

To explore the common understandings of these concepts further, we asked a group of veteran teachers to tell us about situations in their own experiences in which *validity* and *reliability* were at play. But, as a catch, we asked them about situations from *everyday life*—that is, their experiences outside of the classroom. Three of these are presented in the following boxes, called "Teacher-to-Teacher." As you read, keep in mind that this is a fellow teacher *talking* to you in her or his own voice. We have not changed the wording at all, although we have highlighted in bold typeface certain key words that these teachers used in their explanations.

Teacher-to-Teacher

Reliability in Everyday Life: Strep Test
A recent experience my son and I had illustrates the concept of **reliability** and its relationship to **inferences** that may follow a test. In this case, it was

a medical test—the rapid strep throat test used to diagnose the presence of strep throat infection. Is the rapid strep throat test a **reliable** way to **accurately** diagnose the presence of the streptococcal bacteria on the throat? Well, only sort of. As many as 33% of the tests completed report a negative result when the streptococcal bacteria is actually present in the throat. Due to the **unreliability** of the rapid strep test, a throat culture often follows a negative result to ensure a **reliable** diagnosis. So, the rapid strep throat test is adequate for making an initial diagnosis in a clinic, but it is not **dependable** enough to draw a conclusive diagnosis.

Ann
Elementary Teacher

Teacher-to-Teacher

Validity in Everyday Life: *American Idol*

On the television show *American Idol*, each week millions of viewers assess the performances of a variety of singers and vote to determine the next pop artist. The contestants are challenged to sing different songs from different genres. Critiques from the show's judges who work in the entertainment industry may or may not influence the votes of the viewing public. It is **inferred** that the winner of the competition will become a successful entertainer. Because performers are sometimes asked to sing songs that are not suitable for their voices or because they may not have the charisma of others, they may lose favor with the audience and not earn enough votes to keep them in the competition. Some voters may rally for the "underdog" or who they perceive as the least talented competitor. When this happens, the assessment no longer is a **true measure** of vocal talent, stage presence, and other **attributes** that ensure success in the entertainment industry. There is also no information about how the opinions of the voters represent the overall American public. These factors question the **validity** of the competition's results. Although many former contestants, some of whom were not the winners of the competition, have been successful when tested in the real world of entertainment, few have achieved the true status of *American Idol*, so the competition has only limited **predictive value**.

Karen
Middle School Teacher

Teacher-to-Teacher

Reliability in Everyday Life: Referees

As a coach, player, and avid sports fan, I appreciate **reliability** on the field of play within the realm of athletics. In this situation, **reliability** relates to the officials. Most people don't like to say they won or lost because of the officiating, but all would agree they look for **consistency** from their officials. Both teams want **an even opportunity** to compete and win, and they hold the officials accountable to call the game in a **fair** manner. While most home teams rely on the officials for a few calls, I believe most would agree that they would prefer a fair game as opposed to one won with controversy. A game in which the rules of the sport are applied **consistently** is a fair game. This is **reliable** officiating.

Nate
High School Teacher

Validity and Reliability of Teacher-Made Assessments

The principles of validity and reliability function in the realm of teacher-made assessments essentially in the same way as they function in the *everyday life* scenarios just presented. In short, validity is concerned with the truthfulness or appropriateness of decisions resulting from assessments, and reliability is concerned with the dependability or stability of those results. One common means of visually depicting these concepts is by thinking of validity as an archery target and thinking of reliability as the results of shots at the target. This is visually presented in Figure 2.1.

The first picture in Figure 2.1 is a visual metaphor of a valid and reliable assessment. The intended target—the bull's eye in the center of the circular target—is struck shot after shot. This suggests that the correct target is being aimed at and that the target is being hit consistently. Thus, validity and reliability are evident.

In the second depiction, the shots land consistently at a particular location. Thus, the shots are reliable. However, the shots are off target. This illustrates a reliable assessment that is invalid—it consistently hits the wrong target!

The third picture presents another possible scenario. In this case, the shots are aimed at the target; however, they are striking the target in an unpredictable array of locations. In other words, the shots are landing in

Figure 2.1 A Visual Depiction of Validity and Reliability

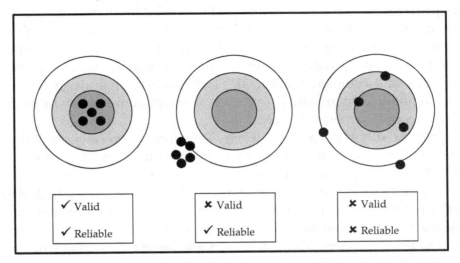

an unreliable pattern. The unreliable pattern of shots—some of which hit the target while others do not—prevents any consistent inferences about performance. In other words, the lack of reliability detracts from the validity.

These illustrations can be quite helpful in thinking about the concepts of validity and reliability. However, as with any metaphor, the depictions in Figure 2.1 are limited in conveying the full meaning of the concepts. There are other attributes of these concepts that teachers, as professionals, should understand. In the following sections, we explore the characteristics of validity and reliability, as well as some practical means of ensuring their presence in teacher-made assessments. We conclude by looking at how validity and reliability interact with and influence each other.

Validity

The attribute of validity is arguably the most important quality of an assessment (Angoff, 1988). As suggested by the examples presented in the prior section, validity is concerned with the appropriateness or meaningfulness of an assessment's target. In other words, validity is concerned with whether a test, quiz, project, or performance assesses what we intend for it to assess. Inherent to this understanding of validity is the supposition that validity hinges on someone rendering *judgments*, making *decisions*, or drawing *inferences* based on results of an assessment (Stiggins & Conklin, 1992). Thus, a more accurate definition of **validity** is the extent to which inferences drawn from assessment results are appropriate.

Typically, when we talk about the validity of a test, we do not do so in absolute terms. Rarely is a test either perfectly valid or utterly invalid. Validity is usually a question of degree. Indeed, we would even argue that no assessment is inherently valid because assessments are, by design, samplings of intended behavior under fixed or simulated conditions and, therefore, are never truly and completely authentic. The important point that classroom teachers should keep in mind is that no assessment, however well-conceived and constructed, is perfectly valid.

Again, validity is a matter of degree. Therefore, when contemplating and discussing the validity of an assessment, it is best to use relative terms, such as *high validity*, *moderate validity*, and *low validity*. For example, rather than saying, "My unit test is valid," you might say, "My unit test has a high degree of validity," thereby accounting for the diminished validity inherent in any assessment. Perhaps you administer a social studies quiz from a commercially produced textbook series. Your intent is to use the results to gauge the degree of student learning so far in the unit, but you are well aware that the quiz requires a good deal of reading. You also know that a portion of your class is one or more grade levels behind in their reading comprehension skills. In this situation, the quiz may have a high degree of validity in assessing social studies content from the unit, but the influence of reading comprehension on the ability of some of your students to demonstrate their knowledge from the unit limits the *inferences* you can draw about their learning in social studies. Thus, the validity of the quiz is reduced somewhat, and you might say, "My assessment has moderate validity for my lower level reading students."

To review, validity is concerned with the confidence with which we may draw inferences about student learning from an assessment. Second, validity is not an either/or proposition; instead, it is a matter of degree.

A third important idea regarding validity that teachers should understand is that validity is a *unified concept*, consisting of four attributes that together comprise the notion of validity. A helpful analogy is to liken validity to a diamond gemstone. A diamond is a beautiful creation of nature. A diamond is also an expensive commodity! How do jewelers decide how to place value on (that is, put a price tag on) a diamond? They consider the four C's: cut, color, carat weight, and clarity. Similarly, when we consider the validity of an assessment, we can also consider four C's, although the C's stand for different concepts than they do for diamonds. When we consider validity, we contemplate evidence related to *construct, content, concurrent,* and *consequential* validity.

You might even consider these components of validity as being like the *facets* of a diamond, as represented in Figure 2.2. A diamond is a single gemstone; however, it is comprised of multiple faces or facets that interact with each

Figure 2.2 Four Facets of Validity

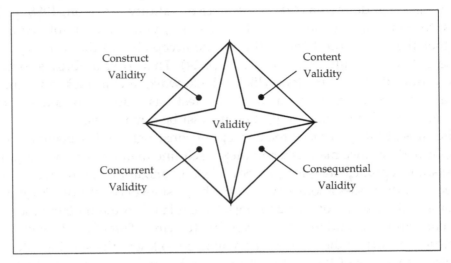

other and with light to create the visual presence for which diamonds are so valued. The attribute of validity as related to a classroom assessment is similar. The validity of the assessment is a function of the multiple facets of the four types of validity evidence, each contributing to the overall degree of validity.

So, understanding that validity is a single concept comprised of four facets, how do you then gauge the validity of an assessment? As previously alluded to, you look for and consider *evidence* of each of the various types of validity. In the next several sections, we describe each of the four facets of validity and ways of gauging the degree of each with teacher-made assessments.

Construct Validity

First, we should clarify that the word "construct" here is the noun form meaning an idea or concept; it is *not* the verb form meaning to build. Construct-related evidence of validity is concerned with how accurately an assessment aligns with the theoretical concept or mental framework of the intended learning outcomes or objectives of the instructional unit. In other words, construct validity asks, "Does the assessment measure what it purports to measure?" Returning to the archery analogy from earlier, construct validity asks, "Are we shooting at the proper target?" When considered in these terms, it is easy to see why construct validity is usually considered the most fundamental and encompassing of the four types of validity (Angoff, 1988).

Construct validity is at once simple and complex to gauge (Embretson, 2007; Gorin, 2007; Lissitz & Samuelson, 2007; Mislevy, 2007; Moss, 2007;

Sireci, 2007). For instance, construct validity is also known as **face validity**, which has been defined as "the *appearance* of validity" (Angoff, 1988, p. 23). Thus, to gauge the construct validity of a test, you could simply consider whether the test "would *look* valid and be acceptable to the test taker and to the public generally" (Angoff, 1988, p. 24). This criterion brings to mind the old quip that if a bird looks like a duck, walks like a duck, and quacks like a duck, then it must be a duck. If a test has math on it and students have to do math to complete it, then it must be a math test.

But it is at this point that the concept of construct validity becomes more complicated because math is a complex discipline made up of myriad points of facts, conceptual principles, procedural skills, and applications. A test, quiz, project, or other assessment—even at the highest levels of study—is going to target a limited scope of learning objectives related to the mathematics that a teacher and her students are currently studying. Therefore, to gauge the construct validity of the assessment, you need to know the specific intended learning outcomes of the unit of study. In other words, you would need to know what content students are intended to learn and the cognitive level at which they are to engage with the content. Now, if you happen to have subject-area expertise in mathematics, a list of such objectives may make perfect sense to you. But if you happen to be an English or social studies teacher, then it may be difficult for you to confidently determine the construct validity of the assessment because you may not have the depth of subject-area knowledge needed. (By the way, the same could be true of a mathematics teacher confronted with an English or social studies assessment!) This is a practical reality, and it is important to realize: At face value, assessments may appear valid; however, to accurately judge the construct validity of a quiz, test, project, essay, or performance-based assessment, you must have a depth of expertise in the subject area itself.

Why should you be concerned about *construct validity* as a classroom teacher? Well, the tricky thing about constructs is that they are not always self-evident or easily understood, and constructs oftentimes are multilayered and dependent upon prior knowledge and skills. The challenge of assessing a student's acquisition of a given construct is to devise some way that the student employs the construct—that is, some way for the student to demonstrate his or her acquisition of the intended learning outcome. For instance, an English teacher may intend for students to know certain literary terms (e.g., metaphor, tone, voice), so asking students to recall or identify those terms on a matching set or even a short answer exercise aligns with the intended construct. But that same English teacher also intends for his students to be able to analyze an author's use of literary devices in order to convey meaning to the reader. You can probably see already that assessing this construct is going to involve a great deal more than matching or listing. Before the construct can be assessed (or even taught!), the teacher needs to clarify for himself what it means to analyze writing for the use of literacy devices and for purposes of the rhetorical intent of an author in employing such literary devices. In other words, ensuring that your assessment has *construct validity* begins with having clarity about what the construct is in the first place. We'll return to this essential point many times in the chapters ahead, as having clarity about the **intended learning outcomes** of instruction (that is, the set of explicit knowledge, skills, and attitudes that the student is to acquire) is essential to creating valid classroom assessments.

Content Validity

Content-related evidence of validity is concerned with how adequately an assessment samples the intended learning outcomes of an instructional unit (Cureton, 1951). Assessments, by definition, are intended to be representative of the assessment taker's knowledge and skills of a given set of intended learning outcomes (Wainer & Braun, 1988). Typically, assessments are limited by the time and resources available for the act of assessing (Stiggins & Conklin, 1992). Thus, an assessment is almost always a *sample* from among a larger set of learning objectives, creating an incomplete but hopefully representative picture of a student's learning.

We know that the term "content" as it applies to content validity is potentially confusing. So, to clarify, "content" as referred to in *content validity* is not the specific subject matter of an assessment, such as fractions, parts of speech, historical eras, or parts of a plant. Rather, content validity is concerned with ensuring that an assessment adequately *samples* from the set of intended learning outcomes of an instructional unit and is, therefore, representative of that complete set of intended learning. We sometimes find it helpful to refer to content validity as **sampling validity**, although we must caution that this is not a broadly accepted synonym.

Content or sampling validity is also related to the proportionality of items on an assessment. The fact is that not all learning objectives are equally important. For example, a high school biology teacher might want her students to learn a long list of anatomical terms and also to understand the interrelated functions of a few key physiological systems. While both learning objectives are important, the teacher needs to ensure that the assessment is representative of the relative importance. If there are 45 terms but only five functions, and the assessment includes exactly 50 equally weighted items in the exact proportion of 45 terms and five functions, then the sampling validity might be weakened. This would certainly be the case if the teacher deems that conceptually understanding the physiological functions is more important than merely recalling the terms. This type of threat to content validity is a frequent occurrence with teacher-made assessments, especially as it is a common mistake to *over-sample* recall knowledge and to *under-sample* complex constructs and skills.

Gauging the content validity of an assessment begins much the same way that gauging construct validity begins: You must first know the intended learning outcomes (or "objectives") of the instructional unit. From there, you then create a **table of specifications** or **blueprint** to account for each of the learning objectives, as well as to ensure that extraneous learning objectives are not unintentionally assessed. We explain the creation of a table of specifications in detail in the next chapter. Suffice it to say here that creating a table of specifications requires a substantial degree of professional knowledge and technical skill. However, in our experience, many current teachers are simply unaware of what a table of specifications is or how to create one whether for a unit test, a performance-based assessment, or any other type of assessment. Yet, once learned, creating a table of specifications is one of the most practical, essential, and easy steps by which to create a valid assessment. Again, we address this competency in detail in the next chapter, but Figure 2.3 summarizes a study that illustrates the unintended negative consequences when content validity (a.k.a., sampling validity) is weakened.

Figure 2.3 The Importance of Content Validity for Teacher-Made Assessments

Are Teachers Testing Higher Order Thinking?

In a study of teacher-made tests in grades K–12 across core subject areas, researchers analyzed individual test items to determine the cognitive level required to respond to each question. They found that 72% of test items functioned at the knowledge level, 11% at the comprehension level, 15% at the application level, 1% at the analysis level, and less than 1% at either the synthesis or evaluation level (using the original cognitive taxonomy developed by Benjamin Bloom and his colleagues). Nearly half of those questions that functioned beyond the knowledge level were on math tests, on which computational (i.e., application) problems were most prevalent. Notably, almost 98% of items on social studies tests were at the knowledge level (Marso & Pigge, 1991).

How are these findings related to validity? Validity concerns whether the inferences drawn from assessment results are appropriate. If a student scores 100% on a typical social studies test from the sample in this study, what can we infer about her learning? Can we infer, for instance, her ability to interpret historical events and relate historical lessons to contemporary experiences? Given that 98% of the test assesses at the knowledge level, we cannot draw such inferences. However, if the teacher, the student, the parent, and next year's teacher all are under the impression that the student's grade on the test is indicative of historical interpretation and critical thinking, then the inferences they each draw about the student's learning are simply inappropriate. In other words, the inferences from the test have a *low degree of validity*, which, in this case, is due to *inadequate sampling* of the intended learning outcomes—a *content validity* issue.

Concurrent Validity

Concurrent-related evidence of validity is concerned with how accurately an assessment equates with another assessment that is intended to measure the same intended learning outcomes. As an example, consider the current state accountability system in Virginia, which is similar in design to the accountability systems in many other states. In Virginia, high school students are required to pass state assessments of the Standards of Learning (SOL) for certain core courses in mathematics, English, history, and science. These assessments are called *end-of-course tests*, and they must be passed for a student to receive credit for designated courses. In this case, two assessments are occurring concurrently (that is, within the same period of time—in this case, the length of the course) to measure student learning: The student earns a grade in the course, and the student also earns a grade on the end-of-course SOL test. Both the course grade and the end-of-course test grade are intended to indicate proficiency in the same set of state standards and at essentially the same time (i.e., at or near the end of study in the course).

Such is the faith in the concurrent validity of the SOL end-of-course tests that if a student passes his course but does *not* pass the related test, he doesn't receive credit for the course. In this scenario a teacher may question the validity of one or the other of the assessments because the assessments are intended to measure the same learning outcomes, but the different results lead to conflicting inferences. The teacher would need to turn to evidence of content validity (as indicated by tables of specifications of the respective assessments) and to evidence of construct validity (by reviewing the appropriateness of the learning objectives on which the assessments are based) to gauge the relative validity of the assessments. Of course, what complicates the concurrent validity of comparing classroom grades to standardized assessment results is that classroom grades presumably assess learning objectives *beyond* the objectives assessed by standardized assessments. Oftentimes, course grades include assessments of knowledge and skills demonstrated most appropriately through projects, labs, participation, and other performance-based activities—elements of learning that standardized tests cannot and do not attempt to tap. Thus, the estimation of concurrent validity becomes quite limited.

Another example of concurrent validity is evident in most schools, although it is not always recognized as such. Consider this hypothetical scenario: A first-year high school mathematics teacher feels very fortunate because her veteran colleagues in the math department are very supportive of her—always providing support, offering advice, and sharing materials. Two of her veteran colleagues have shared with her their unit tests for the unit that she is currently teaching. If she gave half of her students one veteran teacher's test and other half of her students the other teacher's test, could she expect similar results? The tests were designed based on the same curriculum, but would the results of the two sets of students concur? As you might see, concurrent validity has implications for the **horizontal articulation** of curriculum, instruction, and assessment within schools. That is, it is vitally important that the teachers who are responsible for teaching the same grade level and/or subject area have a common understanding of the intended learning outcomes and, therefore, a common understanding of how to assess those learning outcomes accurately.

Granted, the hypothetical example in the previous paragraph was contrived to make a point. The fact is that it is not very common for a teacher to give two or more assessments concurrently. In fact, concurrent validity more often than not occurs at two distinct points in time. This type of concurrent validity is referred to more precisely as **predictive validity**. Returning to the previous discussion of the end-of-course state tests in Virginia, a teacher of such a course might decide to give his students a practice end-of-course test in the weeks prior to the actual state test to predict students' performance on the high-stakes assessment and to plan for further targeted instruction. In this scenario the teacher would gauge the *predictive validity* by reviewing individual students' results on the practice test and comparing those results to performance on the state's end-of-course test. The more consistent the individual students' scores between the two tests, the stronger the evidence of predictive validity of the teacher-made test. The farther apart the actual results from the expected results, the weaker the evidence—and the need to look to *construct* and *content validity* evidence to determine why. With the preponderance of high-stakes standardized assessments in each state, the predictive validity of teacher-made assessments is becoming increasingly important.

Consequential Validity

Consequential-related evidence of validity is concerned with the appropriateness of the intended and unintended outcomes that ensue from an assessment (Linn, 1997; Messick, 1989; Shepard, 1997). Such outcomes can include entry into programs or services, such as honor societies, advanced courses, remediation services, or special education services. They can also include promotion to the next grade level, graduation from high school, and admission to college. Outcomes can also be affective in nature, influencing student motivation, beliefs, or dispositions.

For example, a reluctant and struggling student performs well on a teacher-made test. She felt supported and well prepared by her teacher, and she considers the test to be fair. One important consequence of this scenario may be a more positive attitude on her part toward the teacher, the subject, and learning in general. In this example, the consequence is positive and ultimately leads to improved student learning. The teacher may conclude, therefore, that the test has a high degree of consequential validity for this particular student regarding her sense of self-efficacy for the subject matter and for learning.

Conversely, the consequences of an assessment may be more insidious. If an assessment is perceived to be unfairly difficult, to assess knowledge or skills that were inadequately taught, or to be administered in such a way that students are unable to demonstrate their true learning, negative perceptions and feelings may be engendered. Consider the well-meaning but very busy science teacher. While his class sessions frequently involve inquiring, hypothesizing, and experimentation, his assessments are generated from the automated multiple-choice test bank of the approved textbook series, and the test items tend to focus on recall of distinct facts from the textbook. Many of his students perform poorly on his tests because of the mismatch between the instruction and the assessments. The consequence of the misaligned assessments is that a proportion of the teacher's students become turned off to science, inferring from their test scores that they aren't any good at it, despite their engagement during instruction.

Assessment results—and the inferences that follow—can have profound effects. Some of these effects are intentional and deliberate; others are unexpected and perhaps even unnoticed. Some are productive and affirming; others are insidious and destructive. As is evident from the previous examples, consequential validity can potentially play a significant role in teaching and learning. However, consequential validity is sometimes overlooked. Perhaps this is because the three other types of validity evidence—construct, content, and concurrent validity—are more technical in nature and can be more readily observed. Whatever the case, consequential validity plays a centrally important role in teaching and learning.

Simply put, teachers must come to consider their assessment practices as integral to their instructional practices. Just as most teachers recognize that positive regard, engagement, and relevancy are doorways to student learning, so too must teachers realize that their assessment practices should be engaging, fair, and relevant. Rick Stiggins (2006, p.14), a noted scholar and teacher of classroom assessment, puts it this way:

> Assessment practices that permit, even encourage, some students to give up on learning must be replaced by those that engender hope and sustained effort for all students. In short, the entire emotional environment surrounding the experience of being evaluated must change for all, but especially for perennial low achievers.

Tips for Gauging Validity

Validity is a single, unified concept, comprised of four essential facets. Figure 2.4 explores each of these four distinguishing features and provides some practical questions and evidence that can help teachers ensure the validity of assessments used in the classroom.

Figure 2.4 How to Strengthen the Validity of Teacher-Made Assessments

Facets of Validity	Questions a teacher can ask to gauge validity	Evidence a teacher can gather to determine and strengthen validity
Construct Validity	◆ Can we infer a student's knowledge and skills related to the intended learning outcomes of an instructional unit from the assessment?	◆ Unpack the intended learning outcomes or objectives that the assessment is intended to tap, and determine their appropriateness for the curricular goals of this unit of instruction (see chapter 3). ◆ Create a *table of specifications* and review its adequacy in representing the intended learning outcomes of the instructional unit (see chapter 3).
Content Validity (a.k.a., *Sampling Validity*)	◆ Does the assessment adequately sample the intended learning outcomes? ◆ Does the assessment adequately represent the relative importance of the intended learning outcomes?	◆ Create a *table of specifications* and review it to ensure that the assessment adequately samples the intended learning outcomes, without over-sampling or under-sampling any intended learning outcomes (see chapter 3).
Concurrent Validity	◆ Can we find confirming evidence of learning or predict performance on a related assessment that is designed to measure the same learning objectives?	◆ Compare performance on another assessment of the intended learning outcomes (e.g., a test created by a colleague, state assessments, Advanced Placement exams).
Consequential Validity	◆ What are the consequences of using the assessment for decision-making regarding student learning? ◆ For better or worse, are there any unintended consequences of this assessment for students?	◆ Identify and judge the appropriateness of effects on: ○ Student motivation, attitudes, or beliefs ○ Placement in and/or access to special designations or programs ○ Instructional decisions ○ Inferences drawn by parents, other educators, etc.

Reliability

Closely related to the concept of *validity* is the concept of *reliability*. In fact, the two concepts of assessment are integrally connected and together constitute the core principles of good assessment. So, what is reliability? **Reliability** is the consistency or dependability of the results of an assessment.

Central to the principle of reliability is the relative absence of error. First, let's consider the concept of error in an assessment. **Error** in an assessment is when an assessment item does not adequately distinguish between the student who has truly mastered the intended learning outcome and the student who has not. For example, if a student gets a test question correct, not because she knows it but because of something other than knowledge of or skill in the intended learning being assessed, then there is error in the assessment. Similarly, if a student misses a question for some reason other than a lack of knowledge or skill, then error has occurred.

As with validity, reliability is a matter of degree. Rarely is a single test question or a performance-based assessment perfectly reliable. Rather, a test item or a comprehensive assessment may be relatively free of error—or, put differently, it may be more or less reliable. The fact is that *no* assessment is free of error. Every test has some degree of error. This fact becomes more evident when you consider that there are essentially two types of error to which all assessments are subject: *systematic error* and *random error*. Figure 2.5 depicts these two types of error. In the figure, systematic error is represented by the small sphere, suggesting that sources of systematic error tend to be relatively limited, and, when looked for, sources of these types of error are both detectable and preventable. Random error, however, can be caused by any number of situations, and sources of random error are not always detectable or even knowable. Thus, random error is represented in the figure by the vast space around the sphere of systematic error.

Figure 2.5 Types of Error

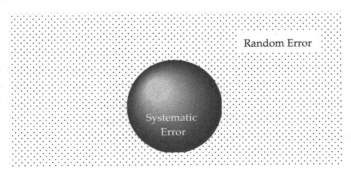

Systematic error is error that is unintentionally built into an assessment and is likely to affect student results, but that may be controlled if detected. Examples of systematic error include the following:

- Culturally biased language, idioms, and references
- Developmentally inappropriate reading level
- Mechanical or grammatical mistakes in assessment items
- Insufficient or unclear directions
- Poor layout of the assessment, causing uncertainty or mistakes in reading the assessment
- Insufficient number of assessment items
- Subjective scoring
- Cheating

Random error is error that influences assessment results but is not easily predicted or controlled. As suggested by Figure 2.5, the possible sources of random error are essentially limitless, but some common examples include the following, just to name a few:

- Illness
- Carelessness
- Luck (or unluckiness!)
- Unhappiness
- Momentary distractedness
- Giddiness
- Fire alarm
- A poor night's rest
- Intercom announcement
- Wobbly desk

Whether assessment error is systematic or random, it can have significant effects on the dependability of the inferences that we draw about student learning. Consider the case of the student presented in Figure 2.6, which we've titled "Subject to Error: The Case of the Hapless High Schooler."

The fact is that scenarios such as the one experienced by the hapless 9th grader—and a myriad of other minor catastrophes—play out every single day in schools. But we don't mean to be melodramatic. Nor are we suggesting that it's incumbent on the teacher to psychoanalyze each student prior to a quiz or test to account for the slings and arrows suffered in the course of normal human interactivity. Instead, our intent is to reduce the *hubris*

Figure 2.6 Subject to Error: The Case of the Hapless High Schooler

Imagine a straight-A, 9th grade student whose day takes a turn for the worse. He walks into his third-period history class expecting to take the test he has dutifully studied for the past three nights in a row. The problem is, in the hallway he just found out that the girl he was going to ask to the homecoming dance just said yes to a rival 10th grader. Our 9th grader is a bit upset but also embarrassed because this is the first dance at his new school and he doesn't have any other prospects.

He's already racking his brain trying to figure out who else he could ask. At the same time, he's trying to decide how to play this off with his buddies at the lunch table during fourth period. They're sure to find out, and they are just as sure to razz him about it.

Preoccupied by the turn of events, he sits down at his desk. There's gum in the chair—just fresh enough to stick to the seat of his pants. Should he try to peel it off? Or should he be nonchalant—as nonchalant as you can be with bright pink bubble gum on your tail-side.

As he distractedly stews over his unlucky situation, the student's history teacher passes around the test and immediately launches into giving oral directions for how to complete the test. Our straight-A student is about to experience error on this assessment of his learning. He misses key directions from the teacher and experiences systematic error because of the teacher's oral directions. This could have been controlled if the teacher had more deliberately facilitated the students' transition into the class and, specifically, into the testing situation. Providing the directions in writing for students to refer to as she spoke would have helped, too. Alas, she was up late last night writing the test as it was.

Of course, our 9th grader also experiences random error. Through no fault of his or of the teacher's (blame the dastardly 10th grader), the student's frame of mind for taking this test has been clouded. He may pull himself together and be able to concentrate, but chances are that his distracted emotional state may cause him to, quite literally, make an error or two in his responses . . . or worse.

In short, this student's results on this particular assessment may not be a particularly reliable indication of what he actually knows about this unit of study in his 9th grade history class. Under different circumstances, he would likely perform better because he knows more than he is able to show on this particular assessment.

with which we, as teachers, sometimes treat assessment in our classrooms. Assessment is an imperfect craft; every assessment is subject to unintended error. We, as teachers, simply need to remind ourselves of this and do our best to control such error.

Reliability is concerned with whether a student's performance on an assessment is a true indication of the student's learning and not unduly influenced by error. Because of the importance of reliability in interpreting assessment results, psychometricians (that is, people who construct, administer, and study assessments for a living) have developed a number of tools for understanding the influence of error on assessments. Through *item analysis* procedures, for example, one can compute *reliability coefficients* on a scale of 0 to 1 that indicate the degree of score stability of an assessment. An assessment can be analyzed to determine the *standard error of measure*, which represents the difference between a student's achieved score and her theoretical *true score*. These and other concepts are especially important when reviewing, analyzing, discussing, and making decisions based on high-stakes assessments. However, each of these also occurs after an assessment has been administered and, therefore, is of less practical use to a classroom teacher. How, then, can a teacher try to strengthen the potential reliability of his or her classroom assessments?

Tips for Ensuring Reliability

Reliability can be defined as *the degree to which a student's performance on an assessment is not unduly influenced by raw chance, systematic error, bias, or cheating.* To the degree that a teacher can control these influences on students, his assessment will be more reliable. In Figure 2.7, we offer several guiding questions and practical steps to strengthen the reliability of teacher-made assessments.

First, the teacher should ask, "Do I have enough questions for each intended learning outcome that I am assessing?" As a general rule of test construction, the more items to which students respond, the more reliable the instrument. Let's say a 4th grade math teacher is giving a test on adding and subtracting decimals. If she puts only one addition problem and one subtraction problem on the test, then how confident can she be in a student's results? If a student misses one out of one addition questions, should the teacher assume the student knows nothing about adding decimals? To account for the possibility of error—that is, to account for the possibility that a student may miss a question for reasons unrelated to knowledge or skills—the 4th grade teacher would be wise to include several addition problems and several subtraction problems. Then, if a student misses all of the addition problems, the teacher can be reasonably confident that the student does not understand how to add decimals. Similarly, if a student gets all the addition problems correct, the teacher could have a relatively high degree of confidence in the stability of the student's performance—that is, the teacher could reliably infer that the student knows how to add decimals.

How many questions on a paper-pencil assessment are enough to ensure reliability? Well, there are no set rules to guide teachers, but some common sense is helpful. Minimally, a teacher would want to *triangulate* each learning objective. Thus, three questions for each main topic of knowledge or specific skill application offers a reasonable guideline from which to begin. More than

Figure 2.7 How to Strengthen the Reliability of a Teacher-Made Assessment

Questions a teacher can ask to gauge reliability	Steps a teacher can take to improve reliability
Do I have *enough questions* for each intended learning outcome that I am assessing?	◆ As a general rule, include three or more test questions or items for each core objective so as to reduce the unintended effects of error on the assessment results.
Are the *questions, directions, and formatting* on the assessment free from systematic error?	◆ Review and proofread individual test questions, prompts, and directions for systematic error, including grammatical or mechanical mistakes, cultural biases, and lack of clarity.
Are the *criteria for grading* the assessment as objective as possible?	◆ Clarify and verify grading criteria for the test, including rubrics. ◆ Ensure *intra-rater* and *inter-rater reliability* by establishing scoring protocols and training.

three questions asked about a specific objective serves to improve reliability still more because the teacher then has a greater number of responses from the student to establish a pattern of demonstrated learning or lack thereof. We refer to this as **repeated trials reliability**. Of course, there is an upper limit to how many questions should be asked on an assessment. A teacher must be aware of the length of assessment that is reasonable for the age of students in the class. After all, if you ask too many questions, then you could unintentionally *decrease* reliability by introducing weariness into the testing situation, leading to error.

A second question a teacher should ask to gauge reliability is, "Are the questions, directions, and formatting on the assessment free from systematic error?" Error can be introduced to an assessment in a variety of ways. If a test question is poorly worded, a student may misinterpret the question and, therefore, answer it incorrectly because of the wording, not because of his degree of learning. If directions for a project are unclear or are unintentionally incomplete, a student who may otherwise perform well on the assignment may miss a critical element. If a multiple choice item requires students to use a map on one page to answer questions stapled to subsequent pages that follow, the very act of flipping back and forth between pages may introduce error. If information in question 3 on a quiz unintentionally provides the answer to 6 on the quiz, the student who does *not* possess the knowledge to answer 6 under different circumstances might get it correct.

With each of these examples, the chain of events is the same: Something in the construction of the assessment itself unintentionally causes a student either to get the question wrong when he or she actually possesses the assessed learning or to get the question correct when he or she actually does not possess the assessed learning. In these examples, the source of the error can usually be detected through careful proofreading, which suggests these instances describe *systematic* error—error that is unintentionally present but can be controlled, if detected by the teacher.

Even in an age of the ubiquitous spell checker and even in a time when commercially produced test banks accompany many textbook series, the introduction of such error is quite common. In our own experiences reviewing teacher-made assessments, we come across such problems quite frequently. Why do such errors in the construction of assessments occur? We have identified three main reasons:

1. Sometimes teachers and commercial test producers do not proofread their assessments carefully for common grammatical and mechanical errors.
2. Sometimes teachers and commercial test producers do not know and follow the guidelines for constructing certain types of assessment items.
3. Sometimes teachers and commercial test producers make incorrect assumptions about students' prior learning, background knowledge, and reading abilities.

How, then, can you as a classroom teacher attempt to ensure against these and thereby improve the reliability of your assessments? Here are a few suggestions:

- ◆ Use your spell checker.
- ◆ Have a colleague proofread your assessment for clarity and correctness.
- ◆ Review and follow the guidelines for constructing different item types, such as multiple choice, true-false, short answer, and essay questions.
- ◆ Consciously consider the cultural and academic backgrounds of your students as you write individual items.
- ◆ Consciously examine your own cultural background and assumptions.
- ◆ Be aware of conditions during assessment that may interfere with students' ability to focus and sustain effort.

Continuing in reference to Figure 2.7, a third question that a teacher can ask to gauge the reliability of an assessment is, "Are the criteria for grading the assessment as objective as possible?" Not only can error be inadvertently built into an assessment when the teacher is creating it, but error can also occur when an assessment is being graded. It could be something as simple as an answer key being incorrect and, therefore, students systematically getting question 15 marked incorrect when, in fact, their answers are correct. Error in grading also occurs when scoring is so subjective that a student's grade comes to depend on factors such as where in the stack his paper was read or the teacher's mood when grading, rather than depending on meeting the criteria of an appropriate response. Written responses such as short answers and essays are especially subject to this, but it can also be the case with a math teacher subjectively awarding partial credit for students showing their work, a choir teacher grading a student's performance, or an art teacher assessing a student's clay project.

To control error in the grading process, a teacher should aim to reduce subjectivity as much as possible and to increase the likelihood that a student's score on an assessment would be the same regardless of when it was graded, in what order it was graded, or under what circumstances it was graded. This principle of assessment is called **intra-rater reliability**, and it means that a scorer consistently applies the scoring criteria to an assessment, thereby resulting in a stable score, uninfluenced by factors that are not the criteria of learning. The same principle applies if two or more teachers have co-created an assessment for their students and the consistent application of the grading criteria by each of the teachers results in accurate scores among students, regardless of which teacher grades which student's work. This is called **inter-rater reliability**.

Appropriately applying criteria when scoring assessments is a critical step in ensuring reliability. This is especially true when using student-created responses, such as computational problems, short answers, essays, projects, performances, and original creations. Such items require a teacher to identify the expected criteria of performance and to determine gradations or levels of possible student work. Techniques for scoring student-supplied responses include *checklists*, *rating scales*, and *rubrics*, each of which we explore and demonstrate in chapter 5.

What Does It Mean to Have a Valid and Reliable Assessment?

If an assessment allows you to draw inferences about the nature and degree of student learning regarding a set of intended learning outcomes, and if the assessment also allows you to distinguish between the student who has truly acquired those learning outcomes and the student who has not, then you have a valid and reliable assessment. If the assessment inadvertently measures a different set of learning outcomes, inadequately measures the various components that make up the intended objectives, fails to predict performance on another assessment that measures the same objectives, or unintentionally infringes on a student's acquisition of the intended learning, then the validity of the assessment is diminished. If the assessment inadvertently allows a student's results to suggest acquisition of the intended learning outcomes when, in fact, the learning has not been acquired, or if a student's results suggest a *lack* of learning when, in fact, the objectives have been acquired, then the reliability of the assessment is diminished.

With the preceding summations of validity and reliability in mind, we conclude our overview of these core principles of assessment by considering several examples. We asked a group of experienced teachers to describe a situation from their own teaching practice that illustrated the principles of validity and reliability in play. The examples come from elementary, middle, and high school settings, as well as from a variety of subject areas and special education. In each case, the teacher shares the application of the concepts of validity and reliability in his or her own words. What's more, each teacher critiques his or her past practice with regard to creating and/or using valid and reliable assessments in the classroom.

Teacher-to-Teacher

Validity and Reliability with My Students
As educators, I'm sure that we could all fill pages about our experiences with **unreliable** or **invalid** assessments. For example, in my current school, teachers must use Cloze tests to determine the reading level of students. Cloze tests are assessments in which students are given a reading passage with a number of words missing from the sentences. The students must read the passage and fill in the blanks with the appropriate words to complete the sentences. I feel that this assessment is **invalid** because a child's reading ability involves a lot more than just ability to fill in the blanks correctly. In no way does this test measure a child's ability to decode text, retell the story or answer questions about it, or self-monitor for breakdowns of comprehension. I feel that this assessment is **unreliable** because giving different versions of the test can result in very different scores. For example, if I give a child a

passage about dinosaurs that is on a 4.0 reading level, and the child loves dinosaurs, then she will have a lot more background knowledge to pull from when it comes to understanding and completing the story and will score higher on the test because of it. On the other hand, if I give that same child a passage about Ancient Rome that is on a 4.0 reading level, and the child knows nothing about the subject, then she will surely score lower than she would have on the dinosaur passage.

Katie
Elementary Teacher

Teacher-to-Teacher

Validity and Reliability with One of My Students

As a special education teacher, I believe I have inadvertently given an assessment that is **unreliable**. This assessment was **unreliable** due to the nature of the test and the situation surrounding the test. This test was to measure a student's ability to read and complete mathematical computations. The student had been given the use of a calculator all year, and, on this particular day, she was asked to complete similar math problems *without* her calculator. The timing was also not conducive to getting quality results. The test was administered the day before Spring Break, with approximately 30 minutes left until the end of the school day. I believe this **skewed the results**, making the test an **unreliable judgment** of this student's ability and thereby leading to **inaccurate inferences** about her learning.

Nate
High School Special Education Teacher

Teacher-to-Teacher

Validity with One of My Students

Recently, a 4th grade student was given a multiple choice history test and received a failing grade. This particular student reads on a 3rd grade level. While analyzing his test, I realized the test questions were written on an end-of-4th grade reading level and that he probably experienced great frustration just trying to read the questions. I re-administered the test orally, and the student was able to answer many of the questions correctly. I felt the initial administration of the test rendered the results **invalid** for this student because the test actually measured his ability to read the test questions and not his knowledge of history, which was the **intended outcome** of the instructional unit.

Ann
Elementary Teacher

Teacher-to-Teacher

Validity and Reliability with My Students

A situation from my own experience in which I gave an assessment that was **invalid** was on a recent weekly spelling test. The purpose of the weekly spelling test was to assess the students' spelling of key terms. Students who memorized the list were able to score very high on the assessment, yet these same students would misspell the same or similar words in their writing assignments the very next week. Not only would the words be misspelled, the students were not able to recognize the misspelled words when proofreading their papers. The weekly spelling tests were more of an assessment of memorization skills than an indication of what I have come to realize was my **true intended learning outcome** for the students: not simply to spell the words correctly, but to do so in authentic writing situations.

Karen
Middle School Technology Support Teacher

Teacher-to-Teacher

Validity and Reliability with My Students

A personal experience as a teacher in which I gave an assessment that was **invalid** and **unreliable** was in summer school when I gave a group of rising 1st graders a pretest that was part of a series we were instructed to use. The series of questions was supposed to test shape acquisition of the square, heart, triangle, and circle. However, the set of questions was written in a table format that the children had never been exposed to. Needless to say, the majority of children got the shape questions wrong. However, when presented another way, all the children could identify those shapes. Another item in this math summer series was a parent guide that went right along with this pre-assessment. It let the parent know what their child needed to work on. In fact it was very specific. If the child missed the shape questions, I had to check a box that said your child could not identify those shapes. So, parents of these children naturally **inferred** that their children could not identify a heart, triangle, square, or circle, when actually it was the table format that gave the child difficulty. Kids who knew their shapes just fine were not able to demonstrate their knowledge due to the format of the questions.

Lindsey
Elementary Teacher

Teacher-to-Teacher

Validity and Reliability with My Students

As a teacher, there have been times in my own assessing of kids' work that I wish I had had greater **validity** and **reliability**. For example, I have often used poster projects as assessments of student learning in social studies, but haven't always clearly defined what a student's individual poster should contain in order to achieve a specific grade. Thus, an artistically pleasing poster that actually expressed very little mastery of content might receive a higher grade than would a blander-looking but more content-rich poster. There is a place for both types of posters in learning and expression, but where I fell short was in not specifying up front what the intention of the poster activity was. Neither my students nor I had any real clarity about *what* was most important for the posters to communicate about their learning. The lack of an assessment anchor such as a rubric also harmed **reliability**. I'm certain that I must have graded one group of posters differently from another because, for one group, I may have been rushed to finish or because I had a more negative or positive view of that class as a whole. Looking back, this is truly regretful, since the kids usually worked hard on their posters and definitely deserved a more professional effort in assessment.

Charley
Middle School Social Studies Teacher

These teachers' reflections on their past practices and experiences with assessments in the classroom illustrate the core principles that should govern how we create and use tests in our classrooms. Teacher-made assessments must accurately represent what we believe them to represent about student learning, and assessments must do so in ways that dependably allow students who have mastery of intended learning outcomes to demonstrate that mastery through knowledge and skill rather than through chance. These core principles that govern the creation of classroom tests are *validity* and *reliability*, and they constitute accurate, dependable, and, ultimately, meaningful assessments of student learning.

3

How Do I Create a Good Assessment?

It's All About Alignment

Have you ever driven a car when its wheels were out of alignment? There are some telltale signs: Driving down a straight road, the car will pull to one side. If the lack of alignment is more severe, you'll feel a jiggling in the steering wheel or even a vibration in the frame of the car itself. When poor alignment is not corrected, tires begin to wear unevenly, which reduces gas mileage and shortens the life of the tires. In the worst case, poor alignment can even lead to structural wear and damage to the suspension, the car frame, or the engine chassis. You do not need to be an auto mechanic to see that when the wheels of your car are out of alignment, you experience a bad ride and your car can become damaged. To state the point more positively, it is important to maintain the alignment of a car so that the car can best serve its purpose of getting you where you want to go.

Alignment is important to creating good assessments as well. In the case of teacher-made assessments, alignment needs to occur among the three foundational elements of teaching and learning that we introduced in chapter 1: curriculum, instruction, and assessment. Think of it this way: What the teacher intends for students to know and be able to do (curriculum) should be what the teacher engages students in so that they will acquire the intended knowledge and skills (instruction), and then the teacher determines the students' acquisition of this set of new knowledge and skills in order to make decisions about what to do next (assessment).

Figure 3.1 Alignment

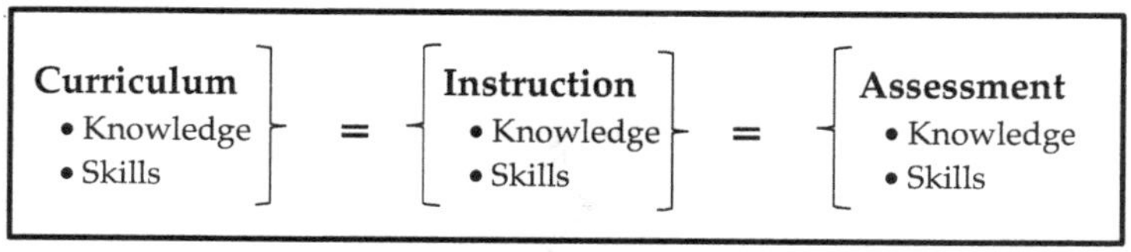

Figure 3.1 illustrates this as a kind of equation, which we oftentimes simplify as a basic tenet: $C = I = A$.

To further illustrate the tenet of alignment, consider this example. Ms. Cahill, a 5th grade math teacher, is responsible for teaching her students how to construct line graphs and stem-and-leaf plots. Through instructional activities in class, students create and interpret information from line graphs and stem-and-leaf plots over the course of a four-day unit. At the end of the unit, Ms. Cahill gives her students a test, which was passed on to her by a well-meaning fellow teacher in her school. The unit test presents a series of line graphs and pie charts, which students are to use to answer a number of multiple choice questions. In this case, the teacher's instruction (I) is aligned to the intended learning for students (C), but the assessment (A) is poorly aligned since the intended content of stem-and-leaf plots is not assessed, while an unintended (and untaught) element of content (pie charts) is assessed. What's more, students demonstrate their ability to read and interpret line graphs, but the intended skill of constructing line graphs is not assessed (exacerbated, of course, by the absence of assessment of any skills related to stem-and-leaf plots). Using our simple CIA tenet, this situation illustrates the following problem with alignment: $C = I \neq A$.

The example of the 5th grade math teacher is one of innumerable examples where the alignment of our curricular intents, our instructional practices, and our assessment methods can be thrown off—sometimes only slightly and sometimes much more severely. You can probably think of examples from your own experiences as a student, if not as a teacher, when what happened during instruction did not seem to relate to what you understood the purposes of the course to be ($I \neq C$) or when the content and skills of instruction were not the same as those that were assessed ($A \neq I$). Such instances can derail the best of intents of a teacher. Since the focus of this book is on classroom assessment and not on instruction, we will focus on the importance of avoiding instances where $A \neq C$, and we will aim to maximize the likelihood of instances where $A = C$, in both the intended knowledge and skills of students' learning.

Seven Steps for Creating a Good Assessment

Keeping the tenet of $C = I = A$ in mind when creating and using classroom assessments can serve as a guide star for teachers as they make important decisions about what to teach, how to teach it, and how to determine the nature and degree of students' learning. However, there are also very practical and defined processes that teachers can take to help ensure alignment of classroom assessments to the intended learning outcomes for students and to strengthen the dependability of such assessments. In this chapter, we will focus on seven essential steps involved in creating classroom assessments so that they are reasonably valid and reliable (Figure 3.2).

Step 1: Unpack the Intended Learning Outcomes

Our aim in creating a good assessment is to ensure that our assessment is aligned with our curriculum. In other words, our aim is that $A = C$. So what becomes evident is that we can't create an assessment until we first deeply and clearly understand what the intended learning outcomes are for students.

In the current accountability era of K–12 education, the articulation of intended learning outcomes begins with formal standards of learning that have been developed at the national and state levels. Currently, all 50 states in the US have content standards in the core subject areas. In most cases, states have drawn on the expertise of subject-matter professional associations at the national level such as the National Council of Teachers of English (NCTE) and the National Council of Teachers of Mathematics (NCTM) to guide the creation of subject standards. Additionally, a majority of states have adopted standards in reading/language arts and mathematics from the

Figure 3.2 Seven Steps for Creating a Good Assessment

☑ Step 1: Unpack the Intended Learning Outcomes

☑ Step 2: Create a Table of Specifications

☑ Step 3: Clarify Your Purposes for and Circumstances of Assessing Student Learning

☑ Step 4: Determine the Appropriate Types of Assessment Items/Activities to Use

☑ Step 5: Determine the Appropriate Number and Weight of Assessment Items

☑ Step 6: Create and Select Assessment Items That Are Valid and Reliable

☑ Step 7: Assemble the Assessment

Common Core of Learning, which represents the most significant step toward a national curriculum in US history (NGA & CCSSO, 2010). Although states have developed these standards, a review of standards in 2012 indicated that not all states provide standards that are course- or grade-specific: Only 33 do so in English/language arts, 31 in mathematics, 26 in science, and 26 in social studies (Education Week Research Center, 2014). Therefore, most school districts develop curriculum materials based on the established state standards so that students have an opportunity to perform well on high-stakes state assessments. School districts further delineate the state standards by breaking them down into a scope and sequence of courses, constituting a program of studies.

This is all part of a system in which state standards are translated into school district curricula and courses. But our focus here is not on the standards movement, nor is it on curriculum development. Our focus is on strengthening teacher-made assessments. Within the system as described earlier, classroom teachers use the school district curriculum to articulate intended learning outcomes or objectives for units of instruction and for lesson planning. In short, intended learning outcomes, which emanate from national and state standards but which ultimately must be explicitly articulated by individual classroom teachers, are the source of what is taught and, therefore, the source of what is assessed in classrooms.

Again, creating a valid and reliable teacher-made assessment must begin with a teacher understanding the intended learning outcomes for students. Unpacking intended learning outcomes is an effective means of doing this (Anderson & Krathwohl, 2001; Chappuis, 2014; Jackson, 2009; Marzano, 2013; Lemov, 2010). **Unpacking** is a common term used to describe the process of reviewing curricular standards or objectives in order to identify the intended content and the intended cognitive levels of learning for students. *Unpacking* intended learning outcomes is sometimes referred to as *deconstructing* or *unwrapping* objectives.

When we unpack intended learning outcomes, for what are we unpacking? Each intended learning outcome is comprised of two basic elements: content and cognitive behavior. The purpose of unpacking intended learning outcomes is for teachers to clearly and deeply understand the content and cognitive rigor of the curriculum of a given instructional unit for students. Let's take a closer look at each of these elements.

Content

Teachers tend to be very good with content. In fact, if you have ever asked a teacher, "What are you teaching this week?" they likely replied in terms of content. A math teacher might say, "I'm teaching fractions"; an English teacher might offer, "I'm teaching *Romeo and Juliet*"; and a history teacher could reply, "I'm teaching the Jazz Age." Each response is a statement of content. There is nothing inherently problematic with this; we are simply pointing out that content naturally tends to hold a dominant spot in most teachers' thinking.

Content is practically synonymous to many teachers' conceptualization of their subject matter. However, our aim in unpacking is to be as clear and specific about the content as possible. To this end, unpacking brings focus to three layers of content: *explicit content*, *implicit content*, and *conditional content*. The subject matter referred to in a standard or an intended learning outcome is the explicit content because it is evident simply by reading the standard itself. But no content exists in isolation; all knowledge is connected with other knowledge. People learn, in part, by assimilating new knowledge into their existing understandings. In other words, students usually need prior knowledge of a topic as a prerequisite to learning more about that topic or before understanding it at a deeper level. When unpacking a curriculum standard, therefore, teachers also must be aware of this implicit content knowledge—that is, knowledge students are presumed to have already and that will allow them to engage in the explicit content. Finally, the content of many intended learning outcomes is also often dependent on certain circumstances or conditions, such as primary sources to be read or situations in which to employ understanding. This type of content facilitates students' engagement with the explicit content of the intended learning outcome and can be thought of as conditional content. In summary, most intended learning outcomes (as well as standards and learning objectives) typically contain three content layers:

1. **Explicit content**—the subject matter directly referred to in a statement of the intended learning outcome;
2. **Implicit content**—the prior knowledge and skills students need to engage with the explicit content;
3. **Conditional content**—specific circumstances, contexts, or materials through which the student will engage with the explicit content.

Let's review an example by looking at an intended learning outcome from elementary mathematics in Figure 3.3. (We have adapted this intended learning outcome from the Common Core Standards [NGA & CCSSO, 2010].)

Our unpacking of content layers can be guided by a few key questions: *What is the "what" of the intended learning outcome? What prior knowledge or skills should they have to engage with the "what"? And what conditions or content*

Figure 3.3 Example of Unpacking the Content Layers of an Intended Learning Outcome

---

The student will use and justify <u>different estimation strategies in a real-world problem situation</u> and determine <u>the reasonableness of results of calculations in a given problem situation.</u>

Analysis of Content Layers within the Standard:

◆ *Explicit Content*—different estimation strategies, reasonableness of calculations;
◆ *Implicit Content*—rounding, adding, subtracting, multiplying, dividing;
◆ *Conditional Content*—in a real-world problem situation, in a given problem situation.

---

is necessary for students to engage with the "what"? As a simple and practical approach to unpacking, we suggest <u>underlining</u> the language from the intended learning outcome that is associated with the content, as shown in Figure 3.3. Returning to our example, there are three questions we ask to identify the layers of content in the standard:

1. *What is the explicit content of the intended learning outcome?* The explicit content contained in this intended learning outcome includes both <u>estimation strategies</u> and <u>reasonableness of results of calculations</u>. This content is explicitly stated in the standard. It is the "what."
2. *What implicit knowledge or skills should students have to engage with the explicit content?* To employ estimation strategies, students need to be able to <u>round numbers</u> and <u>carry out mathematical operations such as addition, subtraction, multiplication, and division</u>. These are the prerequisite knowledge and skills that students need to have to estimate and evaluate the reasonableness of the calculations.
3. *What conditions, content, or materials are necessary or facilitative for students to engage with the explicit content?* In this standard, students must use <u>given problem situations that reflect the real world</u> to demonstrate their ability to employ estimation strategies. This is a condition placed on how the students demonstrate their knowledge and skills; thus, it is conditional content.

To construct a valid and reliable assessment, teachers must have a clear and specific understanding of the content. Understanding the nuances of the explicit, implicit, and conditional content is an important start, but it is not itself sufficient. Teachers must also be clear about the level of cognitive demand.

Level of Cognitive Demand

Human behavior and learning are inordinately complex, so any attempt to simplify our understanding of them ultimately falls short in some regard. Nevertheless, it is helpful to think of learning as a behavior and to think about the different domains in which people's behavior—and, therefore, our learning—can be categorized. A broadly accepted understanding of behavior characterizes learning as taking place in three distinct domains: the cognitive domain, the psychomotor domain, and the affective domain.

Each domain of behavior is critical in its own right. The *cognitive domain* involves thinking and the acquisition of intellectual knowledge and skills. The *psychomotor domain* focuses on perceptual abilities and kinesthetics. In the *affective domain*, the focus is on values and the judgments that are made based on those values.

In formal K–12 education, the cognitive domain is the primary focus. What's tricky about cognition is that it is difficult to "see" what is going on in someone's mind when they are cogitating (that is, thinking). Thus, more than a half century ago, Benjamin Bloom and his colleagues (Bloom, Engelhart, Furst, Hill, & Krathwohol, 1956) developed a means of inferring levels of student cognition based upon students' observable actions. This tool is Bloom's Taxonomy of Cognitive Behavior, more commonly referred to as "Bloom's taxonomy" for short.

Most teachers are familiar with Bloom's taxonomy, with Anderson and Krathwohl's (2001) revised version of it, or with Webb and colleagues' (2005) Depth of Knowledge framework. In our experience, each of these is quite adequate for the task of unpacking intended learning outcomes. What is most important is that a school faculty, if not a school district, select one so that teachers and instructional leaders within the organization have a shared conceptualization and language for engaging in this work. We tend to favor the use of Anderson and Krathwohl's revised taxonomy. We find the renamed and reordered levels, as well as the more robust explanations of the cognitive levels in the 2001 publication, to be more intuitive and more useful. Indeed, we highly recommend Anderson and Krathwohl's (2001) book *A Taxonomy for Learning, Teaching, and Assessing: A Revision of Bloom's Taxonomy of Educational Objectives* as a rich resource for all teachers and school leaders. We have provided an abridged version of Bloom's revised cognitive taxonomy in Figure 3.4.

Bloom's revised taxonomy consists of six cognitive levels: *remember, understand, apply, analyze, evaluate,* and *create.* A brief description of each level is offered in the second column of Figure 3.4. In the final column are samples of behaviors that are associated with each of the six different cognitive levels. Note that these behaviors are all verbs, suggesting actions that could be observed and denoting levels of cognitive demand. Consider

Figure 3.4 Bloom's Revised Taxonomy of Cognitive Behaviors

Cognitive Level	Description *This level of Bloom's taxonomy focuses on . . .*	Samples of Associated Behavioral Verbs		
Remember	Remembering facts, terms, or other specific knowledge by retrieving from long-term memory	Count Define Describe Draw Find	Identify Label List Locate Name	Recall Recite Record State Tell
Understand	Understanding and constructing meaning from oral, written, and graphic communication	Classify Describe Discuss Exemplify Explain	Extrapolate Identify Interpret Outline Paraphrase	Represent Restate Summarize Tell Translate
Apply	Using or carrying out a procedure in a novel, concrete situation	Carry out Classify Compute Demonstrate Determine	Draw Execute Illustrate Implement Prepare	Select Show Solve Transfer Use
Analyze	Breaking down a whole into parts and understanding the role of each part, the relationships among the parts, and the relationship to the overall purpose or structure	Analyze Break down Categorize Characterize Compare	Contrast Deconstruct Differentiate Discriminate Distinguish	Examine Infer Investigate Relate Separate
Evaluate	Making and justifying judgments based on criteria	Argue Assess Choose Conclude Critique	Decide Evaluate Judge Justify Predict	Prioritize Prove Rank Rate Select
Create	Creating a new form with individual parts; putting elements together to form a coherent whole	Adapt Create Design Develop Formulate	Imagine Integrate Invent Make Modify	Perform Plan Predict Produce Propose

the three intended learning outcomes from language arts that follow. How are these different from one another, and how is that difference important?

1. The student will list the five elements of a story.
2. The student will explain the five elements of a story.
3. The student will distinguish among the five elements of a story.

Of course, it is the verb—that is, the cognitive behavior—that is different between each of the intended learning outcomes. While the content of each statement is consistent ("the five elements of a story"), the cognitive demand expected of the students as they engage with the content is different. We can use Bloom's taxonomy to classify the differences: The first learning objective targets *remembering* as students are to *list* the five elements of a story; the second objective targets *understanding* as students are to *explain* the five story elements; and the third objective targets *analyzing* as students are to distinguish each of the five story elements from the others as well as to infer the relationship of each element to the overall story structure.

As another example, let's look again at the elementary mathematics objective that we unpacked earlier for "layers of content." That intended learning outcome is presented again in Figure 3.5. Recall that the content of the objective has been underlined. To complete our unpacking, we have circled the words that indicate targeted cognitive behaviors, and we have used Bloom's taxonomy to identify the cognitive level of each of those behaviors. The three verbs in the standard provide a clue as to the cognitive behaviors that are being asked of students: uses, justifies, and determines. *Use* implies that students apply estimation strategies. *Justify* suggests evaluative thinking because students must be able to defend the use of various estimation strategies. *Determine* requires that students employ (or apply) a process for testing the reasonableness of their estimation. In this example, students are intended to operate cognitively at the *application* and *evaluation* levels with this particular mathematics content.

Let's consider one more example, this one from high school history. After using the district curriculum to plan her unit of instruction on post–World War II America, a teacher articulates the following as one of the intended learning outcomes for her students: *By reviewing posters and slogans from the World War II era, the student will infer and understand changes in economic opportunities for women following the war.* How would the teacher

Figure 3.5 Example of Unpacking the Levels of Cognitive Demand of an Intended Learning Outcome

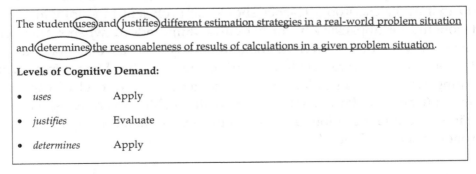

The student uses and justifies different estimation strategies in a real-world problem situation and determines the reasonableness of results of calculations in a given problem situation.

Levels of Cognitive Demand:

- *uses*   Apply
- *justifies*   Evaluate
- *determines*   Apply

Figure 3.6 Sample Unpacking of an Intended Learning Outcome for Both Content and Cognitive Level by a Teacher

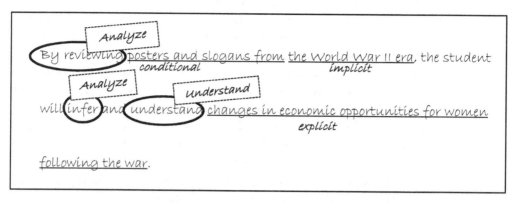

unpack this intended learning outcome? In Figure 3.6, we have illustrated the unpacking as it might appear in the teacher's notes. You will see that the teacher has underlined the content and identified the components of it that are *explicit*, *implicit*, and *conditional* in nature. Additionally, the teacher has circled the words that indicate cognitive behaviors and has identified the corresponding cognitive levels of each of those verbs using Bloom's taxonomy.

Typically, when we work with classroom teachers and school leaders, unpacking intended learning outcomes is done in the way shown in Figure 3.6. Content is *underlined* and categorized using levels of content, and cognitive behaviors are *circled* and classified using Bloom's taxonomy. The technique seems to be intuitive for many teachers. Some teachers, especially when working collaboratively to develop common assessments, will capture their unpacking in a more structured fashion, such as that shown in Figure 3.7.

As already mentioned, Bloom's taxonomy is a useful tool for classifying the level of cognitive demand of intended learning outcomes, and we contend that every classroom teacher should be proficient in employing such a taxonomy for unpacking his or her curriculum. Indeed, when researchers in one study set out to examine the effects of content coverage on student achievement, they were able to account for more of the changes in student learning when they included both the content *and* the level of cognitive demand (Gamoran, Porter, Smithson, & White, 1997). Nevertheless, we offer in Figure 3.8 a few cautions and points to consider about using a cognitive taxonomy such as Bloom's.

Figure 3.7 An Alternate Format for Capturing Unpacked Intended Learning Outcomes

Intended Learning Outcome*	Content	Verbs Used to Indicate Level of Cognitive Demand	Bloom's Classification
Health (Elementary School) The student will analyze the influence of culture, media, technology, and other factors on health by examining an advertisement for a food or health-related product and identify stated and implied messages.	Explicit ◆ Influence of culture, media, technology, and other factors on health ◆ Stated and implied messages Implicit ◆ Knowledge of advertisements and their purposes ◆ An understanding of culture, media, and technology Conditional ◆ Advertisement for a food or health product	Analyze Examine Identify	Analyzing Analyzing Understanding
Music (Middle School) The student will analyze the use of form in a varied repertoire of music representing diverse genres, styles, and cultures.	Explicit ◆ Use of form in a varied repertoire of music including diverse genres, styles, and cultures Implicit ◆ Knowledge of the diverse genres, styles, and cultures Conditional ◆ A varied repertoire of music	Analyze	Analyzing
Culinary Arts (High School) Given a scenario, the student will select and justify time-management principles of mise en place for planning and preparing food.	Explicit ◆ Time-management principles of mise en place Implicit ◆ Planning and preparing food Conditional ◆ A scenario	Select Justify	Evaluating Evaluating
Economics (High School) The student will use basic economic concepts (such as supply and demand; production, distribution, and consumption; labor, wages, and capital; inflation and deflation; market economy and command economy) to compare and contrast local, regional, and national economies across time and at the present time.	Explicit ◆ Basic economic concepts (such as supply and demand; production, distribution, and consumption; labor, wages, and capital; inflation and deflation; market economy and command economy) ◆ Local, regional, and national economies across time and the present time Implicit ◆ Knowledge of types of economies Conditional ◆ Use basic economic concepts	Use Compare Contrast	Applying Analyzing Analyzing

* Intended learning outcomes are adapted from curriculum standards from Nevada, California, Virginia, and Wisconsin, respectively.

Figure 3.8 Cautions When Using a Cognitive Taxonomy such as Bloom's

Benjamin Bloom and his colleagues (1956) provided educators with a way to "see" evidence of student thinking by observing and classifying cognitive behaviors. When teachers are able to do this, they can more effectively align their instructional strategies and their assessments with the intended learning outcomes for their students. However, there are some cautions to keep in mind.

◆ **Standards and objectives cannot always be interpreted literally because different words have different meanings in different contexts.** Consider this intended learning outcome: The student will *identify* the narrator. Depending upon the age of the students, point in the vertical sequence of the curriculum at which this objective occurs (that is, in the K–12 sequence), and the nature of the content itself, the verb "identify" could arguably be at the *understanding, applying,* or *analyzing* level. For example, "identify" could mean to explain what a narrator is (*understanding*). For a child first learning what a narrator is, reading a story and naming who the narrator is could be the *application* level of cognition. Whereas for an Advanced Placement English student who is critically reading a work of fiction with a complex narrative structure such as *Ulysses, As I Lay Dying,* or *Life of Pi,* the verb "identify" connotes the *analysis* level, if not *evaluation.*

This caution points to the need for teachers to understand the developmental characteristics of their students, to understand both the scope and sequence of the formal curriculum, and to possess a deep understanding of their subject areas.

◆ **Cognitive taxonomies should not be viewed as strictly hierarchical in nature.** Bloom's taxonomy is oftentimes portrayed as a staircase or as a pyramid. Unfortunately, such representations imply that the nature of human thinking is that one must be able to recall before one can understand, and one must understand before one can apply, and so on. While there is little question that a strong base of foundation knowledge is essential to effectively and proficiently operate at higher cognitive levels, the fact is that any instance of human cognition can be an exercise in moving up and down the taxonomical levels. Consider this intended learning outcome from science: *The student will observe, record, analyze, and classify clouds in order to understand the similarities and differences among cloud types (i.e., cirrus, stratus, cumulus, and cumulo-nimbus).* In this intended learning outcome, an assumption is made that by engaging in the higher order cognitive processes of observing, analyzing, and classifying, students will come to understand characteristics of cloud types. In other words, the assumption is that *analysis* level thinking can be an entry point to *understanding.* As a general rule, Bloom's taxonomy is ordered from simpler cognitive behaviors (e.g., recalling) to more complex cognitive processes (e.g., critiquing), but this does not mean that one cannot engage in a higher level of cognitive behavior with an imperfect recollection of facts at a lower cognitive level.

This caution points to the need for teachers to understand how students' inherent abilities and inclination to think critically, to argue, and to create can be used as instructional levers to learn facts, concepts, and procedures.

◆ **Bloom's taxonomy is not the only tool for classifying cognitive behavior.** The fact is that educators, psychologists, cognitive scientists, and others have developed innumerable taxonomies and other classification systems for helping humans categorize, understand, and work with human cognition. In the education field, Bloom's (1956) original taxonomy is certainly the most widely recognized. As we've shared, we tend to favor Anderson and Krathwohl's (2001) revised version of Bloom's taxonomy; however, we should note that our introduction and use of that taxonomy in the context of this book is not complete. Most notably, the revised taxonomy includes four distinct dimensions of knowledge

Figure 3.8 (Continued)

(*factual*, *conceptual*, *procedural*, and *metacognitive*) in addition to 19 explicit cognitive processes (which are organized by the six categories that we've described). Other well-known cognitive frameworks include the Depth of Knowledge framework developed by Webb and his colleagues (2005), the Survey of Enacted Curriculum subject-specific frameworks (see Blank 2002 for an early example in mathematics), and the Structure of the Observed Learning Outcome (SOLO) taxonomy developed by Biggs and Collis (1982). There can be good cases to be made for the use of one taxonomy over another, but that is not our main point.

This caution points to the need for the teachers and school leaders of an educational organization (whether a school or district) to have a common framework of understanding about human cognition, as well as a common vocabulary for using that framework for planning curriculum, instruction, and assessment.

◆ **Bloom's taxonomy addresses the cognitive domain only and not the affective and psychomotor domains.** The focus of this book is on the cognitive domain of learning. This is not to say that the other two domains—the affective and psychomotor domains—are any less important. For example, we not only want our students to be able to read, we want them to *enjoy* reading. We want our students to be able to classify types of art as well as develop an *appreciation* for art. Appreciation and enjoyment are affective behaviors. The affective domain addresses aims of education that are oftentimes intangible but critically important—curiosity and patriotism, for instance. These are values or beliefs that get at the heart of schooling, which is to prepare students for life in broader society. However, such intended outcomes of schooling are oftentimes difficult, if not impossible, to assess objectively. The psychomotor domain is no less important. In order to be able to write, a student must be able to hold a pencil in his hand and to manipulate it deftly. Other psychomotor skills include using a lathe to shape wood, measuring with a set of measuring spoons or with a beaker, running, typing or keyboarding, observing using a microscope, and more. We have presented Bloom's taxonomy for *cognitive* behaviors, but there are taxonomies for the affective and psychomotor behaviors, too. While the affective and psychomotor domains are a part of the content and skills that students learn in school, they are less typically assessed using paper-pencil formats and so are not addressed directly in this book on teacher-made assessments.

This caution points to the need for teachers and other school leaders to be cognizant (pun intended!) not only of the cognitive domain of learning but also of the psychomotor and affective domains, which are also central to student learning and development.

Unpacking a Unit of Instruction

The importance of unpacking intended learning outcomes as the first step for creating a valid assessment cannot be overstated. Others agree, including theorists (e.g., Anderson & Krathwohl, 2001; Bloom et al., 1956), researchers (e.g., Blank, 2002; Marzano, 2003; Schmidt, McKnight, Houang, Wang, Wiley, Cogan, & Wolfe, 2001), professional associations (e.g., Kahl, Hofman, & Bryan, 2013), educational pundits (e.g., Schmoker, 2006; Wagner, 2008), professional developers (e.g., Stiggins, Arter, Chappuis, & Chappuis, 2006), and practitioners (e.g., Ferriter, 2009; Jackson, 2009). But there is more to it than simply unpacking.

In each of the preceding examples, we have unpacked intended learning outcomes that have been taken out of context. While this is helpful for purposes of demonstrating the unpacking process, it is not realistic. Teachers break down complex curricula into teachable chunks—that is, units of instruction. Therefore, teachers should unpack the intended learning outcomes for units of instruction, rather than focusing on discrete objectives taken out of context. (As a reminder of this point, revisit the first caution in Figure 3.8.) Let's look at an example of unpacking a unit of instruction from an upper elementary science unit.

Phyllis Phylum teaches 5th grade. She will be teaching a unit on the classification of organisms. Her school district developed objectives based on state standards for 5th grade science. Phyllis uses the district's pacing guide to map out the unit and to determine the number of instructional days that will be spent on specific content. Figure 3.9 shows the intended learning outcomes for the unit and the approximate percentage of instructional time anticipated for each objective.

Phyllis knows the importance of this particular unit in the sequence of the science curriculum. That is to say that Phyllis understands how this unit on the classification and naming system that scientists use will be integral to her students' further learning not only in 5th grade, but also in 6th grade general science, in 7th grade life science, and in high school biology. This is part of the context that Phyllis has kept in mind as she articulated the intended learning outcomes for this unit and as she unpacks them.

Phyllis's unpacking is shown in Figure 3.10. For the sake of our illustration here, Phyllis has unpacked the *content* of her intended learning outcomes simply by underlining it. She has not distinguished between *explicit*, *implicit*, and *conditional* content in this example. She has, nevertheless, taken

Figure 3.9 Sample Intended Learning Outcomes for a 5th Grade Life Sciences Unit

The student will:
1. Compare and contrast key features and activities between organisms. (*Approximately 50% of instructional time.*)
    a. Classify organisms based on physical features.
    b. Arrange organisms in a hierarchy according to similarities and differences in features.
    c. Categorize examples of organisms as representatives of the kingdoms and recognize that the number of kingdoms is subject to change.
2. Explain the binomial nomenclature for naming plants and animals. (*Approximately 30% of instructional time.*)
3. Identify and name examples of major animal phyla. (*Approximately 10% of instructional time.*)
4. Identify and name examples of major plant phyla. (*Approximately 10% of instructional time.*)

Figure 3.10 Sample of an Unpacked 5th Grade Life Sciences Unit

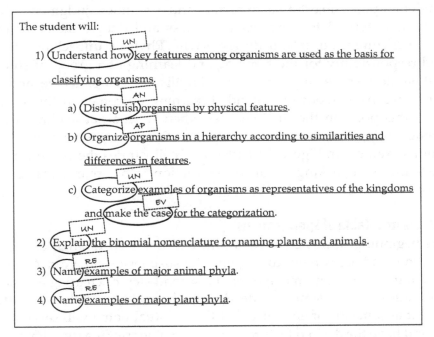

the critically important step of unpacking objectives for cognitive behaviors, and she has used Bloom's taxonomy to identify the corresponding cognitive levels. You'll note that she has used simple abbreviations for the levels, such as "UN" for *understanding* and "AN" for *analysis.*

A few final points about unpacking units of instruction: First, you may note that according to Phyllis Phylum's unpacking, this particular unit targets five of the six cognitive levels. It does not reach the highest level of *creating.* There is nothing inherently wrong about this because the content and cognitive levels are driven by larger decisions about curricular scope, sequencing, developmental appropriateness, and the like. Alas, our focus in this book is not on curriculum development, so we ask that you play along with this example.

Second, you may note that seeing the complete set of intended learning outcomes for this unit helps to interpret some of the targeted cognitive levels. For example, the second part of 1c includes the verb "make," which might suggest the cognitive levels of either *applying* or *creating.* However, seeing that the objective is to "make the case" and see the sequencing of other intended learning that leads to this particular objective, it becomes more evident that the intent is for students to *justify* or *defend* their reasoning, which is an *evaluation* level behavior.

Third, the process of unpacking intended learning outcomes is utterly dependent upon subject-area expertise and grounded judgment. Consequently, it is typical for teachers to discuss and debate their unpacking of the curriculum. So, if you disagree with Phyllis's unpacking and you shared responsibility for the teaching and learning of a group of students, then it would be necessary for you and Phyllis to discuss, debate, and work toward consensus about the intended learning outcomes in this unit. We address this point in the final chapter when we look at leading teachers in strengthening their assessment practices. For now, we hope that Phyllis Phylum's example in Figure 3.10 adequately illustrates the process and the importance of unpacking a unit of instruction rather than isolated objectives or standards.

Step 2: Create a Table of Specifications

At the beginning of this chapter, we likened the need to align curriculum, instruction, and assessment to aligning the suspension on a car. At the risk of drawing on too many metaphors, the second step of creating a valid and reliable assessment is similar to designing a house. An architect will draw a blueprint as a means of ensuring that the eventual home will serve its purposes and have the desired features. In short, a blueprint is a two-dimensional planning tool to guide the creation of a three-dimensional structure. When constructing an assessment, a similar kind of blueprint is necessary, and this tool is referred to as a *table of specifications*. A **table of specifications** is a chart or table that details the content and level of cognitive demand assessed on an assessment, as well as the types and emphases of assessment items. In fact, a table of specifications is often referred to in the assessment field as an "assessment blueprint" (Hogan, 2007).

A table of specifications is essential to addressing both validity and reliability. Validity, as explained earlier, means that the assessment can be used to draw appropriate inferences. A table of specifications provides a way to ensure that the assessment is based on the intended outcomes of learning as articulated in the curriculum. Furthermore, as we know from the previous explanation of unpacking intended learning outcomes, this alignment between the curriculum and the eventual assessment is necessary not only in terms of the intended content of the objectives but also the intended cognitive behaviors.

Reliability means that we can have confidence in the results of the assessment because the assessment guards against sources of error. A table of specifications provides a way of ensuring that the number of items on an assessment is adequate to ensure dependable results that are not likely caused by chance. While this is only one strategy for strengthening the potential reliability of an assessment, any effort to control the influence of error on an assessment is important.

Creating a table of specifications begins with mapping intended learning outcomes onto a grid or chart to show the intersection of the content and the cognitive levels of those objectives, and then it requires consideration of the relative emphasis or importance of intended learning outcomes within the unit. Here we look at creating a table of specifications to guide the design of a teacher-made assessment.

Mapping Intended Learning Outcomes

Phyllis Phylum has written and unpacked the intended learning outcomes for her 5th grade life sciences unit on plant and animal kingdoms. Now she is ready to create a *table of specifications*. Figure 3.11 is a template for a table of specifications. The headings of the columns should look familiar to you from the unpacking process: The major left-hand column is for *content*, while the remaining six columns follow in order of Bloom's *cognitive levels*.

Ms. Phylum now maps her unpacked intended learning outcomes onto this table by writing the content of her unit in the left-hand column and then by indicating the targeted cognitive level of each objective with a corresponding checkmark. (We'll get to the check plusses in a bit.) She has also written the word or words of the targeted cognitive behaviors in the cells.

Figure 3.11 Template for a Table of Specifications

Table of Specifications for _____   Grade_____
(unit of study)

Content	Level of Cognitive Demand					
	Remember	Understand	Apply	Analyze	Evaluate	Create

Figure 3.12 Sample Table of Specifications for Ms. Phylum's 5th Grade Life Sciences Unit

Table of Specifications for ___Plant and Animal Kingdoms___   Grade ____5th Grade____
(unit of study)

Content	Level of Cognitive Demand					
	Remember	Understand	Apply	Analyze	Evaluate	Create
key features among organisms are used as the basis for classifying organisms		✓+ Understand how				
organisms by physical features				✓+ Distinguish		
organisms in a hierarchy according to similarities and differences in features			✓+ Organize			
examples of organisms as representatives of the kingdoms and the case for the categorization		✓+ Categorize			✓ make the case	
the binomial nomenclature for naming plants and animals		✓ Explain				
examples of major animal phyla	✓ Name					
examples of major plant phyla	✓ Name					

As can be seen in Figure 3.12 (Ms. Phylum's table of specifications for her science unit), a table of specifications provides a simple but complete representation of the intended learning outcomes of a unit of instruction, presented in two "dimensions": content and cognitive level. This view of the curriculum for this unit provides a quick visual guide for what the unit assessment should include (that is, items that correspond in content and cognitive demand to the cells indicated by checkmarks) and should *not* include (that is, cells where there is no intersection of content and cognitive level). By including the actual cognitive verbs in the cells, Ms. Phylum is reminded, for example, that the three objectives that are at the *understanding* level actually involve different cognitive behaviors (that is, *understand how*, *categorize*, and *explain*). These differences are important when Ms. Phylum is creating and selecting actual assessment items and activities for each of these intended learning outcomes. Essentially, the table of specifications will serve as a kind of blueprint for the design and construction of Ms. Phylum's assessment for this unit.

Indicating Relative Emphasis

Another consideration in creating a table of specifications is to indicate the relative emphasis of specific intended learning outcomes. This is necessary because some intended learning outcomes might have relatively greater importance than other objectives within a unit of instruction.

In the example from the 5th grade life sciences unit, Ms. Phylum has indicated the relative emphasis on her table of specifications by using check-plus marks (✓+). As shown in Figure 3.12, half of the eight intended learning outcomes are of relatively greater importance in Ms. Phylum's judgment. In this particular example, these intended learning outcomes are at the *understanding*, *applying*, and *analyzing* levels. This is not to suggest that the other four objectives in this unit are not important. Rather, by indicating relative emphasis, Ms. Phylum is more likely to ensure the enduring understandings and skills that are important for her students to acquire through this unit of instruction (Wiggins & McTighe, 2005).

How does a teacher determine the relative importance or emphasis of intended learning outcomes? There are a number of possible considerations. Particularly, a teacher may:

- ◆ Consider what the enduring understandings and the core skills of the unit are, through an instructional planning process such as Understanding by Design (Wiggins & McTighe, 2005).
- ◆ Consider which content and/or skills within the unit are important building blocks for subsequent objectives within the context of the year-long course or within the **vertical articulation** of objectives between grade levels—that is, the intentional sequencing of intended learning outcomes over the course of multiple years and grade levels within a subject area (Porter, 2002). (Recall that Phyllis Phylum knows that understanding scientific naming conventions in the 5th grade is important for subsequent learning in 6th grade general science, 7th grade life science, and high school biology.)
- ◆ Consider which content and/or skills within the unit have interdisciplinary connections to content and/or skills in other subject areas in the **horizontal articulation** of objectives at a given grade level. Drawing on such interdisciplinary connections can gain efficiencies in teaching and can reinforce high-leverage intended learning outcomes that cut across subject areas, such as identifying patterns, drawing connections, representing symbolically, problem solving, and reasoning. (Note how Phyllis has emphasized *distinguishing*, *organizing*, and *categorizing*.)
- ◆ Consider the approximate instructional time that is necessary for each intended learning outcome, which may be evident in the district's pacing guide for the curriculum. (Note in Figure 3.9 that approximately 50% of the instructional time is anticipated for the

first four intended learning outcomes, as Ms. Phylum plans to use an inquiry approach to teaching the content and skills.)

◆ Examine the test blueprints for any external standardized assessment in the subject area that students will take and determine the emphasis given to specific objectives on that high-stakes test. (While this is a practical approach, Ms. Phylum needs to keep in mind the cautions from chapter 1 about *narrowing the taught curriculum*, which can be an unintentional consequence of having external standardized assessments drive a teacher's instructional decisions.)

Typically, a teacher will use a combination of these strategies to determine the relative emphasis given to particular intended learning outcomes in a unit. It may have occurred to you that determining relative emphasis is essentially a process that is related to a teacher making curricular decisions—that is, identifying clearly and deeply the intended learning outcomes for students. For this reason, we contend that there are real advantages to having multiple teachers determine relative emphasis in collaborative teams. Doing so is a concrete step in ensuring that the curriculum is not only relevant and rigorous, but also that every student in the school has the opportunity to acquire the intended learning outcomes of the curriculum (Marzano, 2003).

We should also point out that that the technique of using checks (✓) and check-plusses (✓+) to indicate relative emphasis is just one such system. We have found that some teachers prefer other symbol systems. You might consider these instead of checkmarks:

◆ *H/M/L* to classify intended learning outcomes as having *High, Moderate*, or *Low* emphasis;

◆ Percentages (such as 50%, 25%, 10%) to indicate proportionality of emphasis among intended learning outcomes.

The important point is that a table of specifications should indicate succinctly the relative importance of intended learning outcomes in a unit. (We have even worked with teachers who used smiley faces . . . no kidding! ☺)

How Tables of Specifications Make a Difference

In our experience, the creation and use of a *table of specifications* is a concrete and practical technique for teachers to use when designing and constructing classroom assessments. What's more, creating and using tables of specifications can make a difference in the quality of assessments and, therefore, in strengthening the use of assessment as part of the teaching and learning process.

Recall from chapter 2 our discussion of *content validity*, which we also referred to as *sampling validity*. Sampling validity is concerned with the proportional representation of learning outcomes on an assessment. For instance, if Ms. Phylum devoted 50% of the test of her life sciences unit to naming examples of animal and plant phyla (the last two objectives on her table), then her assessment would have very weak sampling validity. This is because she would be *over-sampling* two intended learning outcomes that are of relatively lesser importance, and she would be vastly *under-sampling* the set of intended learning outcomes that are of greater importance. A table of specifications can ensure against this very typical shortcoming of teacher-made assessments.

In our experience, most classroom teachers are unfamiliar with tables of specifications. Or, if they are familiar with them, their understanding of tables of specifications is in relation only to the construction of standardized assessments. We have found that when teachers begin to create tables of specifications to guide the construction and use of their own classroom assessments, good things follow. For example, one team of scholars has suggested that classroom teachers' use of tables of specifications can be a powerful way of ensuring the alignment of teacher-made assessments to high-stakes accountability measures and outcomes on those measures (Notar, Zuelke, Wilson, & Yunker, 2004). More importantly, though, a table of specifications provides a visually intuitive, two-dimensional blueprint to help teachers align their curriculum, instruction, and assessments. In short, a table of specifications is a means to ensure that $C = I = A$.

Step 3: Clarify Your Purposes for and Circumstances of Assessing Student Learning

Step 1 of the process we are suggesting focused on *what* to assess, with particular emphasis on unpacking the content and cognitive levels of the intended learning outcomes of a unit of instruction. Step 2 introduced a tool called a *table of specifications*, which can serve as a kind of blueprint for planning an assessment. Step 3 requires that a teacher clarify the purpose of assessing student learning and the circumstances under which assessment will occur. Frankly, what we are referring to as Step 3 could arguably be the first step. However, our reason for beginning the seven steps with unpacking intended learning outcomes is because we find it most helpful to have the *intended learning* for students drive the process. In any case, early in the process of creating a teacher-made assessment, the teacher needs to consider a few fundamental questions:

1. Why are you assessing student learning?
2. When are you assessing student learning?

3. Where are you assessing student learning?
4. Under what circumstances are you assessing student learning?

Let's explore these questions as two sets.

Why and When Are You Assessing Learning?

As discussed in chapter 1, assessment is used for three purposes: planning instruction or to establish the level of prior knowledge or skill (pre-assessment prior to instruction), as a learning activity to inform instructional decisions (formative assessment during instruction), and to determine the nature and degree of student learning at some point in time and to communicate that judgment to others (summative assessment after some period of instruction). Being clear about *why* you are assessing student learning (and, as noted in each parenthetical statement in the previous sentence, *when* you are assessing) can have implications for how you will assess. For example, summative assessments tend to be more comprehensive in their coverage of a set of intended learning outcomes than formative assessment techniques, but formative assessments tend to have a greater effect on student learning. We refer you again to Figure 1.4 in chapter 1 for a review of some of the key characteristics of different types of assessments. The other important point here is that the purpose of your assessment will have bearing on the format of your assessment. For the purposes of this book, our focus is on the creation and use of summative assessments; however, we should note that the principles and the techniques we present are relevant to the creation of pre-assessments and summative assessments. In chapter 6, we do provide additional exploration of formative assessment techniques.

Where and Under What Circumstances Are You Assessing Learning?

The format of an assessment will also be influenced by the actual location and circumstances in which students will complete the assessment. For example, an English teacher may wish to assess oral speaking skills. The most appropriate and authentic way to assess these skills is by having each student give a speech in front of an audience and to assess each student's ability based on a rubric of public speaking competencies. This is more authentic than having students answer a series of recall- and comprehension-type questions about public speaking techniques. However, what the teacher will be gaining in authenticity will be lost in efficiency. Such considerations are important because teachers must make practical decisions about the format of assessments, and such decisions will oftentimes necessitate a trade-off among features such as these:

- ◆ Feasibility
- ◆ Efficiency
- ◆ Objectivity
- ◆ Comprehensiveness
- ◆ Authenticity

To further explore this point, consider that teachers need to determine how much time students will have to complete an assessment. The amount of time is influenced by the type of assessment. Some project-based assessments may take a week, two weeks, or even an entire semester. A paper-pencil assessment might be administered in one class period, and a multiple choice assessment may be the best option due to time constraints. The determination of time can also be influenced by how long teachers have to spend on a particular unit of study. Many school districts use pacing guides or curriculum maps that teachers must follow.

Returning to our 5th grade life sciences example, Phyllis Phylum has made some choices in developing her assessment. She will use the assessment for summative purposes to determine whether students have acquired the intended learning outcomes of her life sciences unit. The students receive grades on the assessment, and those grades will be used as one data source to determine the students' nine-weeks grades in 5th grade science. She will also use the completed assessment as a learning activity with her students, having them identify patterns in their own performances (a *formative assessment* use). Because of time constraints, Phyllis has determined that she will use a paper-pencil assessment with objective-type questions. This will make both the taking and the grading of the assessment more efficient. Students will complete the assessment in her classroom. Phyllis has considered why, when, where, and under what conditions this particular assessment will occur. Her decisions contribute to the design of the assessment and, therefore, to the inferences about student learning she will be able to draw from the results.

Step 4: Determine the Appropriate Types of Assessment Items/Activities to Use

Next, teachers must decide what types of items to include on the assessment. There are two basic types of items: select-response and constructed-response. With **select-response items**, the student chooses from answer choices provided by teachers. These items include alternate choice (such as true/false, yes/no, fact/opinion), matching, and multiple choice. Figure 3.13 shows these types of select-response items on a continuum of student response options. True-false questions provide students with only two response options, whereas matching and multiple choice have more

Figure 3.13 Types of Select-Response Items

Figure 3.14 Types of Constructed-Response Items and Activities

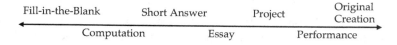

than two response options. Matching is placed in the middle of the continuum, as a matching set typically results in options being narrowed as they are used.

Constructed-response items require that the student provide the answers to questions. Constructed-response items include such formats as fill-in-the-blank, computational problems, short answer, and essays. They also include extended, stand-alone assessment activities, such as performance tasks, projects, and original creations. Figure 3.14 shows the continuum of constructed-response items and activities. As you move toward the left-hand side of the continuum, the responses that students would provide tend to become more *convergent*. In other words, even though students are supplying responses, the responses toward the left of the continuum tend to have a single correct answer or a narrow range of possible correct answers. As you move toward the right-hand side of the continuum, possible responses tend to be more *divergent*, meaning that the possible range of correct answers will be quite varied.

Considering the Utility and Appropriateness of Assessment Items/Activities

The type(s) of items chosen to include on an assessment can depend on a myriad of factors such as the content being assessed, the level of cognitive demand, and the time available to complete the assessment. Let's consider that last point for a moment. Figure 3.15 indicates the amount of time that a variety of common item formats may take to answer and the level of cognitive demand that can be assessed by the item type (Notar et al., 2004). We caution against applying this table without due attention to the footnotes in it and to a more generic caution about considering the age of the students being assessed. Nonetheless, it is important for teachers to consider the utilitarian value that certain item types can provide, such as *efficiency*. Because assessment is always a question of sampling a limited subset of behaviors to represent a broader set of intended learning

Figure 3.15 Item Types by Level of Cognitive Demand and Approximate Time to Respond

Type of Question	Approximate Time to Respond	Level of Cognitive Demand					
		Remember	Understand	Apply	Analyze	Evaluate	Create
Select-Response							
Alternate Choice	15–30 seconds	✔	✔	✔			
Matching	60–90 seconds[1]	✔	✔				
Multiple Choice	30–60 seconds[2]	✔	✔	✔	✔		
Constructed-Response							
Fill-in-the-Blank	30 seconds	✔	✔				
Computation	15–90 seconds[3]	✔	✔	✔			
Short Answer	1–5 minutes[4]	✔	✔	✔	✔	✔	
Essay	5–90 minutes[4]	✔	✔	✔	✔	✔	✔

[1] Depending on the number of matching items
[2] Depending on the level of cognitive demand
[3] Depending on the complexity of required procedures
[4] Depending on comprehensiveness of the topic and complexity of the written form

outcomes, considering the typical amount of time needed to respond is a practical point.

Previously, under Step 3, we mentioned the need for teachers to consider such factors as *feasibility, efficiency, objectivity, comprehensiveness,* and *authenticity* in selecting assessment items and activities. We reiterate and expand upon that point here. Broadly speaking, select-response items tend to be more *feasible* to use, more *efficient* in their use of time both in completion and grading, and more *objective* in their grading, as compared to constructed-response items. By way of contrast, constructed-response items tend to be more *comprehensive* in nature and more *authentic* in their representation of complex intended learning outcomes. Constructed-response items on teacher-made tests most often take the form of open-ended mathematics problems, short answer questions, and essay prompts. However, as noted earlier, constructed-response items can also include stand-alone assessment *activities*. We provide a side note about assessment activities in Figure 3.16.

Figure 3.16 A Note about Assessment Activities

How is an assessment *activity* different from an assessment *item*? Essentially, the differences are between *grain size, number,* and *length of time to complete.*

By *grain size,* we mean the comprehensiveness of an activity or item. Consider items on a conventional paper-pencil test, such as true/false, matching, and even short answer items. Such items typically assess a distinct understanding, concept, or skill. Consequently, such items have specific correct answers. Even if they are constructed-response format, such as a short answer question, the correct answer is typically convergent in nature—that is, the answer is distinct and objective.

For example, a short answer question on a United States history test might prompt students to identify and explain three significant causes of the Civil War. Even though the item is a constructed-response format, its *grain size* is small—that is, the answers are limited in number and can be operationally identified in advance by the teacher. However, we can also assume that this one question alone would not suffice to draw inferences about the nature and degree of student learning in an entire unit on the Civil War. Thus, the teacher is likely to include a series of other small grain size items to assess other content and skills. In other words, there are likely to be a *number* of items that, together, provide an adequate sampling of the intended learning outcomes of the unit. Referring back to Figure 3.15, each of these individual items is likely to require a short *length of time to complete.* In this example, the "test" is comprised of the sum of its individual items, so to speak.

Assessment activities, on the other hand, are essentially stand-alone assessments. By way of contrast to assessment items, assessment activities sample a larger, more complete set of knowledge and skills. For instance, a laboratory exercise in a science class could comprehensively assess students' understanding of a set of content and concepts while also assessing students' application of scientific inquiry skills and reasoning. This comprehensive activity is one assessment performance in and of itself. In other words, this *single* assessment activity would comprise a much larger *grain size* than a single assessment item such as a multiple choice question, but it would also require a much longer *duration of time* for students to complete.

How does a teacher choose between using assessment items and activities? Fundamentally, we follow this principle: *The best assessment item or activity is that which most authentically, efficiently, and fairly provides the student the opportunity to demonstrate his or her acquisition of the intended learning outcome in terms of both content and cognitive level.* Therefore, deciding on the best item or activity always involves a teacher making decisions and trade-offs among issues of feasibility, efficiency, objectivity, comprehensiveness, and authenticity. In early primary grades, the use of assessment *activities,* for example, is often driven by the issue of *feasibility* related to the young age of the students. Alternatively, in upper secondary classrooms, teachers oftentimes need to employ combinations of conventional tests and assessment activities (e.g., essays, labs, debates) to adequately sample complex sets of intended learning outcomes.

Creating a Unit Assessment Plan

Returning once again to our example from 5th grade life sciences, Phyllis Phylum decides to use multiple choice, matching, and short answer items on her assessment. Phyllis reasons that she can assess the multiple cognitive levels identified in her objectives using these types of items. She determines that the assessment item types are appropriate for the content being assessed and that they permit her students to respond feasibly and efficiently within the 50 minutes that she has been allotted for science each day. But what Ms. Phylum also realizes is that her paper-pencil test will not tap into the intended learning outcome in this unit that targets *evaluation* level thinking. What's more, her table of specifications serves to remind her that having students demonstrate their ability to engage in scientific inquiry as a means toward developing their understanding of how scientists classify and name plants and animals is a particularly important set of intended learning outcomes within this unit. With these considerations in mind, Ms. Phylum determines that she needs an assessment activity that will be complementary to her paper-pencil unit test.

Figure 3.17 presents Ms. Phylum's *unit assessment plan*. A **unit assessment plan** is another use of a table of specifications with which a teacher can map out the complementary key assessments within a unit that function together to ensure that all of the intended learning outcomes in a unit are assessed and accounted for. In the example of Ms. Phylum's unit assessment plan, the paper-pencil unit test (consisting of multiple choice, matching, and short answer) will be designed to assess seven of the eight intended learning outcomes at cognitive levels ranging from *remembering* to *analyzing*. A separate

Figure 3.17 Sample Unit Assessment Plan for Ms. Phylum's 5th Grade Life Sciences Unit

Table of Specifications for __Plant and Animal Kingdoms__   Grade __5th Grade__
(unit of study)

Content	Level of Cognitive Demand					
	Remember	Understand	Apply	Analyze	Evaluate	Create
key features among organisms are used as the basis for classifying organisms		✓+ Unit Test Inquiry Activity				
organisms by physical features				✓+ Unit Test Inquiry Activity		
organisms in a hierarchy according to similarities and differences in features			✓+ Unit Test Inquiry Activity			
examples of organisms as representatives of the kingdoms and the case for the categorization		✓+ Unit Test Inquiry Activity			✓ Inquiry Activity	
the binomial nomenclature for naming plants and animals		✓ Unit Test				
examples of major animal phyla	✓ Unit Test					
examples of major plant phyla	✓ Unit Test					

stand-alone, performance-based assessment referred to in the sample unit assessment plan as the "Inquiry Activity" will serve to also assess the first four objectives that are of relatively greater importance in this unit while also tapping the *evaluation* level objective that is not assessed on the unit test.

Creating a *unit assessment plan* can allow a teacher to think strategically about how best to employ assessments as part of the instructional unit. Of particular value is the ability to plan for the complementary roles that conventional paper-pencil assessments and performance-based assessment activities (such as the "Inquiry Activity" in Ms. Phylum's class) can play in ensuring the balanced assessment of intended learning outcomes. For purposes of demonstrating the principles of assessment as they apply to teacher-made assessments, we will continue with our focus on paper-pencil assessments. However, the principles apply similarly when creating constructed-response assessments and extended performance-based assessments, which we will explore further in chapter 5.

Step 5: Determine the Appropriate Number and Weight of Assessment Items

Returning to Ms. Phylum's creation of her unit test, she has determined the types of assessment items she will use. Now she gives thought to the number and relative weight of the items on the test. Keeping the guiding principle of having her assessment (*A*) align with her curriculum (*C*), Ms. Phylum wants to balance her items both in terms of the number of items and the relative weight of each. Ms. Phylum's table of specifications for her unit test is shown in Figure 3.18.

Ms. Phylum's unit test will consist of 33 items, 14 of which will be multiple choice, 13 of which will be matching, and 6 of which will be short answer. By planning for an assessment in which the items align to the intended learning outcomes in terms of both content and cognitive level, Ms. Phylum is strengthening the potential validity of the assessment. In short, she is working to ensure that *A* = *C*. (Remember from the previous discussion of the unit assessment plan that the one cell that does not have any test items indicated will be assessed with the Inquiry Activity assessment.)

Also note that there is some balance among the cells. The number of items within each cell on the table of specifications ranges from 2 (the short answer items for the fifth objective) to 10 (which includes a matching item for eight matches). No intended learning outcome is either under-sampled or over-sampled. What's more, by having at least two items for each intended learning outcome, Ms. Phylum is strengthening the potential reliability of her test through the principle of *repeated trials reliability*, as discussed in chapter 2.

Figure 3.18 Sample Table of Specifications Indicating Item Types for Ms. Phylum's 5th Grade Life Sciences Unit

Table of Specifications for _Plant and Animal Kingdoms_   Grade _5th Grade_

Content	Level of Cognitive Demand					
	Remember	Understand	Apply	Analyze	Evaluate	Create
key features among organisms are used as the basis for classifying organisms		✓+ Understand how 3 MC 2 SA				
organisms by physical features				✓+ Distinguish 8 Mtch 2 SA		
organisms in a hierarchy according to similarities and differences in features			✓+ Organize 3 MC			
examples of organisms as representatives of the kingdoms and the case for the categorization		✓+ Categorize 5 Mtch			✓ make the case	
the binomial nomenclature for naming plants and animals		✓ Explain 2 SA				
examples of major animal phyla	✓ Name 4 MC					
examples of major plant phyla	✓ Name 4MC					

MC = Multiple Choice   SA = Short Answer   Mtch = Matching

Ms. Phylum may also use her table of specifications to decide about the weighting of items. In the absence of a table of specifications, Ms. Phylum might simply reason that since there are 33 questions, each item should be worth 3.33 points. This would conveniently total 99.99, which is close enough to an easily calculable 100. However, using her table of specifications to guide her thinking—and giving particular attention to the relative importance of the intended learning outcomes—Ms. Phylum might reason differently. Figure 3.19 is Ms. Phylum's table of specifications for her unit test indicating the relative weight of each item.

Notice what Ms. Phylum has *not* done. She has *not* simply taken the total number of items and assigned them each the same weight. *Nor* has she simply weighted all of the same item types the same based on the fact that they are the same format (that is, all multiple choice items having the same weight, all matching items having the same weight, and all short answer items having the same weight). Instead, Ms. Phylum has made conscious decisions to weight items differently, dependent mainly on the relative importance of the intended learning outcomes they are assessing. This is not a perfect science. For instance, the total points on Ms. Phylum's test add up to 101, which doesn't make for a perfect percentage. But this is such a minor point

Figure 3.19 Sample Table of Specifications Indicating Relative Weight for Ms. Phylum's 5th Grade Life Sciences Unit

Table of Specifications for _Plant and Animal Kingdoms_   Grade _5th Grade_

Content	Remember	Understand	Apply	Analyze	Evaluate	Create
key features among organisms are used as the basis for classifying organisms		✓+ 3 MC @ 3 pts ea. 2 SA @ 8 pts ea.	_25% of weight_		_25% of weight_	
organisms by physical features				✓+ 8 Mtch @ 1 pt ea. 2 SA @ 8 pts ea.		
organisms in a hierarchy according to similarities and differences in features			✓+ 3 MC @ 4 pts each _12% of weight_			
examples of organisms as representatives of the kingdoms and the case for the categorization		✓+ 5 Mtch @ 3 pts each	_15% of weight_		✓	
the binomial nomenclature for naming plants and animals		✓ 2 SA @ 4 pts ea.	_8% of weight_			
examples of major animal phyla	✓ 4 MC @ 2 pts. each	_8% of weight_				
examples of major plant phyla	✓ 4MC @ 2 pts. each	_8% of weight_				

MC = Multiple Choice   SA = Short Answer   Mtch = Matching

and really of no consequence. The more important point is that the *sampling validity* of the test—meaning the proportional representation of the intended learning outcomes in the unit—is greatly strengthened by Ms. Phylum's guided decision making.

The creation and use of a *table of specifications* to guide the design and construction of teacher-made assessments is a critically important competency of what it means for a teacher to possess *assessment literacy*. (See chapter 1 to revisit this key term.) However, do not let the formality of the tool as presented in these figures mislead you. A table of specifications can be sketched out on a napkin or a scrap piece of paper. Creating a table of specifications is simply a means of showing the intersection between the content and cognitive level of a set of intended learning outcomes and then ensuring that the planned assessment has an adequate and proportional number of items to account for those intended learned outcomes. (Two different templates for creating a table of specifications are offered in Figures 3.11 and 3.20.) Equally important is the use of a table of specifications to ensure

Figure 3.20 Template for a Table of Specifications—Advanced Version

Table of Specifications for _____

(unit of study)

Grade _____

Content	Level of Cognitive Demand					
	Remember	**Understand**	**Apply**	**Analyze**	**Evaluate**	**Create**
	Cognitive Behavior: / Relative Emphasis: # of Items: / Item Types:	Cognitive Behavior: / Relative Emphasis: # of Items: / Item Types:	Cognitive Behavior: / Relative Emphasis: # of Items: / Item Types:	Cognitive Behavior: / Relative Emphasis: # of Items: / Item Types:	Cognitive Behavior: / Relative Emphasis: # of Items: / Item Types:	Cognitive Behavior: / Relative Emphasis: # of Items: / Item Types:
	Cognitive Behavior: / Relative Emphasis: # of Items: / Item Types:	Cognitive Behavior: / Relative Emphasis: # of Items: / Item Types:	Cognitive Behavior: / Relative Emphasis: # of Items: / Item Types:	Cognitive Behavior: / Relative Emphasis: # of Items: / Item Types:	Cognitive Behavior: / Relative Emphasis: # of Items: / Item Types:	Cognitive Behavior: / Relative Emphasis: # of Items: / Item Types:
	Cognitive Behavior: / Relative Emphasis: # of Items: / Item Types:	Cognitive Behavior: / Relative Emphasis: # of Items: / Item Types:	Cognitive Behavior: / Relative Emphasis: # of Items: / Item Types:	Cognitive Behavior: / Relative Emphasis: # of Items: / Item Types:	Cognitive Behavior: / Relative Emphasis: # of Items: / Item Types:	Cognitive Behavior: / Relative Emphasis: # of Items: / Item Types:
	Cognitive Behavior: / Relative Emphasis: # of Items: / Item Types:	Cognitive Behavior: / Relative Emphasis: # of Items: / Item Types:	Cognitive Behavior: / Relative Emphasis: # of Items: / Item Types:	Cognitive Behavior: / Relative Emphasis: # of Items: / Item Types:	Cognitive Behavior: / Relative Emphasis: # of Items: / Item Types:	Cognitive Behavior: / Relative Emphasis: # of Items: / Item Types:

that an assessment does not include items or content at a level of cognitive demand not indicated on the table of specifications.

Step 6: Create and Select Assessment Items That Are Valid and Reliable

An assessment is only as valid and reliable as the items within it. Assessment items should target both the content and the cognitive levels of the intended learning outcomes, as represented in a table of specifications. Here are a few questions to ask as you create and/or select assessment items:

- ◆ Does the item address the appropriate content at the targeted cognitive level?
- ◆ Does the item distinguish between those students who have acquired the intended learning outcome and those who have not?
- ◆ Is the item free from systematic error?

The first question relates to the *construct validity* of the item. In other words, do your assessment items assess what you intend for them to assess? The second and third questions relate to the *reliability* of the item. Because it is important that individual assessment items be both valid and reliable, we devote chapters 4 and 5 to a complete and practical discussion of writing assessment items. Suffice it to say here that you want your assessment questions to assess what you think they assess, and you want them to do so in a way that ensures that a student has every opportunity to demonstrate learning, with minimal influence of chance or error.

Step 7: Assemble the Assessment

The final step may seem obvious, but it is actually critical in ensuring the reliability of the assessment. The physical layout, formatting, and arrangement of your assessment can help ensure that students have the best opportunity to demonstrate their knowledge and skills. A few key guidelines for assembling a teacher-made assessment follow.

Make Sure That One Item Does Not Give Away the Answer to Another Item

Have you ever taken an assessment, struggled with a question, and found the answer to that question later in the assessment? As a student, you were probably delighted that now you had the answer, but, as a teacher, you know that now the reliability of the item is called into question. The student (you, in this case!) had the correct answer because of error in the assessment, not necessarily because of his or her knowledge.

Provide Clear Directions for Each Portion of the Assessment

Clear directions let a student know what to do. For example, on a matching set the directions may state that a student may use an item more than once or that an item may be used only once. These directions are critical for the student to complete the assessment and could mean the difference between demonstrating learning or not.

Place Individual Assessment Items on One Full Page

An item or a set of items should be placed on the same page or on facing pages. If not, a student may not understand that more options are located on subsequent pages. For example, if two of the four answer choices in a multiple choice item are placed on a different page, a student may think that the only two options are those placed under the item stem. Consequently, the student may answer the question incorrectly because of the placement of the answer choices, not because of the student's knowledge of the subject matter.

Organize the Assessment by Item Type Format

Assessments should be organized by item type format. For example, all multiple choice items should be together, all true-false items should be together, and so forth. The type of thinking required for each item type is different. Switching among multiple choice, true-false, and fill-in-the-blank, for example, requires students to readjust their thinking with each type of question. This is unnecessary and easily avoided by grouping questions by item type.

Provide Clear and Adequate Response Spaces

Answer spaces that are clearly indicated are important so that students understand where they are to place their responses. For example, you may provide a line next to each multiple choice item for student responses. For constructed-response items, students need adequate space to supply the response. The space needed is determined by the grade level and the length of response required to adequately answer the question.

Provide Point Values for Older Students

Providing points helps students pace themselves on the assessment and can help students to strategize as they take an assessment. This is true both for select-response type items (e.g., true/false, multiple choice) and for constructed-response items (e.g., short answer or mathematical computations for which partial credit may be given).

In the case of constructed-response items, checklists, rating scales, or rubrics can convey important information about the expectations of responses for students.

Make Sure the Assessment Is Neat and Error Free

An assessment should be organized with clear breaks between sections and space between items to indicate to the student that a new item has begun. A grammatical error on an assessment may give a student a clue about the correct answer in a multiple choice item, or it may confuse the student into thinking that the correct response is incorrect because it does not grammatically complete the item stem. Ask a colleague to review the assessment to make sure the assessment is free from error.

Ensure That the Classroom Environment Is Conducive to Good Assessment

As we know, a good assessment is not only valid but also reliable, meaning that it is relatively free from the influence of systematic and random error. Therefore, it is important for the teacher to ensure that the environment is conducive to providing students the best opportunity to demonstrate their knowledge and skills. Of particular note, teachers should consider the following:

◆ Setting an appropriate tone and atmosphere in the classroom
◆ Minimizing disruptions
◆ Reducing opportunities for cheating
◆ Ensuring adequate time
◆ Addressing student questions about the assessment itself in appropriate ways

Assembling an assessment requires time and thought. The organization, format, and administration of an assessment should contribute to the reliability of the assessment and to student performance—and detract from neither.

Conclusion: A Note About the Seven Steps

This chapter provided a step-by-step process for developing a valid and reliable assessment. When reading this chapter you may think to yourself, "I don't have time to follow this step-by-step process for every assessment that I design." The process may sound time-consuming or cumbersome, but it need not be. Most of the steps occur in quick succession, if not simultaneously. Also, it is important to recognize that the core steps of unpacking intended learning outcomes and creating a table of specifications are learned skills. Similar to how it is with other skills—such as learning to read, ride a bike, or write lesson plans, for that matter—one becomes more proficient with the skills of unpacking and of using a table of specifications with practice.

As one teacher shared with us many years ago after having learned this process, "I just think *differently* about my assessments." Her point was that she keeps the principle of $C = I = A$ in mind, she's cognizant of clarifying the content and cognitive level of her learning objectives, and she uses tables of specifications to construct assessments more intentionally.

4

How Do I Create Good Select-Response Items?

Overview of Select-Response Items

Any teacher who has ever written items for a test, a quiz, or a quick check for formatively assessing student learning at the beginning or end of a lesson will attest to the fact that writing a good question that addresses the content and level of cognitive demand of an intended learning outcome can be difficult and time-consuming. Any teacher who has written select-response items will also agree that writing items that are clear, concise, and relatively free from error can be challenging. This is not to say that teachers should throw up their hands in surrender. By keeping in mind some basic guidelines and principles when writing select-response items, teachers can greatly reduce the potential for error in assessment results, thereby increasing the degree of reliability of an assessment, and teachers can become more proficient and efficient in writing select-response items that address both lower and higher cognitive levels. **Select-response items** are *items that have pre-determined responses from which the student must choose.* With the increased use of technology for assessing student learning, the structure and format of select-response items has changed yet has remained the same. Many states now use "technology-enhanced items," but these technology-enhanced items meet our definition of select-response items as they require students to choose from responses provided. Select-response items addressed in this chapter include binary choice, matching, and multiple choice (Figure 4.1).

Figure 4.1 Types of Select-Response Items

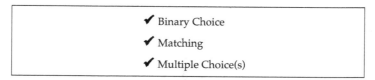

Getting at higher cognitive levels with select-response items can be difficult, but not impossible. As discussed in chapter 3, addressing appropriate cognitive levels is just as important as addressing appropriate content. An item that addresses only one of these compromises the validity of the item and, therefore, the validity of the entire assessment. Binary choice and matching lend themselves to assessing lower cognitive level intended learning outcomes. Multiple choice items are good for assessing lower level cognitive behaviors but are also well-suited for assessing higher level thinking. One misconception regarding state assessments that mainly use select-response items is that the assessment must be assessing only lower level learning. Therefore, teachers may think that select-response items they develop for their own assessments can only measure lower level objectives. We hope to dispel that myth. With that said, the purpose of this chapter is twofold:

◆ To explore the basic guidelines for writing select-response items, with a particular emphasis on writing multiple choice, and

◆ To share principles for writing select-response items that address higher cognitive levels of learning.

Technology-Enhanced Item Types: Something Old, Something New

The advent of technology-based testing has expanded the structure and look of select-response items. States using different item types call these *technology-enhanced items*. These items may be referred to as "click and drag" items, where a student selects from options and moves the options into a diagram. Or students might choose all possible correct answers in which more than one answer is correct. While these are "new" in that the look of the item is new in standardized assessments, we argue that they are not "new" to educators. The "click and drag" example is similar to sorting exercises we have our students do in class activities. Or we provide students with a question in which there are three correct answers out of five possible choices, and we simply ask our students to circle all the right answers. The range of ways these items can be constructed is tied directly to the capability of technology. As technology continually expands, no exhaustive list of technology-enhanced item types can be provided. Two specific benefits of technology-enhanced types of items include the capacity to:

◆ Measure higher order thinking in many content areas (i.e., greater capacity for validity of the item), and
◆ Decrease potential sources of error by reducing the probability that a student could randomly guess the correct answer (i.e., greater capacity for reliability of the item) (Measured Progress/ETS Collaborative, 2012).

Throughout this chapter we have integrated the discussion of technology-enhanced like items that can be used to assess student learning through class activities, quizzes, and tests. Just remember, someone had to first develop the item on paper *before* it was integrated into the technology format. Teachers can use these item types for assessing student learning in the classroom. But here's a caution: These items are still subject to guidelines for construction and have the capacity to assess what they intend to assess (or not) and to be able to distinguish between a student who knows the information and can do the skill (or not).

Some Basic Guidelines for Writing Select-Response Items

By following some basic guidelines in creating select-response items, a teacher can reduce systematic error and therefore increase the reliability of individual items. Put differently, a teacher can have more confidence in asking herself, "Did the student answer a question *correctly* because he truly *knew* the answer and nothing in the item gave the answer away? Conversely, did the student answer a question *incorrectly* because he truly did *not* know the answer and not because something in the item confused the student and caused the student to miss it?" By reducing the potential for error in a select-response question, you can have more confidence that the results of an assessment are true indications of what students *have* or *have not* learned.

In schools, students are taught test-taking skills. Open up any resource in this area and you are likely to find a set of tips such as those found in Figure 4.2.

Figure 4.2 Sample Test-Taking Tips

Binary Choice

☑ If the statement has two parts and one part is false while the other is true, then the entire statement is false.

☑ Guess because you have a 50/50 chance of getting it right.

Matching

☑ Guess if you are not sure and if you will not be penalized for guessing.

☑ Mark out the matches about which you are certain, making it easier to match the remaining items.

☑ Match like types of information.

Multiple Choice(s)

☑ Guess if you are not sure and if you will not be penalized for guessing.

☑ Look for answer choices that grammatically complete the item stem.

☑ If one answer choice is much longer than the others, it is most likely the correct answer.

☑ If an answer choice "All of the above" is provided and you are reasonably sure that two of the answer choices provided are correct, then "All of the above" is most likely correct.

These tips teach students how to spot systematic error and how to take advantage of random error in a test item. While teachers have no control over random error, they can make efforts at reducing systematic error. Reducing systematic error does not "trick" students; instead, it provides students with a chance to truly share what they know and are able to do, and it provides teachers with accurate information as to student achievement.

In this section, basic guidelines of item construction for each type of select-response item are provided. Also for each guideline, a poor example that violates the guideline and a better example that illustrates the guideline are presented, along with a brief explanation. These guidelines were compiled from various assessment sources, as well as from our collective experience as teachers, instructional leaders, item developers, and professors (Gronlund & Waugh, 2013; Hogan, 2007; Popham, 2014; Stiggins & Chappuis, 2012; Taylor & Nolen, 2008).

Most of the guidelines described in this next section relate to the reliability of the item. Before turning our attention to this very critical aspect of item construction, we must emphasize two basic guidelines related to validity that apply to *all* item types. Whether you are creating a binary choice, matching set, or multiple choice item, make sure that the item type is the most appropriate to use for the content and level of cognitive demand. Secondly, make sure that the item does indeed assess the content and the level of cognitive demand you intend for it to assess. (See the discussion of the table of specifications in chapter 3.) An item with a low degree of validity will not provide useful information to you, your students, or anyone else. Now let's take a closer look at the guidelines and principles that govern the three most common types of select-response items.

Binary Choice Items

Binary choice items involve choosing one of two options. These choices might include true/false, yes/no, supported/unsupported, and fact/opinion, to name a few. In fact, binary choice items can be used for practically any learning objective for which distinguishing between two ideas, categories, set of attributes, or the like is the intended cognitive activity. Because the choice is limited between two options, though, the students have a 50% chance of getting it right! These items can be used to assess lower level intended learning outcomes but should be used sparingly and in conjunction with other types of items. Can you imagine a test that had only binary-choice items? The possibility of random error would be so high that you would have very little confidence in the assessment results. When developing binary choice items, there are four guidelines to keep in mind. See Figure 4.3 for a quick reference list of the guidelines.

Figure 4.3 Summary List of Binary Choice Item Construction Guidelines

Guideline 1: Place only one idea in the statement.
Guideline 2: Avoid qualifiers such as *"always"* and *"never."*
Guideline 3: Avoid using negatives in the statement.
Guideline 4: Have as close to an equal number of statements for each option as possible.

Guideline 1: Place only one idea in the statement. Have you ever taken a quiz with true/false items in which there are actually two ideas that may be true or false? What makes the situation even more complicated is when one part of the statement is true and one part is false. How confusing to students . . . and to teachers! Even if the student gets the item correct, the teacher may not be sure whether the student had an understanding of *both* ideas as they were not assessed separately. So the best option is to include only one idea in a true/false statement. Let's look at two examples.

Figure 4.4 Guideline 1: Place Only One Idea in the Statement

Poor Item		
T	F	Condensation turns gases into liquids, and evaporation turns liquids into solids.
Better Item		
T	F	Condensation turns gases into liquids.

In the poor item, the student has to respond to two ideas related to the water cycle. What makes the situation worse is that one part of the statement is true while the other is false. What is a student to do? The student who marks "false" is partially correct, and the student who marks "true" is partially correct. The error in this item prevents the teacher from truly knowing whether the student understands different aspects of the water cycle.

Guideline 2: Avoid absolute qualifiers such as "always," "never," "sometimes," and "usually." Absolute qualifiers such as "always" and "never" oftentimes give the correct answer away. Let's look at two examples from music.

Figure 4.5 Guideline 2: Avoid Qualifiers Such as "Always" and "Never"

Poor Item		
Yes	No	When a sharp comes before a note, you always play the next highest key.
Better Item		
Yes	No	A sharp before a note indicates that the next highest key is to be played.

The poor item includes the word "always" when this qualifying term is not necessary. This word may confuse or trick a student, and he may answer incorrectly or correctly based on the qualifying term rather than responding to the content contained in the statement. The better item deletes "always" as the qualifying term is not needed.

Guideline 3: Avoid using negatives in the statement. Negatives tend to confuse students by requiring them to do mental gymnastics to respond to the item. Use negatives only if they are absolutely necessary and central to the content. Let's look at two examples:

Figure 4.6 Guideline 3: Avoid Using Negatives in the Statement

---

Poor Item

Fact	Opinion	Mahatma Gandhi did not believe that violent protest was the *best* way to bring about social change.

Better Item

Fact	Opinion	Mahatma Gandhi believed that nonviolent protest was the *best* way to bring about social change.

The poor item simply does not make sense and may be confusing to students. They may miss the "not" and read the statement as a positive. There is no compelling reason to write the item in the negative. By writing the item in the positive, the teacher can have more confidence that the item actually measures whether a student understands Mahatma Gandhi's views of nonviolent protest rather than whether the student was confused by the word "not."

Guideline 4: Have as close to an equal number of statements for each option as possible. Just as you try to vary the placement of the correct answer in a multiple-choice item to ensure students do not simply guess "C" because it comes up most frequently, you'll want to do the same for binary choice items by ensuring that one option is not the correct response a majority of the time. If a student determines that "supported" out of options for "supported/not supported" is the correct response on many of the statements, then the student will most likely choose "supported" when encountered with a statement for which she is unsure.

Matching

Matching items serve a purpose of making sure that students can *recall* terms, places, people, events, ideas, and the like. Matching sets typically measure lower levels of cognitive demand and can come in many different configurations:

- ◆ A conventional matching set with two columns of options in which one must match items in one column with items in another column;
- ◆ Fill-in-the-blank statements with a word bank provided;
- ◆ A diagram with processes to label and a word bank of the processes provided.

These are just a few of the ways in which matching can be configured. As discussed earlier in the chapter, technology-enhanced items often make use of the matching set. These items may include a diagram of the water cycle in which students must "click and drag" the names of the processes of the water cycle into the correct slot in the diagram. Regardless of whether items are used in technology format or paper-pencil, the same guidelines apply. As with binary choice items, matching should be used in conjunction with other item types if higher levels of cognitive behavior are identified in the learning objectives that are being assessed. However, truth is stranger than fiction, and, in our experiences as teachers and working with teachers, we have indeed come across assessments that include matching only. When developing a matching set, there are a few basic guidelines to follow. These are summarized in Figure 4.7.

Instead of a matching set to serve as an example for each guideline, Figures 4.8, 4.9, and 4.10 will be used to discuss how each guideline is important. Figures 4.8 and 4.9 show a conventional matching set focused on identifying the contributions of various Americans, symbols of the United States, and United States holidays. Figure 4.10 shows a matching item in which students choose from a word bank to accurately label a diagram. (This item is like

Figure 4.7 Guidelines for Constructing Matching Sets

Guideline 1: Use homogeneous content in a matching set.
Guideline 2: Place item to be matched on the right with the longer prompts on the left.
Guideline 3: Keep the matching set short.
Guideline 4: Use an uneven number of items to match, or allow responses to be used more than once.
Guideline 5: Order items in a logical manner.

Figure 4.8 Poor Matching Set

Directions: Match the following items to the appropriate response.	
1. George Washington 2. Martin Luther King, Jr. 3. Abraham Lincoln 4. Veteran's Day 5. Memorial Day 6. Washington Monument 7. Thurgood Marshall 8. Independence Day 9. Thomas Jefferson 10. Jackie Robinson 11. Statue of Liberty 12. Rosa Parks 13. American flag 14. bald eagle 15. George Washington Carver	a. first African-American Supreme Court Justice b. has fifty stars on it c. the day we celebrate United States independence from Great Britain d. first African-American baseball player to play in the major leagues e. first president of the United States f. the day we give thanks to men and women who have served in the armed forces g. given to the United States by France h. civil rights leader i. refused to give up her seat on a bus j. located in Washington, DC k. founded the Tuskegee Institute l. president during the Civil War m. national emblem of the United States n. the third president of the United States o. the day we remember those who have died fighting war

Figure 4.9 Better Matching Set

Directions: Write the letter of the person described by each statement. You may use each person more than once.	
1. First African-American Supreme Court justice 2. Refused to give up a seat to a white passenger on a bus 3. First African-American baseball player to play in the major leagues 4. Founder of the Tuskegee Institute 5. Led a march on Washington to bring attention to civil rights 6. Led court case *Brown v. Board of Education* to end segregation 7. Found uses for agricultural products such as peanuts and sweet potatoes 8. Received the Nobel Peace Prize for work in civil rights	a. George Washington Carver b. Martin Luther King, Jr. c. Thurgood Marshall d. Rosa Parks e. Jackie Robinson

technology-enhanced items in which students "click and drag" the word to the correct place on the diagram.)

Guideline 1: Use like content in a matching set. The material within a matching set should be homogeneous in nature. In the matching set in Figure 4.8, students are matching three different types of information—famous Americans, American symbols, and American holidays. For example, in

Figure 4.10 Labeling a Diagram

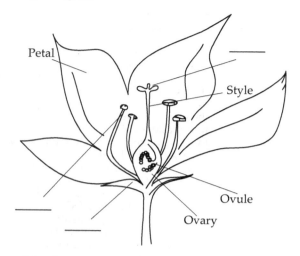

Use the terms below to label the parts of the flower.
Write the correct term on the line provided in the diagram.
One term will not be used.

Pistil

Sepal

Stamen

Stigma

matching any of the people, the student can dismiss many of the responses as they do not refer to people. Furthermore, the student can identify Rosa Parks fairly easily as the only response that refers to a female, thereby finding the match for letter *i*.

In the better matching set, only historical figures are used, and even that set is further narrowed by focusing on African-Americans who influenced civil rights. In Figure 4.10, all options provided are parts of a flower.

Guideline 2: Place items to be matched on the right with descriptions on the left. Take a look at the poor matching set. When a student reads "George Washington," she must read through every response to find a match. This involves a great deal of reading and is an inefficient use of time. The better matching set places the response on the left-hand side. Then, when a student reads "First African-American Supreme Court justice," she needs only to skim the names to find a match.

Guideline 3: Keep the list short. Matching sets should be kept to a minimum. The maximum number of items in a matching set should be 10 for older students and even fewer for younger students (Gronlund & Waugh, 2013;

Hogan, 2007). Notice in the poor matching set that students have 15 items to match and, in the better matching set, have 8 items to match. By using like content, the matching set is kept at a minimum. In Figure 4.10, there are only three parts of the diagram to label, keeping this item at a reasonable number of matches.

Guideline 4: Provide an **uneven** *number of responses to match.* In the poor matching set, there are 15 items to match 15 responses. Therefore, when students get to the end of the matching set, the last few items are usually given to them merely by process of elimination. What's more, if a student answers *incorrectly* for one match, then he will automatically miss a second one as well. In other words, it's not possible to just miss one when the matching sets are even. Matching sets should either have more responses than students can use, or the items should be able to be used more than once. In the better matching set, the directions indicate that each person may be used more than once. In Figure 4.10 students have a part of the flower that is not used in labeling the diagram. Hence, the process of elimination is *eliminated*! Make sure, however, that the directions clearly indicate that items may be used more than once or that some responses may not be used at all.

Guideline 5: Order responses in a logical manner. The items to be matched in a set should be in some type of logical order—numerical order, alphabetical order, short to long, and so forth. In the poor item set, the items to be matched are not placed in any type of logical order and so are quite confusing. Students must switch their thinking from events to holidays to famous Americans. In the better item set and in Figure 4.10, the items to be matched are homogeneous in nature, and they are placed in alphabetical order.

Multiple Choice Items

Multiple choice items are the most commonly used item types on state assessments. In fact, every state and the District of Columbia use multiple choice items to assess student performance, and four states use *only* multiple choice items. This reliance on multiple choice has increased over time, with the number of states using other types of items such as constructed response declining over the past 10 years (Hightower, 2012). Multiple choice is also an icon of classroom-based testing, with this type of item noted in early American education (Shepard, 2000). In addition, use of technology-based testing in state assessments allows for the use of "multiple choices" in which more than one answer choice is correct and students select all correct answers. As stated earlier, however, teachers have been using this format long before technology-enhanced items came on the state assessment scene. For these reasons, we devote a great deal of attention to the development of multiple choice items that are both valid and reliable.

Figure 4.11 Multiple Choice Terms

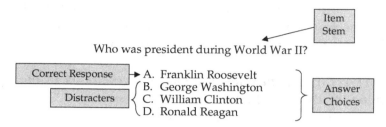

Figure 4.12 Guidelines for Constructing Multiple Choice Items

Stem
Guideline 1: Make the problem clear to the student in the item stem.
Guideline 2: State the item stem in the positive whenever possible.
Guideline 3: Make sure the item stem does not give away the correct answer.
Guideline 4: Emphasize qualifiers such as *"most likely"* and *"best"* in the item stem.

Answer Choices
Guideline 5: Make sure the answer choices are plausible.
Guideline 6: Develop answer choices that are parallel in grammar and in length.
Guideline 7: Avoid using "All of the above" and "None of the above."
Guideline 8: Place the answer choices in a logical order.
Guideline 9: Avoid clues in the answer choices that give away the correct response.
Guideline 10: Make sure that the correct response(s) is/are the *only* correct response(s).

Throughout this section we use some terms to describe parts of multiple choice items. Take a look at the Figure 4.11 so that you have a visual referent for these key terms.

The guidelines for developing reliable multiple choice items are divided into two sections. The first section contains guidelines for developing the item stem, and the second section contains guidelines for developing the answer choices. Figure 4.12 provides a summary of the guidelines for constructing multiple choice items.

Item Stem
The item stem is essentially the question. It serves the purpose of orienting the student to what is being asked. There are two basic formats for a multiple choice item stem:

◆ *Explicit question,* with answer choices from which to select;
◆ *Sentence completion,* with grammatically consistent words, phrases, numbers, or symbols from which to select.

Figure 4.13 Guideline 1: Make the Problem Clear to the Student

Poor Item	Better Item
Antigens	Which of these do antigens attack?
A. Attack memory cells B. Attack killer T cells C. Attack pathogens D. Attack helper T cells	A. Pathogens B. Helper T cells C. Killer T cells D. Memory cells

Regardless of the format used, the following four guidelines apply to constructing the stem of a multiple choice item.

Guideline 1: Make the problem clear to the student in the item stem. The problem should be in the item stem and not in the answer choices. This guideline relates to providing enough information in the item stem to give the student an indication of what is being asked. It also relates to removing unnecessary or confusing information from the question. Let's look at two examples in Figure 4.13.

In the poor example, not enough information is provided. The student does not know what information he is supposed to think about related to antigens. The problem is made clear in the answer choices, rather than the item stem. The question is asking what antigens attack. In the better item, the item stem clearly indicates that this is the focus of the item. The better item still has a concern, however, as only one of the answer choices is a one-word choice while the others are made up of two words and each has the word "cell" in it. This problem is addressed by Guideline 6 later in the chapter.

Guideline 2: State the item stem in the positive whenever possible. As former classroom teachers and test item developers, we recall sometimes becoming frustrated by the challenge of finding plausible distracters when creating multiple choice questions. In response, we found ourselves sometimes converting the item stem to a negative. This conversion was sometimes a cop-out. However, there are instances when a negative in the item stem is necessary. In science class we teach lab guidelines in the negative—*Do not put your hand over the open flame of a Bunsen burner.* You may chuckle when reading this, but how could this lab guideline be stated in a positive manner? The guideline could be "Stay away from flames," but then, in using the Bunsen burner, the student must be near the flame. For some instructional objectives, assessing student knowledge using an item stated in the negative may be very appropriate. However, for the majority of what is taught this is *not* the case. Negatives can confuse students. Also, students may not catch the negative when reading the item. Therefore, for those times when you do

Figure 4.14 Guideline 2: State the Item Stem in the Positive, if Possible

Poor Item	Better Item
Which of these are not reasons why the United States became involved in World War I? More than one response may be correct. A. The United States had economic ties to Great Britain. B. Russia would not intervene on Great Britain's behalf. C. The Germans tried to create an alliance with Mexico. D. President Wilson supported declaration of war in his re-election. E. Germany upheld the Sussex Pledge.	Why did the United States become involved in World War I? Place a check by all the reasons. ☐ The United States had economic ties to Great Britain. ☐ Russia would not intervene on Great Britain's behalf. ☐ The Germans tried to create an alliance with Mexico. ☐ President Wilson supported declaration of war in his re-election. ☐ Germany upheld the Sussex Pledge.

use a negative, be sure to emphasize it in some way, such as by using **bold-face**, *italicized*, or <u>underlined</u> type. Let's look at two examples in Figure 4.14.

This item allows for the student to check all the correct responses and therefore allows for multiple choices. The poor example of the item stem is confusing as students have to sort through the negative in the question. Then, they read the second part of the item stem, which indicates that more than one response may be correct. The better item eliminates the negative altogether. As an aside, note how the responses are not lettered "A, B, C, D . . ." When allowing for multiple correct responses, use check boxes rather than letters. Students who see letters will revert back to the way they've always encountered multiple choice—only one correct response. They are more likely to pick only one response rather than all responses. Lettering the answer choices, in this case, reduces the reliability of the item.

Guideline 3: Make sure the item stem does not give away the correct answer. Sometimes the item stem itself can inadvertently give away the correct answer. For example, one of the most well-known foibles is to end the item stem with the article "an" when only one answer choice begins with a vowel. However, there are other ways that item stems can give away the correct answer. Consider the two examples in Figure 4.15.

If the student knows his constitutional principles, he does not need the newspaper headline to get the poor item correct. Since the correct response is "checks and balances," the phrase "principle of United States government" provides a clue to the correct answer. In the first example, the correct response is the only one that is a principle of United States government. Therefore, the teacher does not know if the student selected the response merely because he knew checks and balances is a principle of government

Figure 4.15 Guideline 3: Make Sure the Item Stem Does Not Give Away the Correct Answer

Poor Item	Better Item
Read the newspaper headline below:	

United States Supreme Court rules that a federal law is unconstitutional.

Poor Item	Better Item
Which principle of United States government is being described in the newspaper headline? A. rule of man B. dictatorship C. checks and balances D. constitutional monarchy	Which principle of United States government is being described in the newspaper headline? A. federalism B. due process C. popular sovereignty D. checks and balances

or if he interpreted the headline correctly. In the better example, each answer choice is a principle of the United States government; therefore, the student would need to know each constitutional principle in order to answer the question correctly.

Guideline 4: Emphasize qualifiers such as "most likely" or "best" used in the item stem. Qualifiers in the stem, such as "most likely," "best," or "least likely," are terms that the student needs to take into account when reading the item. Let's take a look at two examples.

Figure 4.16 Guideline 4: Emphasize Qualifiers Such as "Most Likely" and "Best" in the Item Stem

Poor Item	Better Item
Matthew was paid $20 for mowing his neighbor's lawn. If he spends $5.50 on a movie rental, $6.75 on a pizza, and $2.00 for a soda, which is closest to the amount he will have left?	Matthew was paid $20 for mowing his neighbor's lawn. If he spends $5.50 on a movie rental, $6.75 on a pizza, and $2.00 for a soda, which is *closest* to the amount he will have left?
A. $5.00 B. $0 C. $14.00 D. $9.00	A. $0 B. $5.00 C. $9.00 D. $14.00

In this item the word "closest" is a qualifier that lets students know what is being asked. They are simply being asked to estimate the amount left over, not the exact amount left over. In the poor item, the word "closest" does not stand out to the student at all. A student may miss the word and become confused as the exact amount is not available in the answer choices. In the better item, the word "closest" is italicized and the student is clued in to estimation of the amount.

Answer Choices

The second critical part of creating valid and reliable multiple choice items is to develop quality answer choices. Many times developing the answer choices, particularly the distracters, can be a great challenge and cause much angst. On state assessments, students are typically provided with four answer choices. In developing your own assessments, you will want to have no fewer than three and no more than five answer choices. The next set of guidelines relate specifically to addressing sources of systematic error in answer choices.

Guideline 5: Make sure the answer choices are plausible. Have you ever wanted to bring a little levity to a testing situation? Some of the answer choices may be silly or so ridiculous that students break into a smile when they read them. This isn't such a bad thing when a teacher has rapport with the students in her class, but the teacher needs to be aware that there is a principle of item construction that will be affected. Providing silly or ridiculous answer choices that are not plausible compromises the reliability of items because students can easily dismiss these answer choices.

Mathematics teachers have been writing plausible answer choices for years. A student may add instead of subtract, for example, and an answer choice would be available for this common error. An advantage of having plausible answer choices based on common errors in logic or procedure is that the students' choosing of the incorrect answer choice gives teachers some insight about areas in which students may struggle. Let's look at two examples.

Figure 4.17 Guideline 5: Make Sure Answer Choices Are Plausible

Poor Item	Better Item
Who was president during World War II?	Who was president during World War II?
A. Franklin Roosevelt B. George Washington C. George W. Bush D. Jesse James	A. Dwight Eisenhower B. Lyndon Johnson C. Franklin Roosevelt D. Woodrow Wilson

This item assesses student learning at the recall level. Students must merely know who the president was during World War II to be able to associate specific people with specific events. In the poor item, the possible answer choices are far removed from the event, and the answer choice "Jesse James" is quite silly (especially since he isn't even a past president)! In the better item, the answer choices focus on presidents during the 20th century and those who were president during wartime. The answer choices are much more plausible.

Guideline 6: Make sure answer choices are parallel in grammar and length. Answer choices should begin in the same way and should be about the same length. If the correct response is a one-word noun, then the rest of the answer choices should be one-word nouns. If the correct response begins with a verb, the distracters should also begin with verbs. If one answer choice is quite longer than the others, then it may provide a clue to the correct response. If one answer choice must be long, and one must be short, then a good option would be to have two short answer choices and two long answer choices. Let's look at two examples.

Figure 4.18 Guideline 6: Develop Answer Choices That Are Parallel in Grammar and in Length

Poor Item	Better Item
In English class, Cynthia must write a descriptive essay about the person she admires the most. She wants to write about her father. Which of these would be the *best* way she could begin to write her essay?	
A. Look through old pictures of her and her father. B. She could call her best friend to talk about him. C. By making a list of activities she has done with her father. D. Asking her father to come to her class.	A. by looking at her baby pictures B. by asking her father to come to her class C. by calling her best friend to talk about her father D. by listing all of the things he has done for her and others

In the poor item, the answer choices are grammatically inconsistent and confusing. In the better item, each answer choice begins in the same fashion.

Guideline 7: Avoid using "All of the above" or "None of the above." Have you ever written a multiple choice item with four answer choices and have no problem developing the correct response and two really great distracters but the final distracter is just not there? You may have put in the old faithfuls—"All of the above" or "None of the above"—as the last answer choice.

We have seen many assessments developed by teachers in which "All of the above" or "None of the above" is always the last answer choice and is used with frequency. We have also observed that these are oftentimes *not* the correct choices for the questions in which they are used. In other words, they are not plausible distracters. Let's look at two examples.

Figure 4.19 Guideline 7: Avoid Using "All of the Above" and "None of the Above"

Poor Item	Better Item
Which of these should be used to measure in millimeters? A. A yard stick B. A metric guideliner C. A digital scale D. None of the above	Which of these should be used to measure in millimeters? A. a yard stick B. a metric guideliner C. a digital scale D. a graduated cylinder

In the poor item the last answer choice is "None of the above" when this answer choice is not necessary. The item focuses on measurement and measuring in metric units. Another plausible answer choice is the "graduated cylinder" as it is a tool for measuring and can measure in metric units. The graduated cylinder measures volume rather than length but does offer an attractive option.

It is important to add a caveat about this "guideline"; namely, there is an exception to it! In some cases, "None of the above" and "All of the above" can be plausible options. If they are used throughout a test as answer choices *and* they are, indeed, sometimes the correct answer, then they can be appropriate to use as choices.

Guideline 8: Place answer choices in a logical order. Answer choices should be placed in some type of order, and ordering systems should be consistent throughout any given assessment. Here are a few guidelines:

◆ Place numbers in numerical order.
◆ Place one-word answer choices in alphabetical order.
◆ Order sentences from shortest to longest.

One reason for placing answer choices in a logical order is to ensure random placement of the correct response. When developing multiple choice items, you might begin with the correct response as the first choice, as usually the correct response is the simplest to develop. If the correct response is left as the first answer choice on each item, students will surely pick up the pattern. Figure 4.20 provides examples to consider. In the poor item, the answer choices are not in any logical order, and the correct response is first. In the better item, the answer choices are ordered from the least to greatest. The ordering of the answer choices in the poor item can be confusing for the student.

Figure 4.20 Guideline 8: Place the Answer Choices in a Logical Order

Poor Item	Better Item
What is the next number in the pattern?	What is the next number in the pattern?
54, 53, 52, 51, 50, 49, _____	54, 53, 52, 51, 50, 49, _____
A. 48 B. 50 C. 47 D. 59	A. 47 B. 48 C. 49 D. 50

Guideline 9: Avoid clues in the answer choices that give away the correct response. Sometimes a clue to the correct response can be found in the correct response. The correct response may contain a similar term that is used in the item stem, or the answer choice may be the only choice that grammatically completes the item stem. Be sure to review the correct response to make sure that it does not give away the correct answer. Let's take a look at two examples.

Figure 4.21 Guideline 9: Avoid Clues in the Answer Choices That Give Away the Correct Response

Poor Item	Better Item
Which of the following revolutions resulted in increased business by speeding travel?	Which of the following *best* describes a result of the transportation revolution in the 1800s?
A. industrial B. technology C. textile D. transportation	A. Suburban areas grew. B. Demands for slave labor decreased. C. Manufacturing and production increased. D. People relied less on mass transportation.

In the poor item, a word in the item stem gives a clue as to the correct answer. The word "travel" and the word "transportation" are clearly linked. In the better item, the student must know a result of the transportation revolution, and there are no clues in the item stem that give away the correct answer.

Guideline 10: Make sure the correct response(s) is/are the only correct response(s). This may sound like a silly guideline, but it is paramount to reliability. The correct response(s) should, in fact, be accurate and should be the *only* possible correct response(s). Look at the items in Figure 4.21 that were just discussed with the previous guideline. In the poor item, there is more than one correct response. One could argue that "industrial" is also a correct response as the industrial revolution made it possible for railroads to be built. The better item includes only one correct response.

Select-Response in the Primary Grades Classroom

The examples we have provided for creating select-response items are indicative of questions used at the upper elementary, middle school, and high school levels. Primary grade teachers also use select-response types of assessments to assess student learning. For example, a teacher may lay out four coins and ask a child to point to the nickel. In this case, the teacher is using a multiple choice question to assess the child's ability to identify specific coins. In addition, a teacher may have students match two sets of pictures or sort shapes into categories. All of these are assessments that utilize the select-response format. Therefore, the same guidelines apply in the primary grades classroom.

Another Important Consideration—Bias

Each student comes into the classroom with a wide range of experiences and exposure to ideas, words, and terms germane to specific languages, cultures, societies, and socioeconomic backgrounds. *When writing any type of select-response item, review the item and ask the following question: Are there any words or phrases used in the item that would put a student with limited English proficiency or a student with different sociocultural experiences at a disadvantage?* Consider the following example.

Figure 4.22 Avoiding Bias in an Item

Poor Item	Better Item
Chicago Bears : football :: _____ : baseball A. Anaheim Angels B. Los Angeles Galaxy C. Sacramento Kings D. Tampa Bay Buccaneers	large : big :: triumph : _____ A. loss B. guideline C. small D. success

The two items presented in the examples are analogies. A purpose of analogies is to determine a student's ability to understand the relationship between concepts and ideas. Therefore, a student must have experiences with the concepts or ideas in order to understand the relationships. In the poor item, the student's ability to understand the relationship presented is influenced by her exposure to sports teams, the examples here being teams in the United States. This content is not critical to any subject area, places the student at a disadvantage, and calls into question the *construct validity* of the item. (See the discussion of *construct validity* in chapter 2, but, in short, the intent of the question is *not* to assess knowledge of sports teams.) In the better item, the terms are not tied to popular culture, but rather focus on commonly used vocabulary terms.

Bias can have insidious effects on assessments. By definition, we are often-times *unaware* of our own biases. What's more, it is quite difficult to account for the individual experiences and backgrounds of all of the students in our classrooms. The caution that we raise here is that teachers must attempt to be aware of biases that may influence assessment results and then to control for the influence of those possible biases. After all, reducing the influence of bias is a means of increasing the reliability and the validity of an assessment.

Some Principles for Tapping Higher Cognitive Levels of Learning through Multiple Choice Items

State standards do require that students engage with content at the higher cognitive levels of learning. Select-response item types such as binary and matching are typically not conducive to assessing these higher cognitive levels. A common misconception regarding multiple choice items is that only lower cognitive levels can be assessed. However, these items can assess content at both lower and higher cognitive levels. Therefore, this section addresses only this type of select-response item.

To make the point that multiple choice questions can assess higher cognitive levels, consider the following item similar to items found on state assessments related to physical science shown in Figure 4.23.

In this item, students must interpret not only the stimulus material provided in the diagram, but the students must also interpret each of the answer choices. The student must *remember* and *understand* simple machines, force, the role of a fulcrum, levers, and a host of other terminology and concepts related to simple machines. The student must *apply* what he or she has learned about simple machines, *analyze* and *interpret* the diagram, and then make a judgment regarding the best possible answer. The student

Figure 4.23 Sample Multiple Choice Item That Taps Higher Order Thinking

Jackson needs to help his friend lift a heavy rock. Jackson and his friend are using a board and another, smaller rock. Use the diagram below showing how Jackson and his friend plan to lift the rock to answer the question below.

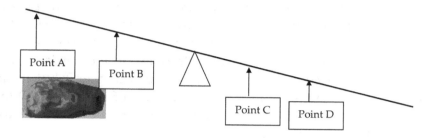

The least amount of force would be needed to lift the larger rock if the smaller rock is placed at –

A. Point A

B. Point B

C. Point C

D. Point D

must also *analyze* the answer choices. This item represents one item similar to state assessments in one subject area. However, reviewing state assessments reveals similar types of items that do, indeed, assess higher cognitive levels of thinking. Therefore, teachers must not only *teach* at higher cognitive levels, but must also *assess* at higher cognitive levels.

There is one disclaimer that we must make at this time. It is very difficult for a multiple choice item to assess at cognitive levels beyond *analyze*—namely, the levels of *evaluate* or *create* (or *synthesize* in Bloom's original taxonomy). By their very nature, multiple choice items are forced choice, meaning the students cannot offer an answer that is not provided. *Evaluate* and *create* require that students construct their own meaning, rather than reasoning an already conceived answer. A multiple choice item could provide various bits of information for students to evaluate, but the creation of meaning for the student is limited to the answer choices. So, our intent here is to show how multiple choice items can tap cognitive levels of *understanding, application*, and *analysis*.

In this section we explore five principles for writing multiple choice items at higher cognitive levels (see Figure 4.24). For each principle, a brief description is followed by a poor item and a better item that illustrates the principle. An explanation of what makes the better item "better" follows

Figure 4.24 Five Principles for Writing Higher Cognitive Level Multiple Choice Items

Principle 1: Refine your understanding of content and cognitive levels.
Principle 2: Introduce novelty.
Principle 3: Focus on complex content.
Principle 4: Use an extended prompt.
Principle 5: Provide stimulus material.

each. We use the term "better" rather than "best" as we recognize that all items have some error and that some items hit the mark in terms of the measurement target while others are very close to the mark. It is virtually impossible to write an item that is free from systematic error. However, steps are taken to reduce that error by following the basic guidelines set forth in the first part of the chapter.

Principle 1: Refine Your Understanding of *Content* and *Cognitive Levels*

Creating multiple choice questions that tap higher order thinking requires that the question creator have a clear understanding of the *content* being assessed and intended levels of student *cognition*. As a reminder from previous discussion in chapter 3, content can be stated explicitly in the intended learning outcome, and content may also be implicit or conditional. Cognitive levels may be lower levels, such as *recall*, or higher levels, such as *analysis* or *evaluation*. For example, *recalling* types of poetry and *analyzing* poetry for figurative language require different cognitive behaviors, although the content may be similar. Let's review examples in Figure 4.25.

Figure 4.25 Refine Your Understanding of Content and Level of Cognitive Demand

State Standard **New York State Standards of Learning – Intermediate Health Education** The student will analyze the multiple influences which affect health decisions and behaviors.	
What is used to measure weight? A. a scale B. a thermometer C. a blood pressure cuff D. a stethoscope	Anna goes to the movies with her friends. Some of them are smoking cigarettes, and so are the actors in the movie. Her parents have discussed the dangers of smoking with her. Her best friend offers her a cigarette, but Anna tells her friend that she does not want a cigarette. Which of these <u>most likely</u> had the greatest influence on Anna's decision? A. the actors B. her parents C. her best friend D. her peer group

The intended learning outcome focuses on the *analysis* level of cognitive demand, and the content relates to the factors that influence health decisions. The poor item misses the mark on both content and level of cognitive demand. The poor item focuses on measuring weight, which can give an indication of health but does not address the intended learning outcome. What's more, the item is written at the *recall* or *remember* level.

In the better item, students are presented with a scenario and asked to determine which of the people presented had the greatest influence on Anna's decision not to smoke a cigarette. This item requires *analysis*, and it also requires students to think about the influences on Anna's health decision. Therefore, it addresses both the content and the level of cognitive demand contained within the intended learning outcome.

This first principle serves as a foundation for each of the other principles. In order to truly teach and assess an intended learning outcome, a teacher must have an understanding of the content and level of cognitive demand contained within the intended learning outcome. This exercise is similar to *Step 1: Unpack the Intended Learning Outcomes* as discussed in chapter 3. The required type of thinking influences the type of item that is written.

Principle 2: Introduce Novelty

Novelty is an essential component of creating higher level multiple choice questions. Novelty requires students to *apply* what they have learned. Merely replicating a task completed in class usually reaches *remember* and *understand* levels of Bloom's taxonomy, even if the task seems difficult on the surface. In social studies, for example, students may analyze primary source documents in order to explore the foundations of constitutional principles. If a multiple choice question asks students to identify a constitutional principle *based on an excerpt from a document discussed in class*, the question may function as a recall question. However, if students are asked to identify a constitutional principle based on an excerpt they have *not* seen, the question presents a novel situation. Let's review the example in Figure 4.26.

The content in this state standard from Texas focuses on literary devices used in various types of genres. The intended learning outcome is written at a higher cognitive level as students must *determine* and *explain* the purposes and effects of literary devices. The identification and interpretation of symbolism in fiction involves higher order cognitive behaviors. One may well imagine most high school teachers leading their students in engaging discussions about symbolism in a variety of pieces of fiction. However, if a teacher helps students identify and interpret a symbol during class discussions, and then, on an assessment, merely asks students to *recall* the symbol that was identified and discussed in class, then the teacher

Figure 4.26 Introduce Novelty

State Standard	
Texas Essential Knowledge and Skills (TEKS) for English Language Arts and Reading, English III	
Literary Genres	
The student analyzes fictional and poetic elements focusing on how they combine to contribute meaning in literary texts . . . by determining and explaining purposes and effects of figurative language, particularly **symbolic** and metaphoric.	
At the end of the novel *The Pearl* by John Steinbeck, the pearl has become a symbol of _____. E. humans' struggle against and eventual triumph over the forces of nature F. humans' ability to survive great emotional pain, although not unchanged G. humans' capacity for love even in the face of death H. humans' triumph over evil through strength	By the end of the novel *The Pearl* by John Steinbeck, the pearl has become a symbol of humans' ability to survive great emotional pain, although not unchanged. What is **most likely** symbolized when Kino throws the pearl into the sea at the end of the story? A. Kino's envy of the upper class B. Kino's hatred of Coyotito's killers C. Kino's acceptance of his status in life D. Kino's willingness to sacrifice for a better future

has inadvertently assessed a lower order thinking skill. By introducing *novelty*—or asking students to interpret a symbol in a way that has not yet been discussed or addressed directly in class—teachers can have students engage in higher order thinking.

Presumably, the poor sample item represents recall of a complex symbol. In the better example, the teacher has not discussed the final symbolism of the pearl in class, thereby reserving the interpretation (or *analysis*) of the symbol in the final scene for the students. This principle reinforces the crucial link between instruction and assessment. Instruction must be examined to determine whether an item does or does *not* present a novel situation.

Principle 3: Focus on Complex Content

The content of questions can be *simple* or *complex*. Simple content is either one-dimensional or consists of relatively few components. Complex content is made up of multiple factors or components. For example, a list of dates of major battles during the Civil War is relatively simple material—it may not be particularly easy to memorize, but the content is rather simple—dates and names. However, an explanation of the interrelated events leading up to any one of these battles could be quite complex. Simple content is often appropriately measured at lower levels of cognitive behavior (e.g., *recall* or *understanding*), whereas complex content often can be appropriately assessed at higher levels of cognition (e.g., *analysis* or *evaluation*). Let's review examples based on 3rd grade science.

Figure 4.27 Focus on Complex Content

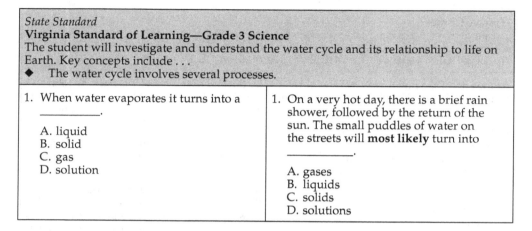

The water cycle is the content contained within this state standard from Virginia. More specifically, students should know the process of the water cycle, including evaporation, condensation, and precipitation. The verbs "investigate" and "understand" indicate that students should engage with this content at higher cognitive levels.

In the poor sample item, the one-dimensional nature of the question amounts to *recall* thinking for students, since they are essentially asked to provide a *definition* of evaporation. In the better sample item, students must *understand* and *analyze* the interrelationship among the states of matter and the environmental context in order to respond to the question correctly. Knowing the definition of evaporation is essential, and the poor item may be clearly legitimate if the purpose of the item is to assess at the *remember* level. However, in order to accurately address the intended learning outcome presented in the example, understanding of the water cycle process is key, of which evaporation is a part.

Principle 4: Use an Extended Prompt

Extended prompts provide students with some background information needed to answer the question and usually involve two or three sentences of text. They introduce complexity by providing contextual information. However, when using extended prompts, be sure to think about whether the student could answer the question *without* the information. If so, the information is not necessary and the question may actually focus on knowledge and comprehension, rather than higher level thinking. Also, make sure

Figure 4.28 Use an Extended Prompt

State Standard	
Wisconsin Model Academic Standards – Grade 12 Social Sciences	
The student will assess the validity of different interpretations of significant historical events.	

Read the excerpts from Atkinson's account and Black Hawk's account of the events at Bad Axe in 1832. Then, answer the question below.

The steamer "Warrior," had escended [sic] the river . . . to warn the Sioux of the approach of the Sacs: - in returning, near the battle ground, a party of Sacs was discovered, and fired upon, when a smart skirmish ensued.

◆ General Henry Atkinson, United States Army, Battle of Bad Axe

We had been [at the Mississippi] but a little while, before we saw a steam boat (the "Warrior,") coming. I told my braves not to shoot, as intended going on board, so that we might save our women and children. . . . I took a small piece of white cotton, and put it on a pole. . . . I told a Winnebago to tell them we were Sacs, and wanted to give ourselves up! A Winnebago on the boat called to us "to run and hide, that the whites were going to shoot!" . . . The firing then commenced from the boat . . .

◆ Black Hawk, Sauk leader, Massacre of Bad Axe

Which of these terms best describes the United States government's policy toward Native Americans at the time of the events at Bad Axe? Circle all correct responses.	Which of these activities would be best to determine whose accounts of the events at Bad Axe are most accurate? Check all correct responses.
A. removal to western lands B. compensation for loss of land C. assimilation into American culture D. purchase Native American land E. preservation of Native American heritage	☐ study relief map of the area from 1832 ☐ interview descendants of Black Hawk ☐ compare eyewitness accounts from both sides ☐ review drawings of the battle created by soldiers on both sides ☐ read government documents written immediately following the battle

that the extended prompt does not provide the correct answer. If so, then the question really measures the students' comprehension of the contextual information, rather than the content being assessed.

Many state standards in social studies focus on the importance of analyzing and assessing the validity of interpretations of events. Wisconsin is no different. The state of Wisconsin expects that by the time a student graduates from high school, he will be able to read excerpts from historical documents and be able to provide evidence of support for or against the interpretation of the event.

In the poor item, a student does not need the extended prompt to answer the question. This is a common issue in using extended prompts, maps, and charts (Suh & Grant, in press). Do students really need the information to respond to the question? In this instance, a student only needs to know government policy toward Native Americans during the early 1800s. The poor item does not measure a student's ability to interpret the primary sources provided or to assess the validity of the interpretations of the battle.

In the better item, students are asked to think about how to go about assessing the validity of an interpretation of a historical event. While they are not yet assessing the validity of the interpretation (which would call for a constructed-response assessment in order to truly do so), they are demonstrating that they know which sources would be best to use to assess the validity of the interpretations. Essentially, what really happened on that day in 1832?

As an aside, this item is an example of one in which students choose more than one correct response. Notice that in the "poor item" the responses are lettered A, B, C, D, and E. Although directions are given to circle all correct responses, having the letters might confuse students. A student might look at the responses and choose one because it looks like the regular multiple-choice questions they encounter. However, in the better item students are asked to check all the correct responses. The check boxes clue students into the fact that this is a different kind of question. In other words, the check boxes improve the reliability of the question.

Principle 5: Engage with Stimulus Material

Stimulus material is similar to an extended prompt in that students must use information given to answer the question. Stimulus material includes diagrams, charts, maps, pictures, excerpts from documents, and so forth. Cautions regarding extended prompts also apply to using stimulus material. The stimulus material should be necessary to answer the question, and the stimulus material should not explicitly provide the correct answer. Instead, stimulus material should require students to *interpret* the information or data presented. Oftentimes, stimulus material can be used as the basis for several questions. Let's review two examples in Figure 4.29.

Patterning begins very early in a child's education. In the state of Florida, by the time students complete the 3rd grade, they should know how to solve problems using the four operations through identifying and explaining numerical patterns. The stimulus material in Figure 4.29 requires students to examine a chart with a sequence of numbers. In the poor item, students are merely reading the chart. The question focuses on *understanding* but not on solving problems, identifying patterns, or explaining patterns. The poor item even fails to hit the intended learning outcome as what is being measured is really the skill of chart interpretation.

Figure 4.29 Engage with Stimulus Material

State Standard
Adapted from the Mathematics Florida Standards – Grade 3
The student will solve problems involving four operations by identifying and explaining patterns.

Manuel wants to save his money. Each week he puts more money into his piggy bank.

Week	Money Put into Bank
1	$0.25
2	$0.50
3	$0.75
4	$1.00
5	?

How much money did Manuel save in Week 1?	If his savings pattern continues, how much money will Manuel put into his bank in Week 5?
A. $ 0.25 B. $ 0.50 C. $ 0.75 D. $ 1.00	A. $1.10 B. $1.25 C. $1.50 D. $1.75

In the better item, students must *analyze* the pattern and solve a problem using the pattern. In order to extend the number pattern, students must analyze the incremental increases in savings to determine the pattern. The better item more clearly aligns with the intended cognitive level of the intended learning outcome as well as the content, including patterns.

Stimulus material offers a way for students to interact with content in a novel way, thereby increasing the level of cognitive behaviors being assessed. By including stimulus material as part of a multiple choice item, teachers can determine whether a student can *apply* or *analyze*. Stimulus material requires students to integrate existing knowledge with a new situation.

Developing Valid and Reliable Select-Response Items: A Science and an Art

The science behind creating items that indeed assess what they intend to assess and are free from systematic error are laid out in this chapter and in chapter 3. You have read about seven steps to creating a valid assessment by assessing both the content and level of cognitive demand. You have also examined guidelines related to constructing selected-response items that serve to decrease systematic error. These guidelines are fairly cut and dry—the science of creating valid and reliable select-response items. However, creating the items also involves art—wordsmithing to get the right wording of the answer choices or choosing just the right stimulus material for students to interact with on an assessment.

This chapter focused on *reliability* as it relates to reducing systematic error by carefully developing select-response items. This chapter also examined how to increase the degree of *validity* by ensuring that questions assess the range of cognitive levels found in state standards. By following the basic guidelines set forth in item construction and the principles of assessing higher level intended learning outcomes, teachers can increase the degree to which their assessments are both *valid* and *reliable*. Finally, with the advent of the use of technology-enhanced items, the types of questions that are considered "select response" has expanded. In this chapter we addressed those types of items and guidelines for creating them.

5

How Do I Create Good Constructed-Response Items?

Assessing the Range of Cognition

Constructed-response items allow teachers to assess a range of cognitive levels, depending on the type of constructed-response item and the complexity of the item. **Constructed-response items** are *items for which the student must provide the answer.* The response can be quite restrictive in that there is one and only one correct response, or the response can be unrestrictive in which the student is synthesizing information and constructing meaning.

As of 2011–12, some type of constructed-response items have been used on many state assessments; 27 states use short-answer items, 38 use more extended constructed-response items in English/language arts (e.g., writing an essay), and 19 use extended constructed-response items in other subjects (Education Week Research Center, 2014). Some states are moving toward adopting assessments aligned to the Common Core State Standards. The Partnership for Assessment of Readiness for College and Careers (PARCC) and the Smarter Balanced Assessment Consortium have included both constructed-response items and items in which a student must perform a task (PARCC, 2014; Smarter Balanced Assessment Consortium, n.d). Constructed-response items are a mainstay of state assessment systems and of the classroom assessment practices of teachers.

Constructed-Response Items and Performance Tasks

The Smarter Balanced Assessment Consortium makes a clear distinction between constructed-response items and performance assessment tasks. They define constructed-response items as those that require students to provide a text or a number to respond to a question. Performance tasks, on the other hand, require more in-depth thinking and analysis, assessing a range of intended learning outcomes within one task (Smarter Balanced Assessment Consortium, n.d.). In addition, they require a more extensive response that may be multifaceted. While we do not focus on making the distinction clear between constructed-response and performance tasks in this book, the guidelines provided here for constructed-response items do apply to developing performance tasks.

In this chapter we focus on general guidelines related to developing any type of constructed-response item (or performance task, for that matter). We provide examples of both poor items and better items to illuminate each guideline. These guidelines are a compilation of our review of assessment experts in the field as well as our own experiences as teachers, instructional leaders, state assessment developers, and, currently, professors (Gronlund & Waugh, 2013; Hogan, 2007; Popham, 2014; Stiggins & Chappuis, 2012; Taylor & Nolen, 2008). The examples provided include common constructed-response formats such as *fill-in-the-blank* or *completion*, *short answer*, and *essay*. These types of items can be used on paper-pencil assessments and are a mainstay of item types for teacher-made assessments. As mentioned in the sidebar, other constructed-response assessments include *performance assessments*, *projects*, and *original creations*. However, these types of assessments do not lend themselves to paper-pencil tests and are usually conducted as part of an overall instructional unit assessment plan that may include paper-pencil tests *and* projects, performance assessments, or original creations.

In chapter 4 we focused on creating select-response items that measure what you intend for them to measure (i.e., validity) and are relatively free from systematic error (i.e., reliability). Then we turned our attention to developing select-response items that tap higher order thinking skills. In the second part of this chapter we follow the same format, providing examples of how to develop constructed-response items that tap higher order thinking skills using the same principles discussed in chapter 4.

Some Basic Guidelines for Developing Constructed-Response Items

When developing constructed-response items, there are three elements of the item that must be considered. Every constructed-response item is comprised of a *prompt* (which provides direction to students on what to do or what is asked of them), *response format* (which are considerations of logistical matters such as where/how do I respond, how much time is available, if certain resources are needed, etc.), and *scoring criteria* (which identify the expectations for performance). Figure 5.1 provides a way of thinking about the relationship among these three elements.

First, notice the arrows that move back and forth between each element. The arrows indicate that in developing constructed-response items a teacher can start with any one of the three elements but that all three must eventually be taken into account and thoughtfully planned. While we can start with any element, typically most teachers begin with the prompt. One of the most common issues we see in our own work is that this is where the development process ends. A teacher develops the prompt but does not necessarily plan for the response format or the scoring criteria. Oftentimes, scoring criteria are developed as an afterthought, when the teacher is about to score the assessment, but this is not best practice.

Second, notice the equal signs between each element. Care must be taken to ensure that the prompt aligns with the response format, the response format aligns with the scoring criteria, and the scoring criteria align with the prompt. More will be discussed about this alignment further in the

Figure 5.1 Elements of a Constructed-Response Item

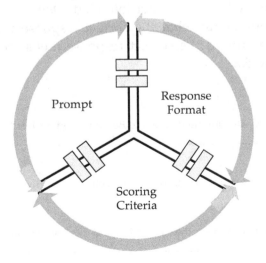

chapter. Attending to these three elements and the alignment among them promotes creating a valid and reliable constructed-response item in such a way that:

1. The item assesses what you as the teacher intend for it to assess;
2. The student can respond in a way that truly demonstrates what she has, or has not, learned;
3. The item does not give away the correct response;
4. The item does not *prevent* a student from providing an appropriate response;
5. The scoring criteria are clear so that the score is truly reflective of what the student knows and is able to do.

For each element of constructed-response items, guidelines are provided along with examples and explanations of the examples.

The Prompt

Every constructed-response item or activity begins with a prompt. Essentially, the prompt provides the student with the problem to be addressed. It could be as simple as identifying a correct term or phrase in a fill-in-the-blank item, or it could be more complex, such as creating a diagram to demonstrate the effects of changes in a food chain in a short-answer item. In both cases, the prompt should be written so that the student understands what he is being asked to do. Here are some basic guidelines when developing prompts:

Guideline 1: Make sure the problem to be addressed is clear to the student. A question that is not clear to students is plagued by systematic error. The student may give a response that makes perfect sense, and may even be correct, but is not what the teacher intended. One way to make the question clear is to think about what the correct response would be and then build the question around the correct response. Let's look at the example provided in Figure 5.2.

Figure 5.2 Guideline 1: Make Sure the Problem to Be Addressed Is Clear to the Student

Poor Item
Discuss synthesis reaction and decomposition reaction.

Better Item
Provide a difference between synthesis reaction and decomposition reaction.

In the poor item, students are given the direction to discuss the two concepts of synthesis and decomposition reaction, when the item really is meant to assess the differences between the two. So why not phrase the question that way? In the better item, students know that they need to think about the differences between synthesis and decomposition reaction and provide one difference. Students can more clearly understand the intent of the question and therefore have a fairer opportunity to respond.

Some Thoughts on Short Answer Items

Short answer items are useful in assessing a range of cognitive levels. They require a bit more than a single word or a phrase as an answer, such as in a completion item, but short answer items are not quite the extensive response required in an essay item. A benefit of short answer items is that they can assess content that cannot be easily assessed on a select-response or fill-in-the-blank item. For example, a teacher may develop a simple addition problem with two-digit numbers in a multiple choice format. However, if the teacher wants to know whether students can carry over in adding two-digit numbers, it would be more useful for students to show their work. Then the teacher can assess whether the students can actually carry out this computation.

Another example can be found in developing a prompt for an essay. In order for a student to provide an appropriate response, the essay prompt must be written in such a way as to elicit an appropriate response. One concern we hear oftentimes with this guideline is, "Aren't we then just giving the answers to the students?" The answer is no. An essay item that is too broadly written, or too narrowly written, puts the student in an unfair situation. If it is too broadly written, students apply their own interpretation to the question, which may not be what the teacher intended. If the item is too narrowly written, then the student may focus in a rote manner only on responding directly to the item rather than employing higher order thinking and developing an insightful response. One way to address this situation is to draft an outline of an exemplary response first and then craft the essay prompt itself. Let's look at two examples of essay prompts in Figure 5.3.

Figure 5.3 Guideline 1: Make Sure the Problem to Be Addressed Is Clear to the Student

---

Poor Item
Discuss how African Americans worked to gain civil rights in the 1950s and 1960s.

Better Item
In a five-paragraph essay, describe how African Americans worked to gain civil rights in the 1950s and 1960s in the following ways: socially, politically, and economically. Include specific historical events in your response to support your ideas.

In the poor item, the students have a wide range of what to discuss in their responses. However, the intent of the item is to assess whether students understand the ways in which African Americans gained civil rights and the specific historical events associated with the civil rights movement. The better item reflects this intent. This item requires higher level thinking as students must *analyze* the events of the civil rights movement and place these events into three distinct categories. The better item also places some conditions on the students' responses. The response must be in the form of a five-paragraph essay and must include historical events. The response format is important, and this element is discussed later in this chapter. Attending to the response format provides clear criteria for students constructing responses and for teachers assessing the students' essays.

Guideline 2: Avoid options within the item. Have you ever taken a test with short answer or essay items in which you have a choice of answering three of the five (or some optional number) prompts provided? You probably wiped your forehead in relief as you could more easily answer some items than others, so you wrote the ones for which you had the most confidence. The two prompts you did not answer were questions for which you may have not had the foggiest understanding or were a bit shakier on your details. What a relief!

In education, we talk a great deal about providing choice to students. While this can allow for differentiation, it poses a problem for assessing student understanding of important intended learning outcomes. If students have a choice among multiple essay or short answer prompts, each of which assesses different content and, possibly, at different cognitive levels of demand, then how can teachers draw inferences about student learning regarding the content of the essays that were *not answered*? It is extremely important for teachers to understand the purpose of the short answer or essay items if options are provided. Let's look at an example:

Figure 5.4 Guideline 2: Avoid Options within the Item

Poor Item

Choose any one of the following three essays. Your response will be based on the story *The Diary of Anne Frank*.

Option 1—Describe the central conflicts in the book, both internal and external, and how the conflicts were resolved, if they were resolved.
Option 2—Choose two of the characters in the book and describe how these characters are developed and how they change throughout the book.
Option 3—Describe how imagery is used in the book.

Better Item

In class, we read *The Diary of Anne Frank*. Throughout the book, Anne describes her family members and the conflicts they faced both with the outside world and among themselves. Using the essay model we have discussed in class, describe the following:

1—Two conflicts, either external and/or internal, faced by Anne and her family
2—How the character traits of the family members influenced how they dealt with the conflicts

Use events from the story to support your ideas.

In the poor item, students can choose from one of three options. The first option focuses on conflict. The second option focuses on character development, and the third option focuses on the use of imagery. First, these types of items may not be the most appropriate given the nature of the story, *The Diary of Anne Frank*. Second, each essay item assesses something different, and so the teacher would have different assessment information for each student. In the better item, the question is more focused and also more appropriate for the novel being studied. The question focuses on integrating both conflict *and* character by intertwining the two. Therefore, the essay assesses a broader range of content and each student writes to the same question, allowing the teacher to make comparisons among student performance and interpret student responses in light of the intended learning outcomes, which are represented on the teacher's table of specifications for the test. Because the better item drops the question related to imagery, the teacher would have to assess that content through some other means.

The Response Format

The response format refers to considerations of logistical matters such as where/how the student responds, how much time is available, resources that are needed, and space provided. Here are some basic guidelines for attending to the response format.

Guideline 1: Clearly state how the student should respond and any resources that might be needed to respond. Many times we assume that students will know how to respond when given a question. However, that assumption can lead to a student not responding in a way that we intended. For example, do we expect the student to write in complete sentences, to draw a diagram, to show computational work? The response format should not be a mystery to students and should be included with the prompt. Look at the example provided in Figure 5.5. The poor item provides a clear problem, but the directions merely indicate to students, "Show your work." The better item more clearly defines accepted formats of how students should show their work through using words, numbers, or pictures. Students have a better sense of an acceptable response format.

Figure 5.5 Guideline 1: Clearly State How the Student Should Respond and Any Resources That Might Be Needed to Respond

---

Poor Item
Jamal made two cookies for each of his kids. He has three kids. How many cookies did Jamal make? Show your work.

Better Item
Jamal made two cookies for each of his kids. He has three kids. How many cookies did Jamal make? Show how you got your answer using words, numbers, or pictures.

In addition, resources may be needed to respond to a question. Will the students need a straightedge, a ruler, graph paper, the periodic table, a sheet of music? Finally, how much time may be needed to respond to the item? It typically takes a student 30 to 60 seconds to answer a multiple choice question. Constructed-response items take more time and can range anywhere from 30 seconds for a fill-in-the-blank to 30 minutes for a more extended constructed-response, such as an essay. When developing constructed-response items, think about the feasibility of being able to complete the entire assessment or test within the amount of time available.

Some Thoughts on Extended-Constructed Response

Some constructed-response items are considered to be more extensive than short answer items. These may include essays in history or English, development of an experimental design in science based on a scenario given, or completion of a detailed graphic organizer showing similarities and differences among the design elements in two pieces of music that are played for students. Extensive constructed-response items provide teachers with the opportunity to assess higher cognitive levels. These items may require students to analyze policies for similarities and differences, synthesize information to formulate a novel understanding, or evaluate the veracity of an argument. They take much more time for students to complete and for teachers to grade. However, they allow teachers not only to assess higher cognitive levels but also to assess a greater depth of content.

Guideline 2: Provide adequate space for the response. Adequate space for the response should be provided to students. Younger students may need more space than older students because they are developing their handwriting skills. Teachers should also consider whether students would be better served by responding in a lined response space rather than a blank response space. It's our experience that if students are provided two lines to provide a response, they will typically write two lines or less. In this case, structure does drive behavior! (In other words, the physical response space can affect the very nature of the students' responses, which could present a problem with the validity of the item itself.) As a general guideline, the response space provided for each short answer item should be equal in size among such items so as not to provide a clue that one short answer item requires more information than another short answer item. If some blanks are longer than others, then the student may be given a clue that the correct response is a longer word or phrase, while shorter blanks may mean that the correct response is a shorter word or phrase. We often see this with completion items in which blanks are different lengths. Figure 5.6 provides an example.

Figure 5.6 Guideline 2: Provide Adequate Space for the Response

Poor Items

The first major agreement between United States officials and Plains Indians was called the _____.

The president can pardon illegal acts by granting _____.

Better Items

The first major agreement between United States officials and Plains Indians was called the _____.

The president can pardon illegal acts by granting _____.

In the poor items, the student knows that the correct response in the first item is longer than the correct response in the second item. In the better items, each blank is equal in length, thereby reducing the possibility of a student gaining a clue to the correct answer based only on the format of the test item, rather than eliciting the answer from the student's understanding of the material. Of course, there is one important caution to keep in mind: If you intend for students to write their answers in the blanks that you provide, then the blanks should be long enough to accommodate the expected answers.

Some Thoughts on Completion Items

Fill-in-the-blank or completion items are useful for assessing lower cognitive levels such as *recall* and *understanding*. They can help eliminate guessing since a student must know the correct answer and cannot choose from a supplied list of possible responses. Fill-in-the-blank items are also fairly easy to grade and allow for an efficient use of assessment time. Some tests use word banks with completion items. Do not confuse these types of items with constructed-response items; they are more akin to matching sets because students *choose* from the possible options offered in a word bank. If using fill-in-the-blank with a word bank, refer to the guidelines to creating matching sets discussed in chapter 4. Here are a few more guidelines to consider when constructing these types of items:

◆ **Position blanks at the end of the statement.** The position of the blank at the end of the completion statement provides the student with an understanding of what is being asked at the beginning. By way of contrast, if the blank is positioned at the beginning of the statement, the student will most likely have to read the statement again, thereby reducing the efficiency of the item.

◆ **Limit the number of blanks.** Have you ever seen a fill-in-the-blank item that is missing so many words that the student would have to be a mind reader to respond correctly? We certainly have. This introduces error into the item by not giving the student enough information to be able to knowledgeably respond.

Scoring Criteria

Each constructed-response item should have clear scoring criteria associated with it. Select-response items are simpler and more objective to score.

The student must choose from one of the answer choices provided, and the teacher grades accordingly. Fill-in-the-blank or completion items are also easier to score, as the answers provided are limited and typically involve little interpretation or variation. Short answer and essay items are more open to interpretation, may allow for more variation, and, therefore, can be more difficult to score. But this need not be the case. By articulating essential criteria, the scoring of an essay or a short answer item becomes a more objective, rather than a wholly subjective, process. We do *not* assert, however, that applying scoring criteria eliminates subjectivity. It does not. Indeed, the creation and use of scoring criteria requires considerable professional judgment and subject-area expertise. Even so, when teachers grade a constructed-response item *without* scoring criteria, the scoring of the response is more susceptible to *uninformed subjectivity*, to *inconsistency*, and to *error*, each of which diminishes the potential reliability and, therefore, the validity of the item.

Types of scoring criteria. Scoring criteria vary in type and sophistication. Some scoring criteria may take a few minutes to construct, and others may take much longer, depending on the content and the level of cognitive demand of the intended learning outcome(s) being assessed. The three types of scoring criteria that are used most often when grading constructed-response items are a *checklist*, a *holistic rubric*, and an *analytic rubric*. Each type of scoring criteria is appropriate in varying circumstances, depending on the type of item and on the level of information teachers need in order to assess student understanding. Each type is briefly explained in the following and an example is provided.

Checklist. A **checklist** is simply that, *a list of behaviors or look-fors in an item response*. Checklists are useful for a quick grading of a response. Checklists focus on certain behaviors that are associated with a task. What the checklist does *not* provide is any degree of how well the items on the checklist were performed. Teachers are simply looking to see that the content and/ or behaviors are present.

With some content and skills, varying degrees of knowledge or ability may not be appropriate. For example, it would be difficult to define degrees of whether a student can perform a simple computational task. Teachers may want to see certain work shown, but varying degrees of completion are not appropriate in this instance. We recommend checklists as a possible tool in evaluating responses to short answer items rather than more complex items, such as essays. Essay items require a more complex response, and thus the checklist is less appropriate. Figure 5.7 shows an example of a checklist that could be used to rate a student's response to the better item in Figure 5.5.

Figure 5.7 Example of a Checklist

____1. The student used pictures, words, or numbers to show the answer. (1 point)
____2. The pictures, words, or numbers portrayed the problem accurately. (2 points)
____3. The correct answer was provided. (2 points)

The checklist provided delineates the task to be completed. Notice that points are awarded for each item in the checklist, making this a five-point question. The first item in the checklist focuses on whether students can use pictures, words, or phrases to depict a problem, an important skill to learn. The next two items focus on accuracy, another critical consideration. So if a student attempts to show her work using pictures but misses the mark, the student still receives one point.

Rating Scales

A common variation of a checklist is a *rating scale*. Like checklists, rating scales are particularly useful and efficient for scoring constructed responses that are comprised of a number of discrete learning outcomes. However, rating scales allow for anticipated variations in the quality or completeness of responses. For example, a teacher may create a short answer item in which students are to explain the difference between the development of two characters in a short story. Student responses could be scored on a four-point rating scale, with 4 indicating a complete and accurate explanation of each of the characters, while 3, 2, and 1 indicate less complete and/or less accurate explanations. A *rating scale* is essentially a hybrid of a *checklist* and a *holistic rubric*. As such, it can provide some of the efficiency of a checklist, while also allowing for anticipated variations in performance of complex learning outcomes.

Holistic Rubric. A holistic rubric is a valuable tool and one that is used by many states to assess student performance on state standardized tests. A **holistic rubric** provides *a defined level of expected performance on constructed-response item that is applied to a student's overall performance but is not indicative of specific components of the performance.* Holistic rubrics typically involve levels of performance. The number of possible levels of performance is associated with a description of the response. The scorer must use the levels to rate the response. A student's response may not fall into more than one category.

The better rubric in Figure 5.8 provides an example of a holistic rubric. Notice that the levels of performance are described as *exemplary, proficient, developing/needs improvement*, and *unsatisfactory*. Each level also has a point value associated with it. The rubric examples provided in Figure 5.8 are

Figure 5.8 Example of a Holistic Rubric

Item

In class, we read *The Diary of Anne Frank*. Throughout the story, Anne describes her family members and the conflicts they faced both with the outside world and among themselves. Using the essay model we have discussed in class, describe the following:

1—Two conflicts, either external and/or internal, faced by Anne and her family
2—How the character traits of the family members influenced how they dealt with the conflicts

Use events from the story to support your ideas.

Poor Scoring Rubric

20 points 10 for each conflict

Better Scoring Rubric

Exemplary (20 points)—The response indicates a clear and insightful level of understanding of the conflicts faced by Anne and her family and how the character traits of the family members influenced how they dealt with the conflicts. Events from the story directly support the description of the conflict and family member character traits. The essay is well written, convincing, and follows the format discussed in class. The essay is generally free from grammatical errors.

Proficient (15 points)—The response indicates an understanding of the conflicts faced by Anne and her family and how the character traits of the family members influenced how they dealt with the conflicts. Events chosen from the book support the description of the conflict and family member character traits, but events that were more directly relevant would have made the essay stronger. The essay is clear and develops a rational position, essentially following the format discussed in class. The essay contains some grammatical errors.

Developing/Needs Improvement (10 points)—The response indicates a limited understanding of the conflicts faced by Anne and her family and how the character traits of the family members influenced how they dealt with the conflicts. Events chosen from the book offer weak support of the description of the conflict and family member character traits. The essay lacks elements discussed in class and contains numerous grammatical errors.

Unsatisfactory (5 points)—The response indicates a weak or inaccurate understanding of the conflicts faced by Anne and her family and how the character traits of the family members influenced how they dealt with the conflicts. Events do not support the description or are not provided. The essay lacks elements discussed in class and contains numerous grammatical errors.

No response (0 points)—The student provides no response or the response cannot be scored.

---

based on the essay from Figure 5.4. The poor rubric in Figure 5.8 is limited and leaves a great deal of room for interpretation. The teacher may also intend to grade on essay format and grammar, but these elements are not taken into account in the poor rubric. In the better rubric, the number of points awarded is clearly delineated, and the teacher knows what she will be looking for when she grades each essay. Essentially she is looking for four items:

- Description of the conflicts and how Anne's family dealt with the conflicts
- Support from the story
- Correct application of elements of a well-written essay
- Correct use of grammar

The holistic rubric is useful for short answer items and essay items, as well as other types of constructed-response items. It provides teachers with criteria to use for grading the item and gives a sense of the entire response, rather than individual pieces of the response, as in a checklist (or rating scale). It also accounts for varying degrees of responses. The holistic rubric, however, does not provide ratings on various processes that may be involved in one item. This type of rubric is called an *analytic rubric*.

Analytic Rubric. The analytic rubric is reserved for the more complex tasks that may involve different processes or skills. An **analytic rubric** is *a scoring key that provides information regarding performance in each of the component parts of the task, making it useful for diagnosing strengths and weaknesses.* Students gain more information regarding their performance, and teachers gain more information regarding a student's level of performance and, therefore, further instruction that may be needed. Developing and applying an analytic rubric can be time-consuming for teachers, but the information the rubric yields can be very valuable. Figure 5.9 provides an example of a rubric that might be used in a writing class. The analytic rubric is not for every type of item. A simple short answer item may require only a checklist or rating scale, but a more involved task may involve a breakdown of the task for both the teacher and the student.

The analytic rubric breaks writing into three component parts: *composing, written expression,* and *usage and mechanics.* Students may perform at the highest level in the first two areas but at a "2" in the *usage and mechanics* area. The student and the teacher then know that the student has the ability to write well but needs to work on grammar. The analytic rubric provides specific feedback to the teacher and to the student. Elements of effective feedback are discussed in chapter 6.

Figure 5.9 Example of an Analytic Rubric Used for Writing

	Unsatisfactory 1	Needs Improvement 2	Proficient 3	Exemplary 4
Composition	The writer demonstrates little or no control of most of the composing domain's features.	The writer demonstrates inconsistent control of several features, indicating significant weakness in the composing domain.	The writer demonstrates reasonable, but not consistent, control of the composing domain's features; the writer may control some features more than others.	The writer demonstrates consistent, though not necessarily perfect, control of the composing domain's features.
Written Expression	The writer demonstrates little or no control of most of the written expression domain's features.	The writer demonstrates inconsistent control of several features, indicating significant weakness in the written expression domain.	The writer demonstrates reasonable, but not consistent, control of the written expression domain's features; the writer may control some features more than others.	The writer demonstrates consistent, though not necessarily perfect, control of the written expression domain's features.
Usage and Mechanics	The writer demonstrates little or no control of most of the domain's features of usage and mechanics.	The writer demonstrates inconsistent control of several features, indicating significant weakness in the domain of usage and mechanics.	The writer demonstrates reasonable, but not consistent, control of most of the domain's features of usage and mechanics.	The writer demonstrates consistent, though not necessarily perfect, control of the domain's features of usage and mechanics.

Guidelines for scoring criteria. Scoring criteria, whether a checklist, a holistic rubric, or an analytic rubric, must be developed deliberately and with careful thought. Here we provide some guidelines for developing scoring criteria to score a constructed-response item.

1. *Unpack the intended learning outcome that the item will be assessing.* This guideline is critical. The scoring criteria must be aligned with both the learning objective and the item that is developed. This step—as with all assessment items—is your first step in ensuring the all-important attribute of *validity*.

2. *Write the prompt for the constructed-response item.* The item itself will provide the starting point for the development of the checklist or rubric. Teachers must know what they are going to assess before they can develop criteria to assess it.

3. *Decide on the most appropriate type of scoring criteria.* The type of scoring criteria is dependent upon the item type, the complexity of the item, and the intended uses of the assessment results. For example, if teachers desire diagnostic information on the students' abilities to apply the skill of comparing and contrasting, then an analytic rubric may be more appropriate. If the assessment will be used primarily for a summative evaluation purpose, then a rating scale or holistic rubric may be not only appropriate but also efficient.

4. *Develop the scoring criteria.* The scoring criteria should be designed based on the elements and anticipated uses of the item itself. Design elements for each type of scoring criteria discussed are provided in Figure 5.10.

5. *Review the item again for alignment between the intended learning outcome, the prompt, the response format, and the scoring criteria.* After developing the criteria, always look at the item again to make sure that the scoring criteria will indeed measure a student's response and to ensure that the item is written in such a way that would provide the opportunity for students to respond correctly. Revisit Figure 5.1 for a visual of this alignment.

Figure 5.10 Design Tips for Developing Different Types of Scoring Criteria

Checklist
- ☑ List the critical elements, facts, or procedures that must be in the response.
- ☑ Assign point values to the critical elements, facts, or procedures.

Holistic Rubric
- ☑ Decide on the number of levels of performance.
- ☑ Describe responses associated with each level of performance.
- ☑ Assign point values to each level of performance.

Analytic Rubric
- ☑ Decide on the number of levels of performance.
- ☑ Define critical elements of the task.
- ☑ Describe the anticipated response for each element at each level of performance.
- ☑ Assign point values to each level of performance.

6. *Apply the scoring criteria after administering the assessment.* It is our experience that applying scoring criteria provides a great deal of information regarding the reliability of the scoring criteria. You may find that the scoring criteria are not quite clear or that some of the elements unintentionally overlap. After applying the criteria, it can be refined for the next use.

7. *Analyze the results.* The results of the assessment provide valuable information regarding student performance and the adequacy of instruction. Checklists may provide information regarding specific elements with which students have difficulty. The holistic rubric provides an overall picture of student performance on a task. The analytic rubric allows the student and teacher to diagnose specific strengths and weaknesses, in varying degrees.

The Importance of Scoring Criteria: A Teacher's Perspective

We have had the great fortune to work with many teachers across the United States and in other parts of the world. We often find that working with teachers provides us with clarity on what is important about assessment and why it is important. In one such instance we were working with a 3rd grade team on developing common assessments to use in mathematics. One teacher wisely offered, "If we do not have common scoring criteria, we do not have a common assessment." He was right! Even if each team teacher used the exact same questions, there would be no common assessment if each teacher scored student work differently. Lack of common scoring criteria would result in different expectations of student performance and therefore different inferences about students' learning.

These seven guidelines provide an outline of how to go about developing scoring criteria. Just as with a table of specifications, scoring criteria need not be a neat, word-processed checklist or chart. It can be written out on a sheet of paper or sketched out on a napkin, for that matter! However, it is only fair to the students that they know how their response will be scored. Scoring criteria should be shared with students (but, hopefully, *not* on a napkin!) as long as the scoring criteria will not "give away" correct responses. Now that we have devoted attention to *developing* scoring criteria, we now turn to *applying* the scoring criteria.

Tips for applying scoring criteria. Following clear guidelines in developing scoring criteria will ensure that the short answer or essay item measures what it is intended to measure and that criteria are appropriate for scoring the item. Just as important is the actual application of the scoring criteria. The criteria you develop may have a high degree of validity in that they are aligned with both the intended learning outcome and the essay item, but it may be applied in such a way that its reliability is compromised. Here are a few tips to consider as you apply scoring criteria to student work. Each tip provides a teacher scenario and then a discussion of the importance of the tip.

Tip 1: Score responses anonymously. Mr. Alonso teaches 8th grade English. The students have been working on how to write persuasive essays while reading a novel in class. The students took a test on the novel that included a persuasive essay item based on the novel. Mr. Alonso is now scoring the essays using a rubric developed by his state in order to prepare students for the state writing assessment. When he gets to Malachi's essay, Mr. Alonso is pleased with what he is reading. Malachi always performs well in class and is a conscientious, hard-working student. When Mr. Alonso gets to Erica's essay, he knows what he is going to find even before he reads the essay. Erica rarely turns in homework, and her essays are usually incomplete. However, this time her essay is complete, and, in fact, her essay is just about on par with Malachi's.

All teachers are human. We develop perceptions of people based on past experiences. In Mr. Alonso's case, he was expecting the "good" in Malachi's essay and was looking for the "bad" in Erica's in order to confirm his perceptions. If Mr. Alonso had scored the essays without knowing the identity of the essay writer in advance, then his bias would have been negated. Bias can even enter into the application of a rubric. By scoring student work anonymously (that is, not knowing the students' identities while scoring), bias is limited, and, consequently, the reliability and validity of the assessment item is improved.

Tip 2: Review responses scored for consistency in scoring. Ms. Rhodes teaches Advanced Placement (AP) American History and administers essays that are comparable to essays that students may encounter on the AP exam. It takes her about 30 minutes to grade each essay, so the process is long. She grades some in the morning, some in the afternoon, and some in the evening. One evening she picks up an essay to grade, not realizing she has already graded the essay earlier in the day since she records comments on a separate piece of paper first. When she figures out her mistake, she finds that the score she had assigned to the student the second time was different from the first time. Ms. Rhodes decides that she needs to go back and spot-check other essays.

Everyone has a different time of the day in which they are more productive and simply more in tune. Teachers are no different. Moods can influence how student responses are viewed. One way to keep yourself objective is to go back and spot-check items that you have already scored to see if you still agree with the rating. This is called *intra-rater reliability* (discussed in chapter 2). Ms. Rhodes has a problem with *intra-rater reliability*, as she found out when she inadvertently scored a paper differently the second time around.

Tip 3: Have someone else score student responses using the scoring criteria. Ms. Bhatia works in a middle school that emphasizes writing across the curriculum. She teaches science and has been using writing both in instruction and in assessment of student work. She recently administered a test on which the last question was an essay item. She used the writing rubric adopted by the school to score the responses. Ms. Bhatia was grading the essays in the teacher's lounge and was having difficulty scoring one student's essay. Another science teacher, Mr. Sams, happened to be in the lounge, and they began talking about the rubric. They decided that they would choose a random number of each other's students to check one another's scoring of student responses.

Sometimes the application of a rubric can be a daunting process, especially if the rubric is externally imposed, as in the case described in the aforementioned scenario. The situation described relates to *inter-rater reliability* (discussed in chapter 2). Ms. Bhatia is concerned with *inter-rater reliability* because she is not sure that she is applying the rubric correctly and would feel better if someone else scored some of her students' work independently. Then she could compare scores to make sure that she is on target with the rubric.

Tip 4: If you have more than one item scored with scoring criteria, score the same item for all students before moving on to the next item. Mr. Sebastiano teaches 5th grade language arts and uses paper-pencil tests to assess students' understanding of various novels and the application of various literary devices found in the novels. On his tests he uses short answer and essay items. For a long time, Mr. Sebastiano graded each student's test completely and then moved onto the next student's test. He went to a workshop on using scoring rubrics, and the presenter recommended that he grade all of the students' responses to each item before moving onto the next item. He was skeptical at first but decided to try it. He found that by doing this he had a better overall picture of the students' responses for each item and that he graded the students' papers more efficiently. He liked that he did not have to re-orient himself to each scoring rubric when he moved on to the next student's test.

Mr. Sebastiano made a time-saving change when he decided to grade all of the students' responses to each item before moving on to the next. This simple change in grading an assessment can provide teachers with an overall sense of student performance on each short answer and essay item. It also is more efficient in that the teacher has the rubric in front of him as he grades each student's paper and is not switching from rubric to rubric with each new item for each new student. More important, though, Mr. Sebastiano also now grades essay items more reliably because he is not having to re-orient himself to the rubric each time he scores a student's test.

Care and consideration must be taken into account in both developing scoring criteria and applying the criteria. The simple guidelines and tips provided help increase the validity and reliability of constructed-response items on a test, thereby increasing the validity and reliability of the test itself.

Putting It All Together: Prompt, Response Format, and Scoring Criteria

In this chapter we have focused on three critical elements of creating any type of constructed-response item: the *prompt*, the *response format*, and the *scoring criteria*. We discussed each of these separately and provided guidelines related to each element. As mentioned at the beginning of the chapter, these three elements are highly interdependent, and alignment among the three must be considered. To further illuminate this alignment, consider the item in Figure 5.11. This item is measuring a student's ability to construct a diagram of a water cycle and then to explain the relationship of the processes to the overall water cycle. Let's examine this item using the three elements for developing a constructed-response item.

The prompt. The prompt is clear, as students know that the question is about the water cycle and the processes involved in the water cycle.

The response format. This is a two-part question in which students must *draw* and *label a diagram* and must *write a paragraph*. The response format is clear to the students, and the teacher would need to ensure that adequate space is provided for students to respond in these ways.

The scoring criteria. The teacher uses an analytic rubric focusing on three criteria: modeling, describing, and the use of paragraph structure. Note that this is a seven-point item and that more points are given for the modeling and describing while only one point would be awarded for the paragraph structure. The teacher is more interested in the students' understanding of the science concepts rather than writing skill, but writing skill is still important in communicating ideas.

The *prompt*, *response format*, and *scoring criteria* are aligned. Students are assessed according to their understanding of the content asked in the prompt and in terms of the response format expected. In addition, the item clearly aligns to the intended learning outcome. All of these considerations increase both the *validity* and *reliability* of the item.

Figure 5.11 Putting It All Together: Prompt, Response Format, and Scoring Criteria

Intended Learning Outcome:

The student will construct a model of the water cycle and will describe the processes of evaporation, condensation, and precipitation as they relate to the water cycle.

Prompt and Response Format:

In the space below, draw and label the water cycle. Then, in a paragraph response, explain the water cycle. Be sure to identify each key stage of the water cycle and describe how each stage leads to the next stage in the cycle. (7 points)

Scoring Criteria:

	0	1	2	3
Model	No drawing	Includes 1 key stage	Includes 2 key stages	Includes 3 key stages
Paragraph response	Single sentence or less written	Two or more sentences written	—	—
Explanation	No description of relationships b/w stages	Accurately describes 1 process and how it transitions to the next stage	Accurately describes 2 processes and how they transition to the next stages	Accurately describes all 3 processes and how they complete a full "cycle"

Another Important Consideration—Bias

Students have varying experiences based on myriad factors. These factors include a student's native language, developmental level, and exposure to concepts and ideas at home, in museums, and in other cultural institutions. Sometimes terms or phrases may be used in a constructed-response item that place some students at a disadvantage because of their background. When writing a constructed-response item, a teacher must review the item to make sure that the language and terms are critical to the content being assessed and do not unfairly penalize students who do not have experiences with the terms or phrases but could demonstrate their understanding of the instructional objective nonetheless. Let's consider the following example.

Figure 5.12 Reviewing Items for Bias

> **Directions:** Correct this sentence.
> **Item:** have you ever read time magazine
> **Student response:** *Have you ever had time to read a magazine?*

The example shows a constructed-response item in which students must correct grammatical errors in a sentence. The student response shows how the student corrected the sentence. The item was intended to measure grammar use, specifically capitalization and punctuation. In particular, the item was measuring whether students know that proper nouns should be capitalized. The student response indicates that most likely the student did not know that *Time* was the name of a magazine, as he had not had exposure to it, so he changed the sentence in a way that made sense to him. Based on how the student corrected the sentence, the teacher does not know whether the student knows that pronouns should be capitalized. Due to bias, the item inadvertently introduced error into the assessment, and, therefore, the reliability and validity of the item are weakened.

Constructed-Response in the Primary Grades Classroom

The examples we have provided for creating constructed-response items are indicative of questions used at the upper elementary, middle school, and high school levels. Primary grade teachers also rely heavily on constructed-response types of assessments to assess student learning. When we work with primary grades teachers we often use the term "assessment activity" rather than "assessment item." The considerations discussed in this chapter for developing a prompt, response format, and scoring criteria also apply in the early grades classroom. For example, a teacher may provide students with a set of bears and ask them to model an addition problem using the bears. The prompt is most likely oral, the response format would be the representation using the bears, and the scoring criteria would be related to accurate modeling. The same guidelines for these elements discussed in this chapter apply in the primary grades classroom.

Principles for Tapping Higher Cognitive Levels of Learning through Constructed-Response Items

In chapter 4, we provided five principles for developing select-response items to assess higher cognitive levels. Typically, constructed-response items, particularly essays, have been used to assess levels of *application, analysis, evaluation,* and *creation.* So you may be wondering why we even address this issue in this chapter. In our experience, short answer and essay questions in some instances may look on the surface as if they are assessing higher cognitive levels, but, in reality, they are assessing *recall* or *knowledge.* The same principles that we discussed with select-response items can be applied to constructed-response items. In this section, we briefly review each principle and provide an example of a poor item and a better item to illustrate the principle. For a more thorough description of the principle, please refer back to chapter 4.

Principle 1: Refine your understanding of content and level of cognitive demand. This principle essentially relates to the validity of an item. Does the item indeed address the content and the level of cognitive demand contained within a state standard or an instructional objective? Perhaps the item addresses the content but not at the level of cognitive demand required. Let's review an example.

Figure 5.13 Principle 1: Refine Your Understanding of Content and Level of Cognitive Demand

State Standard	
Nevada Standards for Advanced Music	
The student will analyze examples of a varied repertoire of music representing diverse genres and cultures by describing the uses of the elements of music and expressive devices.	
Poor Item:	**Better Item:**
Explain the devices used in calypso music.	Listen to the following two pieces of music for elements of music that represent a culture.
	In a paragraph, describe the expressive devices used in the music pieces and how they represent their respective cultures.
	[Students listen to the two pieces of music].

This standard from the state of Nevada focuses on the *use* of expressive devices in various cultures and the *analysis* of music across cultures. Students must be able to listen to musical pieces and explain how certain expressive devices are indicative of a culture. In the poor item, students are merely asked to *explain* what devices are used in calypso music. They do not have to listen to calypso music to identify the devices. In the better item, the students must listen to two pieces of music, identify the expressive devices used, and explain how these devices shed light on the culture from which the music came. The students are analyzing two pieces of music rather than one. The poor item misses the mark on the level of cognitive demand and on the content.

Principle 2: Introduce novelty. Novelty involves students' application of what they have learned to a new situation or thinking about information in a different way. Students must have requisite knowledge and skills to answer the question. Let's consider a high school social studies class in which the students are comparing and contrasting the North and South prior to the Civil War. The teacher teaches the students about the North and South, and the students prepare an extensive graphic organizer detailing the similarities and differences. Figure 5.14 shows two essay prompts built around this content.

The North Carolina state standard here focuses on the issues leading to the Civil War, the events, and the outcomes during Reconstruction. In many history classes, the similarities and differences between the North and South are discussed at length, and, in this particular scenario, the students completed an extensive graphic organizer in class. Because novelty is not introduced in the item, the poor item amounts only to *recall*. On the surface it looks like it is an analysis question. But when instruction is taken into account, the true nature of the cognitive level is revealed. Sure, the students must formulate the response; however, they are merely writing what they have already discussed in class.

Figure 5.14 Principle 2: Introduce Novelty

State Standard	
North Carolina Standard Course of Study for American History	
The student will analyze the issues that led to the Civil War, the effects of the war, and the impact of Reconstruction on the nation.	
Poor Item:	**Better Item:**
Describe the similarities and differences between the North and South prior to the Civil War. Use historical facts to support your response.	Examine the following broadside from the Civil War. [Provide teacher-selected example of a broadside.] In a well-written essay, explain the following: - the issue that is the focus of the broadside - the views of the North and South regarding this issue - the effects of the issue on the Civil War - the resolution of this issue after the Civil War Use historical facts to support your response.

In the better item, the students encounter a broadside selected by the teacher that exemplifies an issue related to the Civil War. They must *interpret* the broadside, *analyze* the broadside for the issue, and then *synthesize* the broadside with the similarities and differences that contributed to the Civil War. The broadside ensures that the students have a level of understanding of the issue and cognitively wrestle with their understanding and the novel prompt . . . a far stretch from *recall*.

Principle 3: Focus on complex content. Content can be viewed as simplistic or complex. For example, describing conflict in an essay may be more simplistic than applying the character traits of those within the novel and how the characters dealt with conflict. Short answer and essay items that address more complex content tend to assess higher level thinking. Consider the examples in Figure 5.15.

This item was built around the Texas Essential Knowledge and Skills for high school English. The state of Texas expects students to be able to not only *identify* conflict but also to be able to *analyze* conflicts for similarities and differences. In the poor item, students must only identify a conflict in the novel *Life of Pi*. This is a very simplistic view of the standard and only scratches the surface of the intent of the curricular objective.

In the better item, the student must not only identify conflicts but must do so for two different types of characters, an idealistic one and a realistic one. The student must then compare the conflict's effect on the characters, thereby tapping into *analytical thinking*. In fact, students even need to *evaluate* the characters to determine whether they are idealistic or realistic. This essay item more closely addresses the complexity of the standard.

Figure 5.15 Principle 3: Focus on Complex Content

State Standard
Texas Essential Knowledge and Skills for English
The student will compare and contrast elements of texts such as themes, conflicts, and allusions both within and across texts.

Poor Item:	Better Item:
Describe a conflict in *Life of Pi* by Yann Martel. Provide evidence from the text to defend your description.	The conflict between an idealistic and a pragmatic response to life is a recurrent theme in *Life of Pi* by Yann Martel. Write an essay in which you analyze the reasons for the conflict between these two ways of responding to life's events and compare their respective effects upon one idealistic character and one more realistic character. Provide evidence from the story to defend your analysis.

Principle 4: Use an extended prompt. An extended prompt provides students with some background information. The students must then link this information with what they already know in order to formulate their responses. A caution when using extended prompts: the information provided should not explicitly give students the answer and should be necessary to answer the question. Let's look at an example.

Figure 5.16 Principle 4: Use an Extended Prompt

State Standard	
Washington State Science Learning Standards	
The student will describe how water and wind cause erosion . . . and describe the most likely cause of the erosion.	
Poor Item:	**Better Item:**
The process of water carrying soil from the plastic boxes into the clear pans is called erosion. Erosion can be caused by more than just water flowing. Describe the process of erosion and explain a cause.	The process of water carrying soil from the plastic boxes into the clear pans is called erosion. Erosion can be caused by more than just water flowing. Describe a cause of erosion other than water flowing. In your description, be sure to: - identify another cause of erosion - describe how and where this other cause of erosion would occur. Use words, labeled diagrams, and/or labeled pictures in your answer.

The state of Washington includes short answer items on its assessments. In this case, students must supply a response to indicate that they understand and can describe the process and causes of erosion. In the poor item, the student is merely restating the information provided in the extended prompt. This item is a reading comprehension item rather than a science item, compromising the construct validity of the item. (Revisit chapter 2 for an explanation of *construct validity*.)

In the better item, the process of erosion is briefly described. Students are then asked to extend beyond the prompt provided and articulate another cause of erosion, while also describing how this cause makes erosion occur. Therefore, they are applying the concept of erosion to a new situation. The extended prompt provides enough information to interpret but does not provide the explicit answer to the item.

Principle 5: Provide stimulus material. Stimulus material is similar to the extended prompt in that students must interact with the information in order to formulate a response. The stimulus material should be necessary to respond to the short answer or essay item but should not explicitly provide clues to the answers for the students. The two examples provided in

Figure 5.17 Principle 5: Provide Stimulus Material

State Standard **Pennsylvania Core Standards**	
The student will represent and solve problems involving addition and subtraction within 20.	

The graph shows how many cookies each person ate.

Poor Item:	Better Item:
How many cookies did Sally eat?	How many more cookies did Stephen eat than Roberto? Show how you got your answer using pictures, words, or numbers.

Figure 5.17 show how stimulus material can be used to raise the cognitive level of an item.

Pennsylvania is a state that has adopted the Common Core State Standards. The state standard focuses on the student's ability to create and solve addition and subtraction problems up to 20. The stimulus material provided sets the stage for students to demonstrate their abilities in this area. In the poor item, the students are merely reading the chart. But—make no mistake—reading a chart for a first grader is difficult. Therefore, interpretation is involved. However, the poor item does not really get at the standard and, in fact, fails to measure whether students can use the information in the chart to add and subtract. In the better item, the students use the information to create a subtraction problem, and then they must show their work. The teacher can adequately measure whether students can interpret the chart, represent a problem, and solve it, indicating cognitive levels of *application* and *analysis*.

Developing Valid and Reliable Constructed-Response Items: A Deliberate Approach

Developing constructed-response items requires a deliberate approach and one that includes attention to the prompt, the response format, and the scoring criteria. If an item has an unclear prompt, an unclear response format, and/or unclear scoring criteria, opportunities abound for error to creep into the teacher's interpretation of the assessment results. You may be concerned that developing scoring criteria for each constructed-response item and scoring each item with the criteria will be time-consuming, and at first it probably will be. However, once criteria have been created for a specific skill or set of content, it can be used with similar content or skills. The application of the scoring criteria can actually reduce grading time as it focuses the grading of the constructed-response item.

A test that includes both select-response *and* constructed-response items can assess a wide range of content at varying cognitive levels, which is why we advocate the use of different item types on tests, depending on the content and level of cognitive demand required in the curriculum. Choosing the most appropriate item types will help you create items that assess what you want to assess and that are relatively free from systematic error. In addition, an overall unit assessment plan that includes a test consisting of select-response items, constructed-response items, *and* performance tasks, projects, and/or original creations ensures that the range of intended learning outcomes are assessed throughout the unit.

6

How Do I Connect Assessment to Student Learning?

Making Use of Assessment

Learning does not stop with assessment. However, one might think otherwise when considering some situations we have seen in our own experiences. Consider, for example, the 9th grade English teacher who administers a unit test to her students, spends two nights at home diligently grading the tests, and hands them back to her students on the third day with final marks of 85, 72, 43, 99, and the like. Incorrect answers are noted with an X, and points are deducted from the short answer and essay questions for factual and grammatical errors. As the teacher hands back the grades, she reminds students this was a "major test" and disappointedly comments, "It's obvious that some of you didn't study the way you needed to." But then she smiles and adds, "The good news is that a few of you aced it!" The teacher concludes by telling students that they must take home their tests for their parents to sign and that everyone who returns the test signed the next day will receive 5 extra points. With that, the teacher instructs the students to put their tests in their notebooks and to open up their textbooks to chapter 8 to begin the next unit.

You probably have some concerns about the teacher's practices in this example. We do, too. Although we commend the teacher for working to grade and return the tests as quickly as she could and for attempting to communicate with parents, we're concerned about the flat feedback of the numeric grades, the generalized admonitions about study habits, and the inappropriate use of bonus points, which imbalance the sampling validity of the test. We're also concerned that the teacher seems to tacitly intend for the test to serve as the end mark on the learning associated with the instructional unit. We don't think the teacher means to communicate this, but her actions seem to say, "We've learned—or, in some cases, not learned—that material, so now let's move on to new material."

Learning should not stop with assessment; in fact, quite the opposite. Assessment, as we suggested in the first chapter of this book, is integral to the teaching and learning process.

Formative Assessment

There is a simple answer to the question that serves as the title for this chapter. *How do I connect assessment to student learning? Use the results of the assessment to draw inferences about student learning and then to make decisions to progress student learning.* In short, the assessment becomes connected to student learning when student performance results are used to help further *form* students' learning. As referenced in chapter 1, this is called *formative assessment*.

A common misconception among many educators and policymakers is that formative assessments are a type of assessment in and of themselves. This is not the case. Rather, what makes an assessment *formative* is the way it is used. For example, many people would consider a quiz a type of formative assessment since a quiz is typically lower stakes in terms of a grade calculation and, more importantly, because quiz results provide both the teacher and the student an indication of where the student is relative to mastery of a set of intended learning outcomes while the study of those intended learning outcomes is still under way. However, if a teacher gives a quiz and does nothing but record a grade for it, never adjusting instruction in response to student performance and never providing feedback beyond a percentage score or a letter grade, then the assessment has no *formative value*.

By way of contrast, a unit test is oftentimes thought of as a *summative assessment*, representing a point-in-time, relatively comprehensive instrument for determining level of achievement on a set of intended learning outcomes. Typically, a unit test then results in a grade that goes into the teacher's grade book, constituting some predetermined percentage of the final course grade. However, if the teacher structures a learning activity through which the students analyze their own performance on the test relative to the learning expectations, process their findings, and then use their inferences to make corrections, demonstrate learning through alternate means, or identify different learning strategies to employ in the future, then the unit test would be functioning as a kind of *formative assessment*.

The distinction between formative and summative evaluation was first referenced in educational literature in the early 1960s. At that time, the distinction was made relative to the use of psychometrics and program evaluation techniques either to strengthen or to judge the merit of curricular and other educational programs (Grant & Gareis, 2014). Since that time, the distinction between formative and summative assessment has developed into that which we have shared by way of introduction to this chapter, as well as in chapter 1. Despite the longevity of these concepts, there is considerable evidence that many educators are not particularly proficient at employing formative assessment practices effectively in the classroom (Grant & Gareis, 2014). Frankly, most teachers know that analyzing and using assessment information is an important part of the teaching and learning process, but *how* to do so—both practically and meaningfully—is not always clear.

Why Teachers Should Analyze Student Learning

In this chapter, we describe and illustrate key techniques for analyzing student learning. Before we turn our attention to that, let's consider *why* teachers should analyze student learning. Succinctly stated, there are five main reasons teachers should analyze student learning on classroom assessments:

1. To garner information about the nature and degree of student learning;
2. To make near-term instructional decisions;
3. To make long-term decisions about curriculum, instruction, and assessment;
4. To communicate the nature and/or degree of learning to others (typically through a grade);
5. To provide feedback to students in order to progress their own learning.

We will expand upon each of these important reasons in the sections that follow as we share a process of analyzing student learning.

Using a Table of Specifications to Analyze Student Learning

Again, most teachers know that analyzing student learning is important to the teaching and learning process. But how? Let's look at the scenario of Mr. Franklin, a middle school social studies teacher. Mr. Franklin and his fellow social studies teachers in his school co-planned a unit they call "The Roots and Principles of Our Government," and they collaboratively created a common unit assessment for it. They began this process by first consulting the district's curriculum framework and then by applying their own subject-area expertise to articulate a clear set of intended learning outcomes for their students. Specifically, through this unit the students would:

- Outline and describe the historical roots of the US governmental system;
- Classify and explain the fundamental principles of consent of the governed, limited government, rule of law, democracy, and representative government;
- Identify and explain the purposes for the Constitution of the United States as stated in its Preamble;
- Identify the procedures for amending the Constitution of the United States;
- Explain the significance of, draw inferences about, and defend positions related to the Declaration of Independence, the Articles of Confederation, and the Constitution of the United States, including the Bill of Rights, in relation to the US governmental system;
- Distinguish between relevant and irrelevant information separating fact from opinion in current events pieces related to the US governmental system.

Through a process of unpacking the intended learning outcomes, they identified the specific content and cognitive levels for this unit, including the relative importance of some of the specific intended learning outcomes. Mr. Franklin and his colleagues then created a table of specifications to serve as a blueprint for their construction of two key assessments. One of the key assessments for this unit was a performance-based assessment activity comprised of a scenario that required students to read and draw inferences from primary source documents and then to use these in addressing a contemporary scenario involving citizen rights. Working in collaborative groups, students established a position on the issue supported by at least two primary source documents and then presented their positions in a "white paper" format. The second key assessment for this unit is a comprehensive test consisting of 25 multiple choice and short answer items. The team's table of specifications for their two common assessments is shown in Figure 6.1.

While Mr. Franklin and his colleagues unpacked the curriculum and then created their two common assessments for this unit, they could not help but talk about, share, and refine some of their most tried-and-true instructional strategies for this unit. That was a nice side benefit of co-creating the two key assessments. Their co-planning not only resulted in tighter alignment among

Figure 6.1 Sample Table of Specifications for Mr. Franklin's 8th Grade Civics Unit

Table of Specifications for _The Roots & Principles of Our Government_   Grade___8th Grade_____

Content	Level of Cognitive Demand					
	Remember	Understand	Apply	Analyze	Evaluate	Create
The historical roots of the US governmental system	✔ Outline 1, 2	✔ Describe 3, 13				
The fundamental principles of consent of the governed, limited government, rule of law, democracy, and representative government		✔+ Explain 5, 10, 16	✔+ Classify 18, 19, 25			
The purposes for the Constitution of the United States as stated in its Preamble	✔ Identify 11, 17	✔ Explain 7, 20, 24				
The procedures for amending the Constitution of the United States	✔ Identify 6, 14					
The significance of the Declaration of Independence, the Articles of Confederation, and the Constitution of the United States, including the Bill of Rights, in relation to the US governmental system		✔+ Explain 9, 12 PBA		✔+ Draw inferences 4, 8, 21 PBA	✔ Defend a position PBA	
Relevant and irrelevant information separating fact from opinion in current events pieces related to the US governmental system				✔ Distinguish between 15, 22, 23 PBA		

#'s represent items on the Common Unit Test   PBA= Performance-Based Assessment

curriculum, instruction, and assessment in their individual classrooms, but also among the team of teachers. We'll expand upon the benefits of creating common assessments in the next chapter; for now, we turn our attention to Mr. Franklin's analysis of his students' learning.

Analyzing Student Learning in the Aggregate

As we pick up with Mr. Franklin, he has recently given his students the common unit test and has graded them. Now, he begins the process of analyzing their learning. His first step is to consider student learning _in the aggregate_. In other words, he analyzes how the class as a whole performed. For this, he calculates a simple _class average_ and finds that the class average is an 84% on a standard grading scale of 100. He thinks, "This is good, but I need to learn more."

Of course, what the average does not tell him is whether all of his students tended to score at or near 84% or whether some students scored very high and some quite low, thus only averaging 84% as a class. To investigate further, he can look at simple statistics such as the _median, mode_, and _range_. In this instance, Mr. Franklin opts to create a _grade distribution_. Here's what he finds:

Figure 6.2 Sample Grade Distribution for Mr. Franklin's 8th Grade Civics Test

	A	B	C	D	F
# of students	14	20	10	1	5

The grade distribution provides Mr. Franklin some additional insight into the performance of his students. He is satisfied that he does not have a bimodal distribution of students who have evidently acquired most of the intended learning and those who did not, although he is concerned, of course, about the 16 students who have achieved below the B level.

Thus far, Mr. Franklin's analysis of student learning in the aggregate has given him some indication of the *degree* of student learning. However, he has not yet learned about the *nature* of student learning.

Conducting an Item Analysis

In order to investigate the *nature* of his students' learning, Mr. Franklin conducts an *item analysis*. While an item analysis can be done with some sophistication, especially when an assessment is scored on a computer or a scanning machine, Mr. Franklin does not have that luxury. A number of the items on the test were short answer format and graded by hand using a four-point rating scale. Therefore, Mr. Franklin decides to undertake a rudimentary (but still useful) item analysis. Counting the multiple choice items as either right or wrong, and counting the short answer responses of three or four points as "correct," Mr. Franklin calculates the percentage of students who got each item on the unit test correct. Here's what he finds:

Figure 6.3 Sample Item Analysis for Mr. Franklin's 8th Grade Civics Test

1) 85%	8) 95%	15) <u>50%</u>	22) <u>45%</u>
2) 85%	9) 100%	16) 80%	23) <u>50%</u>
3) 95%	10) 80%	17) 80%	24) 85%
4) 90%	11) 85%	18) 85%	25) 90%
5) 75%	12) 100%	19) 80%	
6) 75%	13) 95%	20) <u>20%</u>	Average: 84%
7) 85%	14) 90%	21) 100%	

The item analysis provides another layer of insight into his students' learning. For instance, he notes in **bold underline** the items that 50% or more of his students got incorrect: items 15, 20, 22, and 23. Mr. Franklin will review those items to see if there is anything in their construction that might have caused students error, such as an incorrect answer key, unclear wording, or some other issue related to the *reliability* of the item. Similarly, Mr. Franklin will review those items in **bold** that 95% or more of his students got correct. These, too, might have some issue of systematic error that allowed students to get them right not from their knowledge and skills but from something in the construction of the items.

Using an item analysis in this way is a means of strengthening the *reliability* and, therefore, the *validity* of this assessment. That is a practical thing to do because Mr. Franklin and his social studies colleagues will want to re-use versions of this test in the years ahead, and so each year they want to strengthen the technical adequacy of the assessment. In other words, they want to keep making it more valid and more reliable. Doing so is one of the five reasons why teachers should analyze student learning, which we presented at the beginning of this chapter. However, Mr. Franklin still has not completed the first of those five purposes, which is to garner information not only about the *degree* of student learning (such as with the class average, grade distribution, and item analysis), but also the *nature* of student learning.

Viewing Student Learning through the Lens of Curriculum

To garner information about the *nature* of his students' learning, he needs to view their learning through the lens of the curriculum. That is, Mr. Franklin needs to consider his students' performance relative to the intended learning outcomes of this unit. With the *table of specifications* and the *item analysis* in hand, he has what he needs to complete this critically important step. To do this, Mr. Franklin plots the item analysis onto the table of specifications for this unit, as depicted in Figure 6.4.

With the item analysis mapped onto the table of specifications, Mr. Franklin is able to draw certain inferences about the nature of his students' learning. Here we point out just a few key conclusions that Mr. Franklin might draw:

◆ Of the six strands of intended learning outcomes (represented by the rows in the table), the majority of students demonstrated particular proficiency in the first and fifth strands. While Mr. Franklin will want to review certain items (3, 13, 9, 12, 8, and 21) for issues of reliability, the chances of so many items that assess similar objectives having error is slight. In other words, applying the principal of *repeated trials reliability* from chapter 2, Mr. Franklin has confidence

Figure 6.4 Sample Analysis of Student Learning Using a Table of Specifications and an Item Analysis

Table of Specifications for _The Roots & Principles of Our Government_   Grade___ _8th Grade_____

Content	Level of Cognitive Demand					
	Remember	Understand	Apply	Analyze	Evaluate	Create
The historical roots of the US governmental system	✓ Outline 1, 2	✓ Describe **3, 13**				
The fundamental principles of consent of the governed, limited government, rule of law, democracy, and representative government		✓+ Explain 5, 10, 16	✓+ Classify 18, 19, 25			
The purposes for the Constitution of the United States as stated in its Preamble	✓ Identify 11, 17	✓ Explain 7, **20**, 24				
The procedures for amending the Constitution of the United States	✓ Identify 6, 14					
The significance of the Declaration of Independence, the Articles of Confederation, and the Constitution of the United States, including the Bill of Rights, in relation to the US governmental system		✓+ Explain **9, 12** PBA		✓+ Draw inferences 4, **8, 21** PBA	✓ Defend a position PBA	
Relevant and irrelevant information separating fact from opinion in current events pieces related to the US governmental system				✓ Distinguish between **15, 22, 23** PBA		

#'s represent items on the Common Unit Test   PBA= Performance-Based Assessment

that his students have done particularly well in demonstrating their acquisition of these intended learning outcomes. From this conclusion, he might also infer that there is no need to re-teach these in the near term and that his instructional strategies may have been effective and, therefore, would be good to keep for next year.

◆ Item 20 is likely to be an unreliable item. In other words, there is probably some issue of systematic error that caused so many students to get it wrong. Mr. Franklin infers this before ever reviewing the item because of the principle of _repeated trials reliability_. Students performed well on the other two items that assessed this intended learning outcome (7 and 24), which suggests that the issue with 20 is due to error rather than learning.

◆ By way of contrast, items 15, 22, and 23 also proved to be problematic, but the chances of three items that assess the same objective having reliability issues is slight. Although Mr. Franklin will review those items, it is most likely that he has gained an important insight into the _nature_ of his students' learning. The intended learning outcome of being able to _distinguish between relevant and irrelevant information, separating fact from opinion in current events pieces related to the US governmental system_, has evidently not been acquired by many students.

From this insight, Mr. Franklin might make a near-term instructional decision to re-visit this skill, either by re-teaching it explicitly or integrating it into the next unit of study. He might also make a longer-term decision to teach this skill differently in this unit next year.

The example of Mr. Franklin's analysis of student learning using an item analysis plotted onto a table of specifications shows how teachers can use the lens of curriculum (that is, the intended learning outcomes themselves) to (1) garner information about the *nature and degree* of student learning, (2) make near-term instructional decisions, and (3) make longer-term decisions about curriculum, instruction, and assessment. These are three of the five purposes for analyzing student learning that we introduced at the beginning of this chapter. We will turn next to the other two purposes. But we conclude this section by pointing out that the example of Mr. Franklin's analysis depicted in Figure 6.4 is only one iteration of such analysis. You may have already had this realization, but the use of the table of specifications to frame the analysis of student learning could be further deepened in such ways as:

- Including the actual percentage of correct responses on the table item by item;
- Calculating grand averages of student performance within each cell on the table;
- Calculating grand averages of student performance across content rows;
- Calculating grand averages of student performance by cognitive level (columns).

The key point is that a teacher's process of garnering valid and reliable information about student learning and then using that information to make near-term and long-term instructional decisions, as in the example of Mr. Franklin, has been found to have statistically significant effects on student learning (Hattie, 2009). In short, effective use of assessment can promote student learning.

Grading

Despite the understanding that good assessment practices can progress student learning, the fact is that assessment is oftentimes associated more with grading than with learning. In fact, the significance of grading in the minds of students and teachers is evident in the common refrain voiced in classrooms as any given teacher is about to hand back a test to students. "What'd I get?" students are apt to be heard asking.

Whether consciously or unconsciously, students—and even many teachers—seem to consider a test grade the outcome of a transaction within the classroom: You (the teacher) teach me; I (the student) learn; you test me; I get a grade. The grade, therefore, is a representation of the value of the learning transaction (Brown, 1981). Indeed, grading is a type of **evaluation**, which may be defined in the classroom context as a systematic process of making judgments about the nature or worth of student learning. It is important to recognize that grading a test is an evaluative process because it reiterates the critical need to grade in ways that are valid, are reliable, and, ultimately, support student learning.

Let's consider what some noted experts on grading say. According to Guskey (2011), grading is fundamentally an issue of communicating clearly. According to Kohn (2000), poor grading practices can dampen student curiosity, interest, motivation, sense of internal locus of control, and even rote memory. According to Chappuis (2014), the finality of grading is such that a teacher should make every effort to provide adequate opportunities to learn before rendering a grade. Taken together, this sampling of educators' views on grading suggests that the process of communicating the nature and degree of learning should be approached by teachers thoughtfully.

When a grade is put on a test or quiz, the teacher is communicating a judgment about the nature and degree of student learning. Most typically, a test grade is communicated as a percentage correct or a letter grade, but sometimes symbols such as check marks or smiley faces serve as grades, as do numbers such as raw scores. In any case, the function of grading is the same. **Grading** is the translation of student performance on an assessment into a system of relative numbers or symbols to communicate the teacher's judgment about the nature and degree of student learning. In other words, a grade is intended to succinctly represent the nature and degree of a student's learning on a given set of instructional objectives (Gronlund & Waugh, 2013).

The number of ways to grade classroom assessments is as many as the types of assessment that teachers can create and use. What's more, many teachers work within schools and/or school districts that mandate the use of certain grading systems, thus limiting the scope of control that teachers might have in regard to grading assessments. Given this, we address the issue of how to grade an assessment by exploring two basic principles as they apply to grading: validity and reliability. As discussed in chapter 2, validity and reliability are concepts central to constructing appropriate and fair assessments in the classroom. These two concepts are also the central principles for determining how to most fairly and appropriately grade an assessment.

As a reminder, *validity* is the extent to which inferences drawn from assessment results are appropriate. Therefore, as teachers consider the process of grading an assessment, they must aim for grading in a way that allows them to make judgments about student learning that are related to the intended learning outcomes of the instructional unit. Similarly, *reliability* is the consistency or dependability of the results of an assessment. Therefore, the teacher must use a grading process that is not unduly influenced by chance or error, either of which would lead to an inaccurate representation of student learning as measured by the assessment.

In short, the same principles that are used to *construct* a valid and reliable assessment are used to *grade* the assessment. With this in mind, Figure 6.5 draws from concepts presented in chapters 2 to 5 to provide a series of

Figure 6.5 Principles of Grading

Validity	Reliability
1. *Is the assessment adequately aligned with and representative of the intended learning outcomes?* A grade is not valid if the assessment from which the grade is derived has a low degree of validity (Butler & McMunn, 2006). (Refer again to Step 1 of "Seven Steps for Creating a Good Assessment" in chapter 3.) 2. *Are individual assessment items weighted to reflect the relative importance of content and skills?* Alternatively (and preferably), are there more items for learning objectives of greater importance or emphasis compared to those of lesser relative importance or emphasis (Ory & Ryan, 1993)? (Refer again to the discussion of content/sampling validity in chapter 2 and to Steps 2 and 5 of "Seven Steps for Creating a Good Assessment" in chapter 3.) 3. *How will implicit and conditional content be graded?* For example, will composition, grammar, and mechanics be graded on a science test that includes an essay response? (Refer again to Step 1 of "Seven Steps for Creating a Good Assessment" in chapter 3 and to chapter 5 on creating constructed-response items.) 4. *What relative number or symbol will the grade take, and will that meaningfully communicate the nature and degree of student learning to others—most importantly, to students?* As a simple example, a checkmark (✓) on a unit test would likely be quite insufficient to communicate the degree of a student's learning, whereas a ✓, ✓ +, or ✓ − may be an adequate means of conveying learning on a single-question, short answer quiz.	1. *Is the assessment sufficiently free of systematic error?* (Refer again to Step 6 in chapter 3, and also to chapters 4 and 5 on how to construct various test item types.) 2. *Are there a sufficient number of items for each instructional objective to reduce the likelihood of error or chance unduly influencing results?* (Refer again to Step 5 in chapter 3.) 3. *Will partial credit be awarded on responses, and, if so, what specific criteria will be used?* Whether used for short answer, essay, or computational questions, the partial credit requires that teachers and students have a clear understanding about the expectations for showing work or whatever the criteria may be. (Refer again to the guidelines for developing scoring criteria in chapter 5.) 4. *Can the scoring criteria (including the scoring key and any rubrics) be applied objectively?* Although subjectivity is inherent to the assessment creation process (for instance, the teacher decides what to assess and how), the grading system should ensure that the teacher's inherent biases or that conditions such as time of day, setting for grading, and so forth do not influence grades. (Refer again to the tips for applying a rubric in chapter 5.) 5. *Will an item analysis be used to identify potential systematic error on the assessment and, if so, will grading of the assessment be amended accordingly?* An item analysis provides insight into potential error in the construction of test items (Airasian & Russell, 2012).

questions that teachers can use to guide their thinking as they consider their own grading practices.

The intent of Figure 6.5 is to present a conceptual view of grading as being guided by the familiar principles of validity and reliability. In addition, the presentation of nine questions with brief explanations and references back to specific sections in previous chapters is intended to reinforce the centrality of the principles of validity and reliability. Our hope is that teachers can then apply these principles within whatever grading systems, policies, or expectations are characteristic of their particular teaching contexts.

Providing Feedback

The primary intent with any grading system is to clearly, accurately, and fairly communicate the teachers' judgment about the nature and degree of student learning. However, the ultimate purpose of assessment (and, therefore, of grading) is to progress student learning. The glue that binds the assessment process to student learning is *feedback*.

While a grade on an assessment is a type of feedback, grades themselves are typically insufficient to provide the kind of information that students need to progress their learning. This is especially true if student results on an assessment are never translated back into the curriculum from which the test was initially created. Fenwick English (2010), a noted scholar in curriculum, refers to this as *reconnecting*.

We illustrated this earlier in this chapter with the example of Mr. Franklin's analysis of his students' learning on the 8th grade common assessment for the civics unit. By plotting his students' aggregate performance onto the table of specifications for the assessment, Mr. Franklin was able to "view student learning through the lens of curriculum" (as we described it previously), or, as described by English (2010), Mr. Franklin was able to "reconnect" *assessment* to *curriculum*.

Formative Feedback

Ultimately, the purpose of assessment in the classroom is to improve student learning. Teachers test students so that they can have insight into students' acquisition of knowledge and skills, but such insight is gained only by viewing students' performance through the lens of curricular objectives. The same is true for students. If students only view their test grades as symbols, letters, or percentages that summatively represent their performances, opportunities to support student learning are potentially lost. Students need specific, understandable information about their performances that can be constructively used to continue and improve learning (Shute, 2008). Such information constitutes **formative feedback**.

Grades are the most fundamental and common type of feedback derived from classroom assessments (Bangert-Downs, Kulik, Kulik, & Morgan, 1991). However, it is important to recognize that grades carry a great deal of baggage with them. Think of how culturally ingrained the scale of *A-B-C-D-F* is in the United States. In this country, we have a common understanding of what the scale represents: *A* is excellent; *B* is good; *C* is fair; *D* is poor, but acceptable; and *F* is unacceptable—a failure. As evidence of the prevalence of this grading system, consider how we apply the scale to practically anything beyond classroom assessments. We say to a companion, "I give that movie a *C*." Or a parent says to a child, "*A+* on tidying your room today." Grades such as *C* and *A+* convey meaning.

What we don't know in these two examples, however, is what made the movie a *C* and what made the tidying up an *A+*. If we wish to convey instructive meaning about our judgments, we must say something about the expectations or criteria that were met and those that were unmet. The companion might explain to his acquaintance, "I give that movie a *C*. The acting was good, but the plot was too predictable." Or the parent might say to the child, "*A+* on tidying your room today! I appreciate that everything is put back in its place. It will make it easier to find your toys, and now there's plenty of room on the floor to play again!" In both cases—the amateur movie critique and the contented parent—the grades are translated into information that makes the expected criteria explicit. Based on the specific information provided, the acquaintance can make a decision about whether or not to see the movie, and the child may feel reinforced about making the effort to tidy her room and might have a clearer sense of her parents' expectations. These are examples of formative feedback that specifically and constructively reinforce and progress learning.

Does Formative Feedback Support Student Learning?

The role of formative feedback in supporting student learning has long been established but has gained renewed interest and appreciation in recent years. More than four decades ago, Benjamin Bloom identified the statistically significant effect of feedback in mastery learning, which he and his colleagues documented as contributing to an increase in student achievement of more than one standard deviation compared to conventionally taught students (Bloom, 1984; Bloom, Hastings, & Madaus, 1971). A review of several studies from the 1970s and the early 1980s also drew affirming conclusions about the power of feedback in the classroom:

◆ Feedback can promote student learning if students engage with feedback information intentionally.
◆ Feedback can support student motivation.

◆ Feedback can promote students' self-monitoring and metacognition (Bangert-Downs et al., 1991).

Focusing on the instructional intent of feedback, Butler and Winne (1995) identified five purposes of feedback in the classroom:

1. To confirm understanding
2. To add information
3. To correct incorrect understandings
4. To fine-tune current understandings
5. To restructure a student's conceptual framework or schemata regarding the intended learning outcomes

The case for using formative feedback based on classroom assessments has grown still stronger through the work of the Assessment Reform Group (1999) in England. Through a series of studies, these researchers established increasing evidence that teachers' formative assessment practices in the classroom can significantly contribute to improved student learning (Black, Harrison, Lee, Marshall, & Wiliam, 2004). Similarly, another team of researchers have identified feedback as an essential component of effective teaching. In a popular meta-analysis of empirically researched instructional strategies, Marzano, Pickering, and Pollock (2001) identified *providing feedback* as one of a number of high-yield instructional strategies with a statistically proven evidence base correlated with improved student learning. In a chapter titled "How We Teach," Schmoker (2011) distilled more than 40 years of research on the design elements of effective teaching and concluded that the simple strategy of *checking for understanding* (the important first step of garnering and providing feedback) is one of the most powerful and "indisputable" (p. 57) elements of effective instruction. And in one of the most comprehensive reviews of research on variables associated with student learning, Hattie (2009) concluded that *feedback* is one of the "essential ingredients of learning" (p. 24).

What Are the Characteristics of Effective Feedback?

In chapter 1, we defined *teaching* as the intentional creation and enactment of activities and experiences by one person that lead to changes in the knowledge, skills, and/or dispositions of another person, and we defined *learning* as a relatively permanent change in knowledge, skills, and/or dispositions precipitated by planned or unplanned experiences, events, activities, or interventions. These definitions suggest that there is an interaction between the learner and her environment. In a review of literature on the role of feedback in learning, a team of researchers posited this:

Any theory that depicts learning as a process of mutual influence between learners and their environments must involve feedback implicitly or explicitly because, without feedback, mutual influence is by definition impossible. Hence, the feedback construct appears often as an essential element of theories of learning and instruction.

(Bangert-Downs et al., 1991, p. 214)

The realization that feedback is central to learning is echoed by other researchers, as well. Consider these statements:

Students are high on the list of people who make decisions on the basis of classroom assessment results.

(Stiggins & Conklin, 1992, p. 184)

The most noble purpose of assessment is to provide feedback to both the student *and* the teacher.

(Wilson, 2005, p. 100)

Assessment for learning must involve pupils, so as to provide them with information about how well they are doing and guide their subsequent efforts. . . . The awareness of learning and the ability of learners to direct it for themselves is of increasing importance in the context of encouraging lifelong learning.

(Assessment Reform Group, 1999, p. 7)

To be effective, feedback should cause thinking to take place.

(Black et al., 2004, p. 14)

If you take a careful look at the definition of formative assessments, you'll see that the evidence elicited by assessment procedures is used either by *teachers* to adjust their ongoing *instruction* or by *students* to adjust their current *learning tactics* (that is, the procedures students are using in an effort to learn what they are supposed to be learning).

(Popham, 2014, p. 292)

As illustrated by the preceding comments, feedback is a vital aspect of improving student learning through classroom assessments (Brookhart, 2007/2008). So what are the characteristics of good formative feedback? Figure 6.6 presents five essential features of feedback that can support and promote student learning.

Figure 6.6 Characteristics of Effective Formative Feedback*

Honest Honest feedback is both genuine and forthright (Brookhart, 2007/2008; Brophy, 1981). This criterion almost suggests that a teacher may be *dishonest* or may intend to deceive. We don't think that's likely to happen purposefully among teachers. But is it possible that feedback may *unintentionally* deceive students? Is it possible that feedback could be *intellectually dishonest*? For example, generic or disingenuous praise (e.g., "Good work") can convey a false sense of mastery to a student who, in fact, has made fundamental and correctable errors in her work. What we are suggesting is that feedback must be *truthful*. It must represent *what is* and not lead to other inferences.
Accurate Accurate feedback is fair (Brookhart, 2007/2008; Stiggins & Conklin, 1992). It is, in essence, feedback that is reflective of the learning objectives (i.e., valid) and based on dependable information that is not subject to error or chance (i.e., reliable). Therefore, teachers must clearly know and understand the expected criteria for student performance, and they must use assessments to gather information that provides an appropriate reflection of students' acquisition of the curricular objectives.
Specific Specific feedback is necessary; otherwise, efforts to support student learning become over-generalized and unfocused (Brookhart, 2007/2008; Brown, 1981; Shute, 2008). Specific feedback, therefore, is precise and selective, using what evidence is available from test results to target instructional objectives for re-teaching, remediation, or other ongoing instructional activities. Specific feedback tends to be more easily understood by students (Butler & McMunn, 2006). It is also more germane to criteria of achievement (Stiggins & Conklin, 1992). For example, stock phrases such as "Well done!" and summative letter grades do not communicate specific elements of strength or shortcomings in a student's thinking or application of skills. A comment such as "Remember to provide examples from the text to support your generalization" does. Specific feedback helps to focus on learning objectives.
Constructive Assessment feedback is strongly associated with student motivation. Feedback, therefore, should be positive in tone (Brown, 1981), and feedback should also provide information that a student can use to progress his or her own learning (Brookhart, 2007/2008). If feedback negatively affects learning, it is not formative (Shute, 2008). A comment such as "Think about the definition of a control variable; which variable in the experiment fits this definition?" is much more constructive than "You obviously didn't study!" This is not to say that feedback should forsake honesty for constructiveness. Rather, by combining honesty, accuracy, specificity, and constructiveness, feedback can provide students with a realistic and feasible sense for *how* to improve learning.
Timely Feedback must also be timely (Brookhart, 2007/2008; Brown, 1981; Shute, 2008). In other words, feedback must occur within a time frame reasonably associated with the assessment activity; otherwise, feedback will lose its relevance. Feedback that is separated from performance by days or even weeks of time (such as often happens with teachers marking major projects or tests and also with most standardized tests) becomes meaningless and, thus, largely useless to students.

*Adapted from the Assessment Reform Group (1999).

It must be noted that these five characteristics of feedback represent distinct, but interrelated, aspects of effective formative feedback. Teachers should understand that in order for feedback to be used effectively in the classroom to support learning, each of the five characteristics bears importance. It is not enough, for example, to provide accurate and specific feedback. To maximize the instructive effect of feedback, it must also be honest, constructive, and timely. Teachers, therefore, are wise to consider practical ways to provide formative feedback to students in their own classrooms.

How Can I Provide Formative Feedback to Students?

When the results of classroom assessments are purposefully employed by teachers to support and promote student learning, then teachers are engaged in using **assessment** *for* **learning**. This turn of phrase is widely used in contemporary educational literature to suggest a distinction from the conventional use of assessments in the classroom, namely assessment *of* learning. Assessment *of* learning seeks to determine the nature and degree of student learning, whereas assessment *for* learning is the intentional use of assessment strategies and instruments by teachers to direct and contribute to students' learning activities.

Assessment for learning is a compelling concept. As noted in the earlier review of research associated with feedback, it is a powerful means of supporting student learning. Assessment for learning can occur in the classroom in a variety of ways, including the use of pretests, checking for understanding during instruction, and disaggregating standardized assessment results. However, given the focus of this book, we turn our attention to practical techniques for providing formative feedback to students using the results of teacher-made assessments in the classroom. In other words, after a teacher has *administered* and *graded* a class's set of assessments, what are some practical approaches for *returning* and *reviewing* students' assessment results? We explore six such techniques that are supported by previous research and our own experiences. Note the common theme throughout these techniques: to prompt students to think about their own learning (Assessment Reform Group, 1999).

1. Explain to Students How the Assessment Was Scored

As suggested in the earlier scenarios of the amateur movie critique and the contented parent, summative representations of students' performances on tests (such as letter grades and percentage scores) are of limited value to students. For the results of an assessment to convey instructive information, students must understand the *criteria* by which their performances are assessed (Hogan, 2007). Thus, a simple and effective technique for providing formative feedback to students is to explain to students how the assessment was scored. For students to make use of feedback, they must know the criteria for expected performance (Wilson, 2005). This can include, for example, reviewing scoring rubrics for short answer, computational, or essay responses. It can also include explaining not only how items on the test are weighted, but why they are weighted in particular ways.

For any age of students, reviewing the table of specifications for an assessment with their teacher can be a relatively quick and visually intuitive way of conveying the criteria for performance in terms of curricular objectives. Let's briefly return to the example of Mr. Franklin's civics test in Figure 6.4. Imagine two students, each of whom scored the class average of 84%. We might infer that they learned the same thing in this unit. However, one of these students, Lori, missed items 1, 11, 17, and 14. The other student, Jamal, missed items 5, 16, 18, and 19. By having the students circle the items they missed and identify the pattern (Lori, recall-level items; Jamal, the content of fundamental principles of our governmental system), Mr. Franklin and these two students can quickly draw inferences about the different *nature* of their learning, although the *degree* is the same.

This provides students the information necessary to view their test results in specific and constructive ways. We also offer one additional caveat about explaining to students how assessments were scored: It is important to communicate with students about assessment results in language that is familiar to them. This means referring back to specific terms, concepts, facts, or skills from previous instructional activities and doing so in the context of discussing assessment items, assessment activities, and student responses. In this way, assessment results can be reconnected to instruction.

2. Limit the Amount of Feedback Provided to Students

A practical reality in many classrooms is that time is a rare commodity. It is, therefore, not always feasible to orally review tests with a class comprehensively, question by question. This is not necessarily a bad thing, however. Research on feedback has shown that the sheer amount of feedback is not correlated with increased student achievement (Bangert-Downs et al., 1991). Therefore, an effective technique for providing formative feedback is to limit the amount of feedback. Teachers should concentrate on essential understandings rather than elaborating on details or information that is "nice to know," as suggested by Wiggins and McTighe's (2005) instructional planning approach known as Understanding by Design. The same holds true for providing written feedback. By providing a limited amount of focused feedback both to individual students and to whole classes, teachers are attending to the feedback principle of *specificity*. What's more, by giving less attention to the comprehensiveness of feedback, teachers are able to provide greater *depth* of feedback, an approach that supports the aims of providing *specific* and *constructive* feedback to students.

3. Provide Written and Oral Commentary First, Then Provide the Grade at a Later Time

A common phenomenon when handing back assessment results in a classroom is that students immediately look at the grade. Then, any written feedback that is provided on the assessment—whether simple indications of multiple choice questions that are incorrect or extensive written commentary on an essay response—is viewed through the lens of the summative grade. A practical technique to mitigate this phenomenon is to return assessments with written and oral commentary but not with summative grades.

This practice helps engage students in the feedback and to interpret their own performances in light of the feedback rather than through the lens of the grade. Feedback is generally more effective if it is accompanied by explanation, but the explanation can be lost if it is overshadowed by a summative grade (Bangert-Downs et al., 1991). As a variation on this technique, teachers can provide written or oral commentary first and then require students to respond (in writing or orally) before receiving the grade. Such techniques are particularly effective when providing feedback on short answer and essay responses, especially if students have their teacher's written feedback and a rubric with which to review their own writing. Feedback is then more *specific* and *constructive* because it is interpreted by the students.

4. Give Students the Opportunity to Ask Questions

Whether providing written feedback, oral feedback, or a combination of both, it is important to provide students with the opportunity to ask questions. A common error that teachers make, however, is to provide insufficient time for students to think before asking their questions. Providing feedback too quickly—that is, before students are prompted to and have the opportunity to reflect on their performance themselves—can actually dampen, if not preclude, the potential positive effects of feedback on learning (Bangert-Downs et al., 1991). Therefore, teachers should precede an invitation to ask questions with a structured time for students to review and reflect on written and oral feedback, such as described in technique 3. Then, during the question-and-answer time available, teachers should consider some possibilities for the best way to allow for questions while balancing the constraints of time and the fact that taking time to answer an individual student's question may or may not be helpful to the rest of the class.

For example, as suggested in techniques 1 and 2, teachers can use their item analyses to frame which test questions to review. In this way, teachers retain some control over time in class, while also serving the needs of a larger proportion of the class. As time allows, individual questions can be addressed. Also, depending on class sizes and the types of assessment items (such as a heavy use of constructed-response items), teachers may consider individually conferencing with students. In instances when teachers of high school students use extended written responses on assessments and individual conferencing is not planned, teachers may invite students to ask about their written responses but let them know in advance that they (that is, the teachers) may need to reread the response to provide students the best feedback possible. This is because it can be quite difficult to recall the intricacies of one essay out of a class of 25, not to mention several classes of 25 students each. The use of the techniques associated with prompting student questions about their assessment performances can support the use of feedback that is *honest, specific, constructive,* and *timely.*

5. Allow for Student-to-Student Discussion

An effective means of informal formative assessment within classrooms is teacher-facilitated discussion. This instructional strategy can be adapted for providing formative feedback to students using results from classroom-based assessments. Marilyn Burns (2005) suggests a number of ways to prompt and facilitate student-to-student discussion, and the following list is adapted from her ideas:

1. Ask students to explain their answers, whether or not the answers are correct.
2. Ask students to share their solution strategies with the group.
3. Organize small groups to review specific test items, being sure to provide directions for which items to review, how to review them, and how to report to the larger group.
4. Ask students to restate others' ideas.

There are at least three distinct advantages to using student discussion to review formative feedback on assessments. First, students often benefit from engaging with other students in a structured, collaborative activity. In other words, students can effectively learn from each other (Marzano et al., 2001). Second (and related to the first point), helping others to learn can reinforce one's own learning. Third, student discussion provides teachers excellent opportunities to identify the nature of students' thinking and possible misunderstandings, thereby providing teachers with richer information from which to make instructional decisions (Ory & Ryan, 1993). Indeed, for teachers who intentionally listen to what students are saying to each other during collaborative reviews of assessments, student discussions can provide a number of *teachable moments* of which teachers can take *timely* and *constructive* advantage.

6. Provide the Opportunity to Redo or Revise

Feedback is most effective when it allows students to re-engage with the content and skills associated with a particular assessment item, series of items, prompt, or performance-based assessment. As suggested in the previous five techniques for providing formative feedback, teachers can re-engage students in a number of ways, all intended to get students thinking. However, there is evidence that feedback becomes even more powerful when it is *applied*. Schmoker (2006) argues, for example, that "students need . . . feedback—and they need it quickly, with the opportunity to correct or revise" (p. 169). Black and his research associates (2004) concluded that "comments become useful feedback only if students use them to guide further work, so new procedures are needed" (p. 13).

Indeed, the idea of providing students the opportunity to rewrite essays or retake entire tests is new to many teachers or, at least, an idea that is somewhat uncomfortable to consider. Nevertheless, it is an idea that strongly reflects the notion that the ultimate purpose of assessment is not grading, but *improving student learning*. Here's how one practicing teacher illustrated his insight into using formative feedback to provide students opportunities to re-engage with the content and skills of his curriculum, rather than focusing solely on grades:

> If students are allowed to raise their grade through extra-credit work that is independent of essential learning, then that raised grade reinforces the view of grades as a commodity to be earned. When a student asks for an extra-credit assignment to raise his or her grade, I remind the student that the purpose of grades is to assess and promote learning. A low grade simply communicates a learning gap; the way to raise the grade is to learn more. I explain that although I do not believe in extra credit, I do believe in opportunities for further learning. A student who scored low on a formal paper, for example, may seek extra writing help, rewrite the paper, and try for a higher grade. If a student received a low quiz grade, he or she may take the quiz again to demonstrate mastery of the material. This approach helps reinforce the view that grades are a communication tool, not the goal.
>
> (Winger, 2005, p. 64)

Summing Up What We Know About Providing Feedback

Using formative feedback from classroom assessments can be a powerful instructional tool for teachers. The techniques described in the previous section provide practical and proven ways to help teachers harness the potential to use assessments *for* learning. However, teachers must exercise considerable professional judgment when planning for providing formative feedback to students. For example, teachers are wise to consider their students' ages, grade levels, and learning needs when deciding what techniques or variations of techniques to use. Teachers should also consider differences in the use of these techniques among various subject areas. Although feedback is positively correlated with student learning in all core subject areas, the specific demands of providing feedback on essay responses in an English class differ from those required of a series of computational problems in a physics course (Bangert-Downs et al., 1991).

Regardless of the specific techniques that teachers use to provide formative feedback, the guiding principle remains the same: *to prompt students to think about their own learning* (Assessment Reform Group, 1999). More specifically, teachers' intentions should be to guide students to answer three essential questions, based on the formative feedback given to them:

1. What have I set out to learn?
2. How am I progressing?
3. What do I need to do to continue my progress?

Therefore, a teacher's feedback—be it written or oral, presented to the class or individually—should provide students insight into the answers for these questions.

Assessment *as* Learning

Formative feedback is, indeed, a powerful means of supporting and improving student learning. This is certainly important for the immediate and short-term objectives associated with formal curricula in typical courses of study. For example, formative feedback can help students improve their understanding of historical facts, their application of the order of operations in solving equations, their composition of persuasive essays, or their analysis of data tables. But students' frequent and ongoing engagement with formative feedback can lead to longer-range outcomes, as well.

Figure 6.7 presents five long-range outcomes for students that can be collectively described as *assessment as learning*. Assessment *as* learning suggests

Figure 6.7 Tacit Long-Range Learning Outcomes: Assessment as Learning

By engaging with formative feedback frequently and over time, students will be able to:

✓ Accurately articulate criteria of achievement, learning, and success;
✓ Ask meaningful questions as a means of learning;
✓ Constructively provide feedback to others;
✓ Effectively respond to feedback from others;
✓ Actively reflect on learning.

Adapted from Assessment Reform Group (1999); Black et al. (2004); Chappuis (2005); Earl (2013); Leahy, Lyon, Thompson, & Wiliam (2005); Stiggins (1999); Stiggins (2005).

a distinction from both assessment *of* learning and assessment *for* learning. The term **assessment *as* learning** refers to students' disposition for and ability to self-assess and, ultimately, their ability to self-direct learning.

Assessment *as* learning suggests that one of the larger aims of formal education is to enable students to become *lifelong learners*, capable of formulating and pursuing interests and needs associated with continuous learning well beyond the 12th grade. This long-range curricular aim is articulated by many educators.

> We must constantly remind ourselves that the ultimate purpose of evaluation is to enable students to evaluate themselves. Educators may have been practicing this skill to the exclusion of the learners. We need to shift part of this responsibility to students. Fostering students' ability to direct and redirect themselves must be a major goal—or what is education for?
>
> (Costa, 1989, pp. 2–3)

> [One of the key, empirically supported factors for using assessment-related techniques to improve student learning is] the active involvement of pupils in their own learning . . . and the need for pupils to be able to assess themselves and understand how to improve.
>
> (Assessment Reform Group, 1999, p. 5)

> Only by abdicating some control in the classroom can teachers empower students to monitor and make decisions about their own learning. . . . If students are to become reflective practitioners and autonomous learners, they must be given opportunities to develop these skills.
>
> (Butler & McMunn, 2006, pp. 151 and 153)

Many teachers who have tried to develop their students' self-assessment skills have found that the first and most difficult task is to get students to think of their work in terms of a set of goals. Insofar as they do so, they begin to develop an overview of that work that allows them to manage and control it for themselves. In other words, students are developing the capacity to work at a metacognitive level.

(Black et al., 2004, p. 14)

Teaching students to assess their own work helps them better understand the skills that are valued in a particular field and develop the general life skills of being able to look honestly at and improve their own work.

(McGonigal, 2006)

When teachers focus on assessment *as* learning, they use classroom assessment as the vehicle for helping students develop and practice the necessary skills to become critical thinkers who are comfortable with reflection and the critical analysis of their learning.

(Earl, 2013, p. 28)

As we consider the intention that the inclination and ability to self-assess are important, longer-term aims of formal education, it is interesting to note how the three fundamental elements of formal education become conjoined. *Assessment as learning* brings together curriculum, instruction, and assessment. Thus, assessment cannot be thought of as *that thing teachers do to students at the end of instruction*. Instead, assessment itself becomes an important component of our teaching, an important learning tool for our students, and an intended outcome of learning in its own right.

7

How Can I Constructively Influence Professional Practice in My School?

Leading for Assessment Literacy

The answer to the title of this chapter is twofold: *A teacher can influence the professional practice of teachers and instructional leaders in a school first by developing the competency of assessment within him- or herself and then by becoming a teacher-leader in the area of classroom assessment practices.* Throughout this book, we have emphasized and drawn on an understanding that assessment is integral to teaching and learning. Whereas *curriculum* identifies the knowledge and skills students are intended to acquire and *instruction* provides the means by which students engage with these objectives, it is the role of *assessment* to ascertain the nature and degree of students' learning. Furthermore, it is from assessments of learning that teachers and students can then make informed decisions about past experiences, current needs, and future learning activities.

Given the important role of assessment in teaching and learning, it is vital that teachers possess and apply the knowledge, skills, and dispositions associated with this professional competency. When teachers gain these, they can serve both formally and informally as leaders in their schools to improve the assessment practices—indeed, the teaching practices—of their colleagues, thereby also improving student learning, as well.

Assessment as a Professional Competency

In chapter 1, we reviewed the licensure requirements of a number of states, which suggested a widespread appreciation of the importance of assessment within the profession. However, the descriptions of assessment as a profes-sional competency vary considerably among state licensure requirements; therefore, we offer here a summary of our view of the three essential aspects of the professional competency of assessment. In brief, teachers must be good *creators of*, *consumers of*, and *communicators about* assessment.

Teachers Must Be Effective *Creators of* Assessments

Even in a standards-based curriculum, in which the learning objectives for students are articulated within state curriculum frameworks, it is the role of classroom teachers to translate standards into accessible and relevant instruc-tion for students. In other words, curriculum and instruction must necessarily be particularized by teachers for the students they teach any given academic year. This means that teachers must also particularize assessment—that is, they must be able to develop assessments of student learning that are not merely reflective of the standards-based curriculum for which they are accountable, but assessments that are responsive to *how* and *how much* they have taught. This is not easily accomplished by simply lifting a commercially produced test from a textbook series, test-generating software, or released test items from the state department of education. Rather, teachers themselves must be able to create assessments that are fair to students, are feasible to employ in the classroom setting, have practical purpose regarding continued student learning, and result in accurate indications of student performance (JCSEE, 2003). This is not to say that outside resources cannot be integrated into teacher-made tests; they can, if checked for validity and reliability.

In addition (and as suggested again and again by teacher licensure stan-dards and professional literature), teachers must be able to create *a variety of assessments* appropriate to the grade level of students and for the subject matter being taught. The variety of assessments can include quick checks for understanding in the midst of instruction, quizzes to inform student progress and highlight areas of need, and tests to gauge cumulative learning over some period of time. Furthermore, the variety of assessment types may range from select-response items such as true-false, matching, and multiple choice to constructed-response items such as practical mathematics problems, short written answers, extended essays, or even projects, performances, or original creations. As we hope we have conveyed in the previous chapters of this book, teachers must master certain knowledge and skills to effectively create assessments to collect information about student learning in their classrooms. For example, teachers must understand and be able to apply the principles of validity and reliability, create tables of specifications, select and construct different types of assessment items, and analyze assessment results to make instructional decisions. These are some of the essential knowledge and skills associated with effective and appropriate assessment practices of professional teachers in the classroom.

Teachers Must Be Intelligent *Consumers of* Assessments

A central purpose of assessment is to collect information about student learning. But too often in classrooms the outputs from assessments follow a very predictable path. For example, students take a test, the teacher grades it, the students receive the test back, and a grade is entered in the grade book. In this common scenario, information about student learning is collected, but it is used primarily—if not solely—as a source for a grade.

It is incumbent on teachers not only to gather information about student learning, but also to meaningfully interpret that information, both for individual students and in the aggregate for classes. Assessment information can be used to identify patterns of strengths and struggles among students, within specific content strands, and at various levels of cognition.

Understanding the purpose and structure of the assessment itself is a critical step in interpreting and *consuming* the information about student learning that the results of a quiz, a test, a project, or any other type of assessment can provide. But this is true not only of teacher-made assessments in the classroom. It is equally important that teachers be able to interpret and use the results of standardized assessments. Such assessments can provide critical information regarding the progress of a class toward meeting the standards required by a state. However, being handed reams of student score reports (or a password-protected digital file, as is oftentimes the practice these days) is insufficient for making *data-driven decisions* about student learning, as we would want teachers to do (Miller, 2009). One problem with the standardized assessment results is that a reconnect to specific state standards is not made from these assessment results (English, 2010). Another issue is that standardized assessments tend to be "instructionally insensitive" (Popham, 2008, p. 135). In other words, a teacher may receive information that a student has reached a certain achievement level, but specific curricular objectives may not be evident.

Again, as with teacher-made assessments, a first step for the teacher in interpreting and using standardized test results is to understand the purpose and structure of the test itself. Teachers must be intelligent *consumers* of assessments and the information about student learning that both teacher-made and standardized assessments can provide. Here are three fundamental cautions that teachers should keep in mind regarding state standardized assessments:

◆ *State assessments are well suited for drawing inferences about the achieve-ment of populations but not particularly well suited for drawing inferences about individual students' learning.* State standardized assessments are less reliable indicators of *individual achievement* because such assess-ments typically assess a large number of curriculum objectives with a relatively small number of questions. State assessments also usu-ally represent an individual's performance on a given day, without repeated measures. For these reasons they tend to be less reliable indicators of individual achievement than they do as indicators of a group's achievement (e.g., a school or district).

◆ *State assessments tend to be well aligned with curriculum state standards, but they typically do not assess many of the most important objectives from the curriculum.* For example, oral language skills, such as pub-lic speaking, are often integral to the English/language arts cur-riculum; however, state assessments do not assess this important strand of learning objectives simply because oral language is not readily assessable in a standardized testing format. The same is true for important subject-specific skills that involve extended, complex cognitive behaviors, such as scientific inquiry, historical analysis, and applied mathematical reasoning. Teachers must be cautious not to draw sweeping inferences about student learning in the absence of explicitly assessed intended learning outcomes (Polikoff, Porter, & Smithson, 2011).

◆ *State assessments assess a range of cognitive levels but not the highest lev-els of cognition.* State standardized assessments have been criticized for being nothing more than simple tests of recall. However, this is not the case. Most state assessments assess higher order thinking beyond recall, such as *comprehension, application*, and even *analysis*. Nevertheless, a fairer criticism of standardized assessments is that they do not tap the *highest levels* of cognition, namely students' abil-ity to evaluate and create. The reason for this is evident in chapter 4: Most state standardized tests use a select-response item format, which can efficiently assess a broad range of learning objectives but has limited ability to assess the *highest levels* of cognition. Therefore, many important curricular objectives that include students' abilities to synthesize, evaluate, and create simply are not assessed on state tests (Polikoff, Porter, & Smithson, 2011).

Classroom teachers create assessments to gauge their students' learning, and teachers can use the results of commercially produced tests to inform their teaching. Therefore, teachers should be good *consumers* of assessment results from both their own classroom-based assessments and standardized assessments.

Teachers Must Be Effective *Communicators about* Assessments

The acts of creating assessments and interpreting assessment results are very much within the purview of teachers. However, assessment results—that is, information that represents the nature and degree of student learning—is not of interest only to teachers. Other people involved in the educational process have strong interests in assessment results as well—namely, students, parents, and other educators. Yet *why* teachers communicate about assessment with these other people is different. Let's consider the essential purposes of communication about assessment for each of these groups.

Why should teachers communicate about assessment with students? The primary purpose must be to support and improve student learning, as described in chapter 6. When a teacher shares assessment results with students intentionally and conscientiously, that feedback *about* student learning can become a powerful instructional strategy to support student learning (Dean et al., 2012; Hattie, 2009). In addition, students need to know where they stand in terms of summative evaluations of their learning. The fact remains that test scores, course grades, grade point averages, and the like *mean something*. They are intended to communicate the worth or value of student achievement, and such grades are used by teachers, students, and others to make decisions. Therefore, summative indications of student learning must be communicated as well.

Why should teachers communicate about assessment with parents? Again, as with providing feedback to students, the ultimate aim of communicating about assessment with parents is to support and improve student learning. Parents are the first and most important teachers of their children. Therefore, it is incumbent on teachers to provide useful information about student learning to parents in the most constructive ways feasible. This means, for example, that teachers may need to translate assessment results from *educationese*—the jargon-laden language of our profession that we educators comfortably use among ourselves but which is less accessible to the typical parent. It may mean that teachers should rely less on the age-old convention of *A-B-C-D-F* to communicate the degree of student learning and more specifically talk about a student's competencies in, for example, composing essays and spelling, as well as weaknesses in sentence construction and sentence variety. In other words, teachers must consider ways to provide feedback from assessments that is less summative in favor of providing information that is more *informative* (Guskey & Bailey, 2010). This is information about student learning that parents can better understand and, therefore, potentially use to support their children's learning.

Why should teachers communicate about learning with other educators? There are a host of reasons:

◆ *Principals and other building-level instructional leaders* use assessment results from teachers to monitor student learning, to identify patterns of strengths and weaknesses among students, and to provide an important additional perspective on student learning that standardized assessments cannot offer. In other words, wise instructional leaders value and use classroom-based assessment results as valid and reliable information about student learning and, therefore, the effectiveness of educational programs in the school.

◆ *Teachers in the next grade level* use the previous year's or previous semester's assessment results as the initial and important indicator of a student's prior achievement, as well as of their current knowledge and skills. Teachers can then begin to plan for instruction based on valid assessment data.

◆ *School counselors* at all school levels use classroom assessment results to help students and families make decisions about courses of study and future educational and career paths.

◆ *Child study teams* use classroom assessment results to help make decisions about interventions or services that may be necessary and important support for individual students.

◆ *Program coordinators, honors committees, and admissions committees* use classroom assessment results (namely in the form of course grades and grade point averages) as important factors in making decisions about entry into educational programs, awards and recognitions, and for entry into post-secondary education.

Teachers communicate information about student learning to a number of people—namely, students, parents, and other educators—for a number of reasons. This fact suggests one clear need: The information that teachers communicate about student learning must be information that is relevant and dependable. If assessment information is inappropriate and inaccurate, people's impressions and decisions about student learning will be misguided and maybe even harmful.

Assessment is integral to the process of teaching and learning. Indeed, assessment is the means by which teachers can determine the nature and degree of student learning and through which instructional decisions can be knowledgeably and effectively made. It is imperative, therefore, that every teacher exhibit competency in creating, consuming, and communicating about student assessment and learning. This has been our primary aim throughout this book. More specifically, we hope to help teachers improve their ability to assess student learning in their classrooms in ways that are valid, reliable, meaningful, practical to employ, and, ultimately, supportive of student learning.

Teacher Leadership: Constructively Influencing the Professional Practice of Others

Being able to create, use, and communicate about student learning through meaningful assessment practices in the classroom is central to what it means to teach. As teachers individually develop and master the competency of assessment, teachers can help lead other teachers to do the same (Guskey, 2009). The act of teachers serving as leaders to other teachers is known as **teacher leadership**, which we define as the constructive influence of one teacher on the professional practice of one or more other teachers. Within the professional domain of classroom assessment, there are several ways that teachers can positively contribute to the improved practice of their colleagues.

Lead by Example

First and foremost, teachers influence the practice of other teachers through their own examples. Therefore, a first step in teacher leadership around the competency of assessment is to create, use, and communicate about assessment in ways that are *legally responsible*, *feasible*, *useful*, and *accurate* (JCSEE, 2003). Teachers lead by their spoken and observed example, whether in the classroom, teachers' lounge, or any other settings in which teachers are engaging with each other. Demonstrating principles of assessment through one's own professional practice can be a powerful model and motivator for other teachers to want to learn more and improve on their own skills.

Collaborate with Other Teachers

An increasingly recognized means of professional development is through teacher collaboration (Northwest Evaluation Association, 2014). In Japan, for example, educators have demonstrated notable success with the use of lesson study. In a lesson study, a team of teachers jointly plans for a lesson or a series of lessons on a topic. Then one of the teachers delivers the planned lesson in his or her classroom while the other teachers on the study team observe. Following the demonstration lesson, the entire team of teachers critiques the design and efficacy of the lesson itself (as opposed to the focusing on the particular teacher's delivery of the lesson). Through this approach, the team of teachers develops a series of collaboratively designed and proven lessons.

Teachers can take a similar approach in the area of assessment. Collaboratively designed assessments can be powerful tools in supporting grade levels, departments, or interdisciplinary instructional teams to develop shared assessments, ranging from quizzes to unit tests to performance-based assessments (Fisher, Grant, Frey, & Johnson, 2007/2008; Wiliam, 2007/2008). Whatever the level of assessment, the creation of collaboratively designed and constructed assessments requires a team of teachers to jointly unpack the shared curriculum, identify essential understandings, select the means of assessing student learning, recognize the inherent limitations of the assessment, and thereby be better prepared to interpret and use the results of the common assessment.

Advocate for Professional Development in the Area of Assessment

As described in the opening chapter of this book, the assessment practices of many teachers in today's schools have been developed inconsistently at best and haphazardly at worse. Our concern from our own experiences both with and as classroom teachers is that classroom-based assessment is an extraordinarily important component of teaching and learning that has long received insufficient attention. Although our suspicion is that this has been the case for decades, the current era of standards-based accountability has brought the situation to light. In short, many teachers need support in developing their professional competencies in the domain of assessment (Mertler, 2000; Stiggins, 2004; Zhang & Burry-Stock, 2003). Therefore, teacher leaders can constructively influence the professional practice of other teachers by advocating for and, indeed, by providing professional development opportunities in assessment.

In this book, we have sought to present a case for improving teachers' classroom-based assessment abilities; however, professional development in assessment can go still further. For example, the principles and techniques of assessment described in this book are generic to students in elementary, middle, and high schools, but the specific application of the principles of assessment vary for students of different ages. Targeted professional development can address important points such as this. Similarly, the application of the principles of assessment varies for different subject areas (Brown, 1981). Teachers must have *pedagogical content knowledge* to be effective classroom teachers, meaning that teachers must have a combination of depth of subject matter and depth of understanding about how best to teach that subject (Shulman, 1986). Pedagogical content knowledge should include practical understandings of common errors and difficulties in the subject area, as well as the ability to interpret and respond to individual students' difficulties in learning the subject area, which are made evident through appropriate assessments germane to the subject (Black et al., 2004).

Teaching is a profession, which suggests that the act of teaching requires the ongoing exercise of learned decision making to anticipate, respond to, and meet the needs of learners. Thus, professional development within the important domain of assessment is imperative for teachers throughout their service in classrooms.

Constructively Develop and Critically Review Assessments Used by School Districts

With the advent of high-stakes state standardized assessments has come an increased use of *interim assessments* by school divisions. Also referred to as *benchmark assessments*, **interim assessments** are intended to indicate progress toward the acquisition of a set of learning objectives that will be summatively assessed on a subsequent grade-level or end-of-course accountability assessment. In theory, interim assessments are intended to serve a formative purpose, whereby a student's performance on an interim assessment is to inform a teacher's instructional decision making in order to progress the student most effectively toward the learning goals that will be measured at a later time.

Despite the intuitive appeal that interim assessments hold for many administrators as a means of progressing students toward higher achievement on accountability tests, their efficacy is inconclusive, at best (Brookhart, 2014; Slavin, Cheung, Holmes, Madden, & Chamberlain, 2013). This may be for any number of reasons, including weaknesses in the validity and reliability of such assessments (especially among poorly aligned, commercially produced assessments), inconsistent and ill-informed administration of the assessments, and teachers' and administrators' lack of knowledge about how to use interim assessment data (Cizek & Bunch, 2007; Goertz, Oláh, & Riggan, 2009; Slavin et al., 2013).

As an alternative to large-scale interim and benchmark assessments, many schools and school districts are engaging teachers in professional learning communities to develop and use *common assessments*. **Common assessments** are formal assessments developed collaboratively by a team of teachers and typically focused at a unit or semester scope of intended learning outcomes. Given the smaller scope of intended learning outcomes that are assessed, the closer alignment to those intended learning outcomes, and the instructional sensitivity they are likely to provide teachers to inform decision-making (Popham, 2008), common assessments offer a promising alternative to large-scale interim and benchmark assessments.

According to Wagner (2008), the creation of common assessments and the ensuing professional discussions about student performance by teachers is a practice that characterizes the highest performing countries. Indeed, the very process that we have outlined in chapter 3 and expounded upon in chapters 4, 5, and 6 can be very effectively used by teachers to develop common assessments (Chappuis, 2014; Young, 2009), namely:

1. Unpack the intended learning outcomes for the unit of instruction.
2. Create a table of specifications to guide the construction of the assessment.
3. Clarify the teaching team's purposes for and circumstances of assessing student learning.
4. Determine the appropriate types of assessment items/activities to use, including complementary performance-based assessments that may be necessary to cover the full scope of the intended learning outcomes.
5. Determine the appropriate number and weight of assessment items, including developing common performance criteria.
6. Create and select assessment items that are valid and reliable.
7. Assemble the assessment, including clarifying directions for the conditions of administering the assessment across classrooms.

Of course, other important steps must follow these: for instance, administering the assessment among a team, grade level, or department of students and then analyzing the results of the assessment in order to garner information about the nature and degree of student learning. Such steps can lead to making near-term and long-term instructional decisions, communicating about learning, and strengthening the validity and reliability of the assessment in anticipation of future uses of it.

In our experience working with grade-level teams, departments, schools, and districts, the creation of common assessments is a particularly powerful professional practice as the process itself not only results in more valid and reliable assessments, but, in the collaborative work of developing such assessments (A), teachers inevitably talk about and strengthen their understanding of curriculum (C) and instruction (I). In short, the development of common assessments is a means for teachers within a professional learning community to strengthen the alignment of curriculum, instruction, and assessments: $C = I = A$.

Inform Policy Regarding the Use of Assessment in the Classroom

As we have suggested previously, much of what many teachers know about assessment has been learned through their own experiences both as former students themselves and as practicing teachers. How, then, are assessment policies in schools, districts, and states developed? One study concluded, "Often, testing and grading policies are written by educators who have little formal background in sound assessment practice. This can lead to the implementation of policies that can have a detrimental influence on the nature and quality of classroom assessment" (Stiggins & Conklin, 1992, p. 185). This caution from more than two decades ago rings even truer today when one considers the unintended consequences of the accountability era, which we described in chapter 1.

Policy is developed to express the beliefs of an organization and to guide the work of the professionals within that organization. Policies regarding assessment practices are found at all levels of the K–12 educational system, including the school, district, and state levels. Given this fact, teacher leaders can constructively influence the professional practice of other teachers by using their understanding of the principles of classroom assessment to inform school and district policies. For example, does a school require that certain types of assessments be used by teachers, such as quizzes, tests, and projects, or does the school require that grades be assessed and reported by objectives rather than by types of assessments? Does the school mandate the relative percentages that each of these types of assessments is worth in calculating a final grade? Does the school have a traditional letter-grade scale, or does the school use a developmental rubric? Does the school have a homework completion policy or a provision for not assigning zeros for assignments that students do not complete? Does the district or state require teachers to demonstrate impact on student learning as part of the teacher evaluation system (Popham, 2013)?

Although the number of policies that may govern assessment in schools is myriad, our point here is that teachers who have developed competencies associated with appropriate classroom assessment principles can and should use their knowledge to inform the practices of others. Contributing to the development, review, and revision of policy is a powerful means of promoting best practices within the domain of assessment.

Summing Up Teacher Leadership of Assessment

By providing an example of professional competency in the domain of assessment, collaborating with others to construct assessments, advocating for teachers' ongoing professional development, and influencing policy, teacher leaders constructively influence the professional practice of others in their schools and school districts. The longer-range aim of such efforts is to change the culture of assessment within the profession. In other words, by positively contributing to the improved practice of other teachers, teacher leaders can change the way that assessments—whether teacher-made or standardized—are viewed and used by teachers. The intended effect of this is that teachers are more willing and more able to discern the nature and degree of their students' learning; to draw more valid and reliable inferences about their students' learning; and, therefore, to better make instructional decisions about what to teach and how to teach, thereby resulting in improved student learning.

We are strong believers in the power of teacher leadership. We believe that when teachers are empowered with a genuine base of professional knowledge and skills and when they have the opportunity to enact their professionalism through collaborative efforts and authentic classroom practice, then great things can happen in terms of student learning.

We also believe that the process of teaching and learning in contemporary educational settings such as K–12 schools is fundamentally comprised of three elements: curriculum, instruction, and assessment. We see these as three manifestations of the same thing, that thing being the broad aim of *student learning*—that is, the knowledge, skills, and dispositions that we intend for students to acquire through their educational experiences. Since curriculum, instruction, and assessment are in essence manifestations of this, then it follows that aligning curriculum, instruction, and assessment is necessary for both an effective and efficient educational process.

With these beliefs in mind, we hope that we have conveyed a sense for how classroom assessment practices—when employed intentionally—can be a means of connecting curriculum, instruction, and student learning. At the beginning of this book, we posited that there is a core set of knowledge and skills that all teachers should possess relative to classroom assessment. We referred to this as **assessment literacy**—the ability to create and use valid and reliable assessments as a classroom teacher to facilitate and communicate student learning. More specifically, we hold that assessment literacy fundamentally involves a teacher's ability to:

◆ Articulate and unpack intended learning outcomes;
◆ Understand and appreciate the purposes and various forms that classroom assessment can take;
◆ Ensure the alignment of classroom assessment instruments and techniques to the content and cognitive demand of intended learning outcomes;

- ◆ Ensure the representative balance of intended learning outcomes on assessments;
- ◆ Create and use selected- and constructed-response assessment items and activities appropriately;
- ◆ Ensure that student performance on classroom assessments are not unduly influenced by systematic and random error;
- ◆ Use formative assessment techniques and feedback to progress student learning;
- ◆ Use student performance on assessments to communicate student learning to others and to make instructional and curricular decisions.

We recognize that there are other important knowledge and skills associated with educational and psychometric assessment practices. However, our hope is that the ideas, techniques, examples, and perspectives that we have presented here are practical and meaningful to classroom teachers and instructional leaders. By strengthening classroom assessment practices, teachers are better able to connect curriculum, instruction, and student learning.

Glossary of Terms

analytic rubric—a scoring key that provides information regarding performance in each of the component parts of a task, making it useful for diagnosing specific strengths and weaknesses

assessment—the process of using tools and techniques to collect information about student learning

assessment as learning—students' dispositions for and ability to self-assess and, ultimately, their ability to self-direct learning

assessment for learning—the intentional use of assessment strategies and instruments by teachers with their students to direct and contribute to learning activities

assessment literacy—the ability to create and use valid and reliable assessments as a classroom teacher to facilitate and communicate student learning

blueprint—a commonly used synonym for a *table of specifications*; a chart or table that details the content and level of cognitive demand assessed on a test as well as the types and emphases of test items (also see *table of specifications*)

checklist—a list of behaviors or look-fors in a supply-response item

common assessments—formal assessments developed collaboratively by a team of teachers and typically focused at a unit or semester scope of intended learning outcomes

concurrent validity—how accurately an assessment equates with another assessment that is intended to measure the same learning outcomes, standards, or objectives (also see *predictive validity*)

conditional content—specific circumstances, contexts, or materials through which the student will engage with the explicit content

consequential validity—the appropriateness of the intended and unintended outcomes that ensue from an assessment

construct validity—how accurately an assessment aligns with the conceptual or theoretical framework of the intended learning outcomes, standards, or objectives of the instructional unit

constructed-response items—types of assessment items that require that the student supply an answer to a question or prompt; responses may be convergent in nature or divergent

content—the subject matter with which students engage in the learning process

content validity—how adequately an assessment samples the intended learning outcomes, standards, or objectives of an instructional unit

curriculum—a set of intended learning outcomes for students

error—when an assessment item inadequately distinguishes between the student who has truly mastered the intended learning outcome and the student who has not

evaluation—a systematic process of making judgments about the nature or worth of student learning

explicit content—subject matter directly referred to in an intended learning outcome (i.e., a standard or objective)

face validity—the appearance of validity without explicit evidence

formative assessment—the assessment of student learning integrated into the act of teaching

formative feedback—specific, understandable information about student performance that can be constructively used to continue and improve learning

grading—the translation of student performance on an assessment into a system of relative numbers or symbols to communicate the teacher's judgment about the nature and degree of student learning

holistic rubric—a defined level of expected performance on a supply-type item that is applied to a student's overall performance but is not indicative of specific components of the performance

horizontal articulation—the intentional drawing of interdisciplinary connections between subject areas that can result in accentuating the relevance of content and skills across intended learning outcomes; the common understanding of the intended learning outcomes among teachers who teach the same subject and/or grade level

implicit content—prior knowledge and skills students need to engage in the explicit content of the curriculum

instruction—planned and unplanned experiences provided by a teacher that are intended to result in the acquisition of a set of intended learning outcomes by students

intended learning outcomes—the set of explicit knowledge, skills, and attitudes that the student is to acquire through instruction and ultimately demonstrate through one or more assessment activities; the term "objectives" is closely synonymous to "intended learning outcomes"

interim assessments—assessments intended to indicate progress toward the acquisition of a set of learning outcomes that will be summatively assessed on a subsequent standardized assessment; also known as *benchmark assessments*

inter-rater reliability—the consistency with which two or more scorers apply the grading criteria of an assessment, thereby resulting in stable assessment results among students, uninfluenced by factors that are not the intended criteria of learning

intra-rater reliability—the consistency with which a scorer applies the grading criteria of an assessment, thereby resulting in stable assessment results uninfluenced by factors that are not the intended criteria of learning

learning—a relatively permanent change in knowledge, skills, and/or dispositions precipitated by planned or unplanned experiences, events, activities, or interventions

level of cognitive demand—expected level of thinking when engaged with specific content

pre-assessment—assessment of student learning prior to teaching

predictive validity—a particular type of *concurrent validity*, the degree to which the results of one assessment can foretell results on another assessment that is intended to measure the same learning outcomes, standards, or objectives

random error—chance events or circumstances that influence assessment results but are not easily predicted or controlled

reliability—the consistency or dependability of the results of an assessment; the degree to which a student's performance on an assessment is not unduly influenced by chance, systematic error, bias, or cheating

repeated trials reliability—the use of multiple items on an assessment for each intended learning outcome in an effort to control for error and thereby strengthen the potential reliability of the assessment

sampling validity—a useful synonym for *content validity*, although the term "sampling validity" is not commonly used in scholarly literature on assessment

select-response items—types of assessment items that have predetermined responses from which the students choose

summative assessment—assessment of student learning at the end of some period of instruction

systematic error—flaws that are unintentionally built into an assessment and that likely affect student results, but that may be controlled if detected

table of specifications—a chart or table that details the content and level of cognitive demand assessed on a test as well as the types and emphases of test items (also see *blueprint*)

teacher leadership—the constructive influence of one teacher on the professional practice of one or more other teachers

teaching—the intentional creation and enactment of activities and experiences by one person that lead to changes in the knowledge, skills, and/or dispositions of another person

test—a deliberately designed, representative set of written questions and/or prompts to which students respond in written form, intended to measure the acquisition of certain knowledge, skills, and/or dispositions

unit assessment plan—another use of a table of specifications with which a teacher can map out the complementary key assessments within a unit that function together to ensure all the intended learning outcomes in a unit are assessed and accounted for

unpacking—the process of reviewing curricular standards or objectives to identify the intended content and cognitive levels of learning for students

validity—the extent to which inferences drawn from assessment results are appropriate

vertical articulation—the intentional sequencing of intended learning outcomes over the course of multiple years and grade levels within a subject area, usually conveyed in the formal, written curriculum of a school or district

References

Airasian, P. W., & Russell, M. (2012). *Classroom assessment: Concepts and applications* (7th ed.). Dubuque, IA: McGraw-Hill.

Anderson, L. W., & Krathwohl, D. R. (Eds.). (2001). *A taxonomy for learning, teaching, and assessing: A revision of Bloom's taxonomy of educational objectives.* New York: Addison Wesley Longman.

Angoff, W. H. (1988). Validity: An evolving concept. In H. Wainer & H. I. Braun (Eds.), *Test validity* (pp. 19–32). Hillsdale, NJ: Lawrence Erlbaum Associates.

Assessment Reform Group. (1999). *Assessment for learning: Beyond the black box.* Cambridge, UK: University of Cambridge School of Education.

Atkin, J. M., Black, P., & Coffey, J. (Eds.). (2001). *Classroom assessment and the National Science Education Standards.* Washington, DC: National Academy Press.

Au, W. (2007). High-stakes testing and curricular control: A qualitative meta-synthesis. *Educational Researcher 36*(5), 258–267.

Axtman, K. (2005). When the test's cheaters are the teachers: Probe of Texas scores on high stakes tests is the latest case in a series of cheating incidents. *Christian Science Monitor*, January 11, 2005. Retrieved January 22, 2007, from http://www.csmonitor.com/2005/0111/p01s03-ussc.htm.

Bangert-Downs, R. L., Kulik, C. C., Kulik, J. A, & Morgan, M. (1991). The instructional effect of feedback in test-like events. *Review of Educational Research 61*(2), 213–238.

Biggs, J. B., & Collis, K. F. (1982). *Evaluating the quality of learning: The SOLO taxonomy.* New York: Academic Press.

Black, P. (2013). Formative and summative aspects of assessment: Theoretical and research foundations in the context of pedagogy. In J. H. McMillan (Ed.), *SAGE handbook of research on classroom assessment* (pp. 167–178). Los Angeles, CA: SAGE.

Black, P., Harrison, C., Lee, C., Marshall, B., & Wiliam, D. (2004, September). Working inside the black box: Assessment for learning in the classroom. *Phi Delta Kappan 86*(1), 9–21.

Blank, R. K. (2002). Using surveys of enacted curriculum to advance evaluation of instruction in relation to standards. *Peabody Journal of Education 77*(4), 86–121.

Bloom, B. (1984). The search for methods of group instruction as effective as one-to-one tutoring. *Educational Leadership 41*(8), 4–17.

Bloom, B. S., Engelhart, M. D., Furst, E. J., Hill, W. H., & Krathwohl, D. R. (1956). *Taxonomy of educational objectives, Handbook I: The cognitive domain.* New York: David McKay.

Bloom, B. S., Hastings, J. T., & Madaus, G. (1971). *Handbook on formative and summative evaluation of student learning.* New York: McGraw-Hill.

Brookhart, S. M. (2007/2008). Feedback that fits. *Educational Leadership 65*(4), 54–59.

Brookhart, S. M. (2014, October). *Millman Award Address.* Presented at the annual meeting of the Consortium for Research on Educational Assessment and Teaching Effectiveness, Williamsburg, VA.

Brophy, J. (1981). Teacher praise: A functional analysis. *Review of Educational Research 51*(1), 5–32.

Brown, F. G. (1981). *Measuring classroom achievement.* New York: Holt, Rinehart, and Winston.

Burney, M. (2007). Camden's probe: Rigging at Brimm. *Philadelphia Inquirer,* January 19. Retrieved September 10, 2014, from http://articles.philly.com/2007–01–19/news/25221986_1_test-answers-answer-sheets-pagan.

Burns, M. (2005). Looking at how students reason. *Educational Leadership 63*(3), 26–31.

Butler, D. L., & Winne, P. H. (1995). Feedback and self-regulated learning: A theoretical synthesis. *Review of Educational Research 65*(3), 245–281.

Butler, S. M., & McMunn, N. D. (2006). *A teacher's guide to classroom assessment: Understanding and using assessment to improve student learning.* Hoboken, NJ: John Wiley & Sons.

Chappuis, J. (2005). Helping students understand assessment. *Educational Leadership 63*(3), 39–43.

Chappuis, J. (2014). Thoughtful assessment with the learner in mind. *Educational Leadership 71*(6), 20–26.

Cizek, G. J., & Bunch, M. B. (2007). *Standard setting: A guide to establishing and evaluating performance standards on tests.* Thousand Oaks, CA: Sage.

Clarke, M., Shore, A., Rhoades, K., Abrams, L., Miao, J., & Li, J. (2003). *Perceived effects of state-mandated testing programs on teaching and learning: Findings from interviews with educators in low-, medium-, and high-stakes states.* Report from National Board on Educational Testing and Public Policy. Boston: Boston College.

Costa, A. L. (1989). Re-assessing assessment. *Educational Leadership 46*(7), 2–3.

Cureton, E. E. (1951). Validity. In E. F. Lindquist (Ed.), *Educational measurement* (pp. 621–694). Washington, DC: American Council on Education.

Dean, C.B., Hubbell, E.R., Pitler, H., & Stone. B.J. (2012). *Classroom instruction that works: Research-based strategies for increasing student achievement* (2nd ed.). Alexandria, VA: Association for Supervision and Curriculum Development.

DeLuca, C., & Bellara, A. (2013). The current state of assessment education: Aligning policy, standards, and teacher education curriculum. *Journal of Teacher Education 64*(4), 356–372.

Earl, L. (2013). *Assessment as learning: Using classroom assessment to maximize student learning* (2nd ed.). Thousand Oaks, CA: Corwin Press.

Education Week Research Center. (2014). *District disruption and revival: School systems reshape to compete and improve.* Bethesda, MD: Editorial Projects in Education.

English, F.W. (2010). *Deciding what to teach and test: Developing, aligning, and auditing the curriculum* (3rd ed.). Thousand Oaks, CA: Corwin Press.

Embreston, S.E. (2007). Construct validity: A universal system or just another test evaluation procedure? *Educational Researcher 36*(8), 449–455.

Ferriter, W.M. (2009). Yes, I can: Responsible assessment in an era of accountability. In T.R. Guskey (Ed.), *The teacher as assessment leader* (pp. 54–86). Bloomington, IN: Solution Tree Press.

Fisher, D., Grant, M., Frey, N., & Johnson, C. (2007/2008). Taking formative assessment schoolwide. *Educational Leadership 65*(4), 64–68.

Gamoran, A., Porter, A.C., Smithson, J., & White, P.A. (1997). Upgrading high school mathematics instruction: Improving learning opportunities for low-achieving, middle income youth. *Educational Evaluation and Policy Analysis 19*(4), 325–338.

Goertz, M.E., Oláh, L.N., & Riggan, M. (2009, December). Can interim assessments be used for instructional change? *CPRE Policy Briefs* (RB-51). Philadelphia, PA: Consortium for Policy Research in Education.

Good, T.L., McCaslin, M., Tsang, H.Y., Zhang, J., Wiley, C.R.H., Bozack, A.R., et al. (2006). How well do 1st-year teachers teach: Does type of preparation make a difference? *Journal of Teacher Education 57*(4), 410–430.

Gorin, J.S. (2007). Reconsidering issues in validity theory. *Educational Researcher 36*(8), 456–462.

Grant, L.W., & Gareis, C.R. (2014). Formative assessment. In L. Meyer (Ed.), *Oxford bibliographies in education*. New York: Oxford University Press.

Gronlund, N.E., & Waugh, C.K. (2013). *Assessment of student achievement* (10th ed.). Boston: Pearson.

Guskey, T.R. (2003). How classroom assessments improve learning. *Educational Leadership 60*(5), 6–11.

Guskey, T. R. (Ed.). (2009). *The teacher as assessment leader*. Bloomington, IN: Solution Tree Press.

Guskey, T. R. (2011). Five obstacles to grading reform. *Educational Leadership* 69(3), 16–21.

Guskey, T. R., & Bailey, J. M. (2010). *Developing standards-based report cards*. Thousand Oaks, CA: Corwin.

Guskey, T. R., & Jung, L. A. (2013). *Answer to essential questions about standards, assessments, grading, & reporting*. Thousand Oaks, CA: Corwin.

Hattie, J. A. C. (2009). *Visible learning: A synthesis of over 800 meta-analyses relating to achievement*. New York: Routledge.

Hightower, A. M. (2012). *On policy, student achievement, states pressing to measure up*. Bethesda, MD: Editorial Projects in Education.

Hogan, T. P. (2007). *Educational assessment: A practical introduction*. Hoboken, NJ: Wiley Jossey-Bass.

Jackson, R. R. (2009). *Never work harder than your students and other principles of great teaching*. Alexandria, VA: Association for Supervision and Curriculum Development.

Johnson, M. (1965). *American secondary schools*. New York: Harcourt, Brace, & World.

Joint Committee on Standards for Educational Evaluation. (2003). *The student evaluation standards: How to improve evaluations of students*. Thousand Oaks, CA: Corwin Press.

Joyce, B., Weil, M., & Calhoun, E. (2015). *Models of teaching* (9th ed.). Boston: Pearson.

Kahl, S. R., Hofman, P., & Bryant, S. (2013). *Assessment literacy standards and performance measures for teacher candidates and practicing teachers*. Dover, NH: Measured Progress.

Kohn, A. (2000). *What to look for in a classroom . . . and other essays*. San Francisco, CA: Jossey-Bass.

Kozol, J. (2005). *The shame of a nation: The restoration of apartheid schooling in America*. New York: Crown.

Leahy, S., Lyon, C., Thompson, M., & Wiliam, D. (2005). Classroom assessment: Minute by minute, day by day. *Educational Leadership* 63(3), 18–24.

Lemov, D. (2010). *Teach like a champion: 49 techniques that put students on the path to college*. San Francisco, CA: Jossey-Bass.

Linn, R. L. (1997). Evaluating the validity of assessments: The consequences of use. *Educational Measurement: Issues and Practices* 16(2), 14–16.

Lissitz, R. W., & Samuelsen, K. (2007). A suggested change in terminology and emphasis regarding validity and education. *Educational Researcher* 36(8), 437–448.

Magnunson, P. (2000). High stakes cheating: Will the focus on accountability lead to more cheating? *Communicator.* Retrieved January 22, 2007, from http://www.naesp.org/ContentLoad.do?contentId=151&action=print.

Manna, P. (2006). *School's in: Federalism and the national education agenda.* Washington, DC: Georgetown University Press.

Marso, R. N., & Pigge, F. L. (1991). An analysis of teacher-made tests: Item types, cognitive demands, and item construction errors. *Contemporary Educational Psychology 16,* 279–286.

Marzano, R. J. (2003). *What works in schools.* Alexandria, VA: Association for Supervision and Curriculum Development.

Marzano, R. J. (2013). Cognitive verbs and the common core. *Educational Leadership 17*(1), 78–79.

Marzano, R. J., Pickering, D., & Pollock, J. (2001). *Classroom instruction that works.* Alexandria, VA: Association for Supervision and Curriculum Development.

Maxwell, L. A. (2014, May 14). Philadelphia educators charged in test-cheating scandal. *Education Week,* p. 4.

McGonigal, K. (2006, Spring). Getting more "teaching" out of "testing" and grading. *Speaking of Teaching, Center for Teaching and Learning 15*(2), 3.

McMillan, J. H. (Ed.). (2013). *SAGE handbook of research on classroom assessment.* Los Angeles, CA: SAGE.

Measured Progress/ETS Collaborative. (2012). *Smarter balanced assessment consortium: General item specifications.* Los Angeles: Author.

Mertler, C. A. (2000). Teacher-centered fallacies of classroom assessment validity and reliability. *Mid-Western Educational Researcher 13*(4), 29–36.

Messick, S. (1989). Validity. In R. L. Linn (Ed.), *Educational measurement* (3rd ed., pp. 13–103). New York: Macmillan.

MetLife. (2013). *The MetLife survey of the American teacher: Challenges for school leadership.* New York: Author.

Miller, M. (2009, August). *Achieving a wealth of riches: Delivering on the promise of data to transform teaching and learning* (Policy brief). Washington, DC: Alliance for Excellent Education.

Mislevy, R. J. (2007). Validity by design. *Educational Researcher 36*(8), 463–469.

Moss, P. A. (2007). Reconstructing validity. *Educational Researcher 36*(8), 470–476.

National Commission on Excellence in Education. (1983). *A nation at risk: The imperative for educational reform: A report to the nation and the secretary of education, United States Department of Education.* Washington, DC: Author.

National Governors Association Center for Best Practices & Council of Chief State School Officers. (2010). *Common core state standards.* Washington, DC: Authors.

Nichols, S. L., & Berliner, D. C. (2005). *The inevitable corruption of indicators and educators through high-stakes testing* (EPSL-0503–101-EPRU). Tempe, AZ: Education Policy Studies Laboratory.

Northwest Evaluation Association. (2014). *Make assessment matter: Students and educators want tests that support student learning.* Portland, OR: Author.

Notar, C. E., Zuelke, D. C., Wilson, J. D., & Yunker, B. D. (2004). The table of specifications: Insuring accountability in teacher made tests. *Journal of Instructional Psychology 31*(2), 115–129.

Office of the Press Secretary. (2009, November 4). *Fact sheet: The race to the top.* Washington, DC: The White House. Retrieved September 26, 2014, from http://www.whitehouse.gov/the-press-office/fact-sheet-race-top.

O'Leary, M. (2008). Towards an agenda for professional development in assessment. *Journal of In-Service Education 34*(1), 109–114.

Ory, J. C., & Ryan, S. E. (1993). *Tips for improving testing and grading.* Newbury Park, CA: Sage.

PARCC. (2014). *PARCC task prototypes and new sample items for math.* Retrieved October 3, 2014, from http://www.parcconline.org/samples/math.

Polikoff, M. S., Porter, A. C., & Smithson, J. (2011). How well aligned are state assessments of student achievement with state content standards? *American Educational Research Journal 48*(4), 965–995.

Popham, W. J. (2005). "Failing" schools or insensitive tests? *School Administrator 62*(3), 6.

Popham, W. J. (2008). *Transformative assessment.* Alexandria, VA: Association for Supervision and Curriculum Development.

Popham, W. J. (2009). Assessment literacy for teachers: Faddish or fundamental? *Theory into Practice 48*(1), 4–11.

Popham, W. J. (2013). *Evaluating America's teachers: Mission possible?* Thousand Oaks, CA: Corwin.

Popham, W. J. (2014). *Classroom assessment: What teachers need to know* (7th ed.). Boston: Pearson.

Porter, A. C. (2002). Measuring the content of instruction: Uses in research and practice. *Educational Researcher 31*(7), 3–14.

Schmidt, W. H., McKnight, C. C., Houang, R. T., Wang, H. C., Wiley, D. E., Cogan, L. S., & Wolfe, R. G. (2001). *Why schools matter: A cross-cultural comparison of curriculum and learning.* San Francisco, CA: Jossey-Bass.

Schmoker, M. (2006). *Results now: How we can achieve unprecedented results in teaching and learning.* Alexandria, VA: Association for Supervision and Curriculum Development.

Schmoker, M. (2011). *Focus: Elevating the essentials to radically improve student learning.* Alexandria, VA: Association for Supervision and Curriculum Development.

Shepard, L.A. (1997). The centrality of test use and consequences for test validity. *Educational Measurement: Issues and Practice 16*, 5–24.

Shepard, L.A. (2000). *The role of classroom assessment in teaching and learning.* Report published for the Center for Study of Evaluation (CSE Technical Report #517). Retrieved September 26, 2014, from https://www.cse.ucla.edu/products/reports/TECH517.pdf.

Shulman, L.S. (1986). Those who understand: Knowledge growth in teaching. *Educational Researcher 15*(2), 4–31.

Shute, V. (2008). Focus on formative feedback. *Review of Educational Research 78*(1), 153–189.

Sireci, S.G. (2007). On validity theory and test validation. *Educational Researcher 36*(8), 477–481.

Slavin, R.E., Cheung, A., Holmes, G.C., Madden, N.A., & Chamberlain, A. (2013). Effects of data-driven reform model on state assessment outcomes. *American Educational Research Journal 50*(2), 371–396.

Smarter Balanced Assessment Consortium. (n.d.). *Sample items and performance tasks.* Retrieved October 10, 2014, from http://www.smarterbalanced.org/sample-items-and-performance-tasks.

Stiggins, R. (2004). New assessment beliefs for a new school mission. *Phi Delta Kappan 86*(1), 22–27.

Stiggins, R. (2005, December). From formative assessment to assessment FOR learning: A path to success in standards-based schools. *Phi Delta Kappan 87*(4), 324–328.

Stiggins, R. (2006, November/December). Assessment for learning: A key to motivation and achievement. *Edge 2*(2), 14.

Stiggins, R., Arter, J., Chappuis, J., & Chappuis, S. (2006). *Classroom assessment for student learning: Doing it right—Using it well.* Upper Saddle River, NJ: Pearson.

Stiggins, R.J. (1999, November). Assessment, student confidence, and school success. *Phi Delta Kappan 81*(3), 191–198.

Stiggins, R.J., & Chappuis, J. (2012). *An introduction to student-involved assessment FOR learning* (6th ed.). Boston: Pearson.

Stiggins, R.J., & Conklin, N.F. (1992). *In teachers' hands: Investigating the practices of classroom assessment.* Albany: State University of New York Press.

Stronge, J.H. (2007). *Qualities of effective teachers* (2nd ed.). Alexandria, VA: Association for Supervision and Curriculum Development.

Suh, Y., & Grant, L.W. (in press). Analysis of the use of images as historical evidence and student performance in the NAEP U.S. history assessment. *History Teacher*.

Taylor, C.S., & Nolen, S.B. (2008). *Classroom assessment: Supporting teaching and learning in real classrooms* (2nd ed.). Upper Saddle River, NJ: Pearson.

Tierney, R.D. (2006). Changing practices: Influences on classroom assessment. *Assessment in Education: Principles, Policy & Practice 13*(3), 239–264.

Tucker, P.D., Stronge, J.H., Gareis, C.R., & Beers, C.S. (2003). The efficacy of portfolios for teacher evaluation and professional development: Do they make a difference? *Educational Administration Quarterly 39*(5), 572–602.

Wagner, T. (2008). *The global achievement gap*. New York: Basic Books.

Wainer, H., & Braun, H.I. (Eds.). (1988). *Test validity*. Hillsdale, NJ: Lawrence Erlbaum Associates.

Webb, N.L., Alt, M., Ely, R., & Vesperman, B. (2005). *Web alignment tool (WAT): Training manual 1.1*. Wisconsin Center of Education Research, University of Wisconsin. Retrieved July 18, 2014, from http://wat.wceruw.org.

Wenglinsky, H. (2000). *How teaching matters: Bringing the classroom back into discussions of teacher quality*. Princeton, NJ: Educational Testing Service.

Wiggins, G.P., & McTighe, J. (2005). *Understanding by design* (2nd ed.). Alexandria, VA: Association for Supervision and Curriculum Development.

Wiliam, D. (2007/2008). Changing classroom practice. *Educational Leadership 65*(4), 36–42.

Wilson, L.W. (2005). *What every teacher needs to know about assessment* (2nd ed.). Larchmont, NY: Eye on Education.

Winger, T. (2005). Grading to communicate. *Educational Leadership 63*(3), 61–65.

Young, A. (2009). *Using common assessments in uncommon courses*. In T.R. Guskey (Ed.), *The teacher as assessment leader* (pp. 134–153). Bloomington, IN: Solution Tree Press.

Zhang, Z., & Burry-Stock, J.A. (2003). Classroom assessment practices and teachers' self-perceived assessment skills. *Applied Measurement in Education 16*(4), 323–342.

Zubrycki, J. (2012, October 17). Cheating scandal lands ex-superintendent in prison. *Education Week*, p. 6.